THE GREAT BARNATO

Books by
STANLEY JACKSON

Mr Justice Avory
Guy de Maupassant
The Aga Khan
The Life and Cases of Mr. Justice Humphreys
Laughter at Law
The Savoy
The Sassoons
The Great Barnato

M REMACLE
Feb 91

Stanley Jackson

THE
GREAT BARNATO

PENGUIN BOOKS

PENGUIN BOOKS

Published by the Penguin Group
27 Wrights Lane, London W8 5TZ, England
Viking Penguin Inc., 40 West 23rd Street, New York, New York 10010, USA
Penguin Books Australia Ltd, Ringwood, Victoria, Australia
Penguin Books Canada Ltd, 2801 John Street, Markham, Ontario, Canada LR3 1B4
Penguin Books (NZ) Ltd, 182-190 Wairau Road, Auckland 10, New Zealand
Penguin Books, Amethyst Street, Theta Ext 1, Johannesburg, South Africa

Penguin Books Ltd, Registered Offices: Harmondsworth, Middlesex, England

First published by William Heinemann Ltd in 1970

This edition published by Penguin Books in 1990

Copyright © Stanley Jackson

ISBN 0 14 0126902

Printed and bound by National Book Printers, Goodwood, Cape

FOR
Diana Barnato Walker

'More men have been knocked off balance by gold than by love'

DISRAELI

CONTENTS

▬

Contents

FOREWORD

Financiers, however powerful in their day, rarely outlast the ashes of dead companies or the plaques commemorating their benefactions. The name of Barney Barnato has proved exceptionally durable for reasons beyond his spectacular triumphs—and failures —in the world's money markets. Although De Beers and 'Johnnies' are today among the bluest of Stock Exchange chips, his pioneering rôle in these and other still-powerful groups is far less remembered than the legends that have gathered about him.

As a rags-to-riches story it is astonishing enough. Few novelists would risk a facsimile of a semi-literate cockney Jew quickly making his way from a barrow in Petticoat Lane to the Mansion House, as the Lord Mayor's guest of honour, still less reaching a position from which he could successfully issue an ultimatum to the President of the Transvaal Republic. His short life and violent death have all the obvious elements of a classic cautionary tale, but its lasting fascination stems from a dynamic personality who inspired both affection and hatred during his life and posthumously.

Unfortunately, it has also created a massive but unreliable body of folk-lore. Over the years the picaresque story has become a magnetic field for surmise and rusty half-truths. They derive from three main sources. Through vanity and often from motives of expediency, Barnato liked to romanticize himself. By contrast, Rhodes's admirers have consistently sought to glorify their hero at the expense of his old opponent. Finally, the few biographical studies so far attempted have suffered either from special pleading or a lack of documentary evidence.

In 1897, within a few months of Barnato's death, a 'Memoir'

was hurriedly rushed into print by Harry Raymond, a South African journalist who had often interviewed him and dutifully incorporated most of his fanciful self-assessments. His book, while valuable as source material, demonstrates the subject's notorious weakness for justifying himself to shareholders as well as his guile in laying smoke-screens.

Louis Cohen, his first partner in Kimberley, had much to say about him and others in his highly-coloured reminiscences, but for reasons which will become apparent he must be treated as a hostile witness. It has been rightly said that 'if Barnato had been in the very least like the portrait of him by Cohen, he could never have achieved what he did'. Indeed, Cohen's scurrilous attacks on other victims finally landed him in the Courts.

Raymond's book apart, the only attempt to set out the details of Barney's career is Richard Lewinsohn's biography, published over thirty years ago and translated from the French. It narrates many of the then-known facts without attempting to assess Barnato's character or offer much enlightenment on his complicated relations with Rhodes, Kruger, the Joels and other key figures in the story.

In attempting to fill some of the gaps, I have assessed the often conflicting data by checking it for accuracy against every available source, together with new supplementary material from various members of the family and many others who have been associated, directly or indirectly, with the Barnatos and Joels. This has been particularly helpful in dealing with Barney's marriage, the still-puzzling circumstances of his death and the dynastic convulsions that followed.

I owe a special debt to Barney's granddaughter, Diana Barnato Walker, and his great-nephew, Stanhope Joel, who both gave me access to their private libraries and papers which made my task easier and more rewarding. Among many others who kindly furnished advice, information, letters and pictures, I must thank H. J. Joel; Mrs Audrey Taylor, daughter of Barney's would-be rescuer, W. T. Clifford; Richard Haxton; Sir Richard Jackson; G. C. Shaw; Jane Pithey; H. J. Franklin; W. G. Colegate; John Furber; Mrs H. W. Jamison; S. Crook; Peter Brightman; A. B. Levy; Robin Barnard; A. B. Fincham; Arthur Calder-

Marshall; Gillie Potter; Miss N. E. Rule; Percy Baneshik; Jon Beverley of the *Diamond Fields Advertiser*, and A. L. Harington of the Department of History, University of South Africa.

In addition to generous help from various archivists in Johannesburg, Cape Town, Kimberley and Pretoria, I am much indebted to the librarians and staffs of the British Museum; South Africa House, London; the *Jewish Chronicle*; the London *Evening News*; the *News of the World*; and the *Daily Express*. Finally, I have received useful guidance and co-operation from Howard Vaughan of De Beers Consolidated Mines Ltd., and owe a special debt to Brian Roberts who very kindly read my manuscript and offered many helpful suggestions.

South Africa in the mid-nineties

THE BARNATO-JOEL DYNASTY

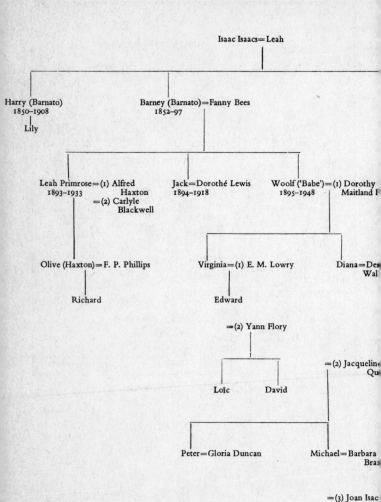

A CONDENSED VERSION

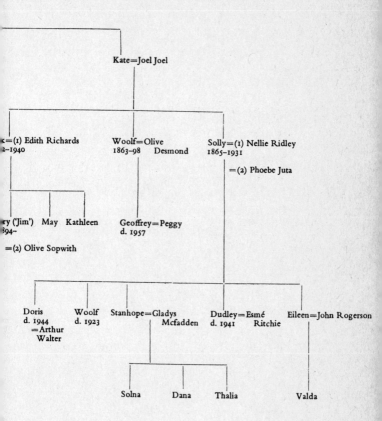

Kate=Joel Joel

=(1) Edith Richards
2–1940

Woolf=Olive
1863–98 Desmond

Solly=(1) Nellie Ridley
1865–1931

=(2) Phoebe Juta

ry ('Jim')   May   Kathleen
894–

=(2) Olive Sopwith

Geoffrey=Peggy
d. 1957

Doris
d. 1944
=Arthur
Walter

Woolf
d. 1923

Stanhope=Gladys
Mcfadden

Dudley=Esmé
d. 1941 Ritchie

Eileen=John Rogerson

Solna   Dana   Thalia

Valda

Part One

PETTICOAT LANE
and
KIMBERLEY

1

───

IN THE MID-NINETIES when the Kaffir share boom had almost reached its feverish climax, Barnato was possibly the richest and, without doubt, the most powerful financier in South Africa. His real estate and mine holdings had a market value of over £20m and it was estimated that, in the summer months of 1895, he earned a five-pound note for every minute of his working day.

The Rand boom had made him such an international force that brokers on the London Stock Exchange, who had once sniffed at all gold scrip as too speculative and a trap for the unwary, began almost affectionately to label shares in his companies as 'Barneys'. He was already a Life Governor of De Beers which controlled almost the whole of the world's diamond output. He had been re-elected unopposed to the Legislative Assembly at the Cape and had given his name to both a park and a bank. He was, moreover, founder-chairman of the flourishing Johannesburg Consolidated Investment Company with valuable interests in land development, gold mines, breweries and newspapers.

The mansion he was then building in Park Lane, on a site purchased from the Duke of Westminster and adjacent to 'Rothschild Row', seemed such a natural setting for his social and commercial grandeur that legend tactfully transformed the stucco of his background into marble. One sycophantic penny-a-liner declared that he was 'the younger son of Isaac Isaacs Barnato, Esquire, of Devonshire Terrace, Hyde Park, and related on his mother's side to Sir George Jessel, Master of the Rolls. He was educated at private scholastic establishments by special tutors.'

Barnato himself used to hoot his derision at all such attempts to invest him with a spurious pedigree. For good or ill he would remain a true son of the ghetto to the end of his days.

Barnett Isaacs was born in the very heart of London's East End on 5 July 1852, a year to the day before Cecil Rhodes's birth in the Vicarage at Bishop's Stortford. His home was a ramshackle shanty in tumbledown Cobb's Court at the corner of Middlesex Street (long known as 'Petticoat Lane' through its associations with the old clo' trade) and Wentworth Street. It was located in the network of mean alleys, cul-de-sacs and arched passage-ways that straggled like varicose veins between Spitalfields and Whitechapel. The house with a shop on the ground floor, two grimy bug-infested rooms above and a wretched cellar, rarely rat-free, was no different from scores of others that reeked of poverty in a quarter where immigrant Jews had customarily settled just outside the City limits when they crossed the North Sea to escape persecution. It had been the haven of poor refugees from Cromwell's days. Here for generations they earned a bare livelihood as pedlars, tailors, hatters and artisans. Only a tiny minority followed the aristocratic fringe of scholars, bankers, musicians and wealthy merchants— mainly of Spanish or Portuguese origin—to the more salubrious suburbs. The banker David Salomons had become London's first Jewish Lord Mayor in 1855; three years later, Baron Lionel de Rothschild entered the House of Commons.

The Isaacs boys, Harry and Barney, raised in a slum long reputed to be the most vicious annexe of London's underworld, had more prospect of appearing in the dock than gracing the Chancery Bench like Sir George Jessel, with whom their mother claimed a vague kinship. Rising from the rickety bed shared in a corner of their father's shop, they would snatch a hunk of black bread and sluice it down with a mug of dark brown tea before running to answer the clanging bell of the Jews' Free School in nearby Bell Lane. A hard-pressed headmaster, assisted by a dozen apprentice teachers, taught a thousand boys to read and write Hebrew and English, leavened by some potted history and geography. Leaving shortly after his thirteenth birthday, Barney narrowly missed the generosity of Sir Anthony de Rothschild who endowed the school with more classrooms, a new gymnasium and four playgrounds. His arithmetic was exceptionally good but he had no other qualifications for the Rothschild Scholarship which Israel Zangwill, the future novelist and playwright, was later awarded.

Barney left Bell Lane with the blessing of his kindly teacher plus a new penny which he added to his hoard. Already a huckster in embryo, he had traded among his schoolfellows in licorice, laces, toffee, monkey nuts, brass buttons and a variety of beer-bottle labels salvaged from the refuse bins at Truman's Brewery. He was unusually quick with his fingers and excelled at marbles, but more robust talents were demanded in a quarter notorious for thieves, gin-sodden bullies, fences and prostitutes. ('Jack the Ripper' would find many of his victims in Flower and Dean Streets and Frying Pan Alley where the Isaacs boys played as children.)

They were taught from the cradle that the Messiah would surely come one day, at any time and without advance notice, to restore the rich inheritance of God's chosen. Meantime, however, it was prudent not to venture alone into the largely Gentile area of Shoreditch or risk running into a gang of drunken Irishmen in Buck's Road, Whitechapel. Numerical superiority was also essential when meeting boys from the Wentworth Street Ragged School who might not like one's nose and insist on changing its shape.

Mrs Isaacs kept her kettles and saucepans simmering on the stove for twenty-four hours from Friday sunset, after which it was ritually forbidden to light a fire or even strike a match. Her husband, a man of piety who dutifully closed his shop on the Sabbath, was not blinded to everyday realities. Practical experience had taught him that an eye-for-an-eye philosophy was vital in Spitalfields. Two nights a week he rigged up a ring in his backyard or cleared a space in the shop during the winter months. There he taught his sons the elements of boxing and imparted a piece of advice which was long cherished: 'Never let a man put his hand on you without giving him what for, and always 'it 'im first.' He nailed a sketch of the last bare-knuckle fight to the lavatory door in the yard and advised his boys to model themselves on Tom Sayers and the immortal Aldgate-bred champion, Daniel Mendoza.

They were usually joined by a cousin, David Harris, who walked four miles daily to and from his home in Canonbury to save fares on the new horse trams. He often arrived at school soaked through and clutching a scarecrow umbrella. A quiet, well-mannered boy, he always had a clean handkerchief tucked up his sleeve.

He took most of the punishment in those sparring bouts. Harry, the oldest of the trio, had a long reach and moved adroitly, flicking out punches with some skill. Barney had the heavier fists but his jug-like fleshy ears usually ended up red from his brother's attentions. Small for his age—he would never stand over five foot three—he was of stocky build and exceptionally strong in the shoulder. His main disability was short sight which made his timing a little erratic, although he compensated with the grace of a natural acrobat. One of his favourite tricks was to walk the top rope of the ring in imitation of Blondin crossing Niagara Falls.

He was something of a physical oddity among the darker-skinned and weedier boys of his race. The butter-yellow hair, blue eyes and chubby pink cheeks hinted at some remote Baltic ancestor, and few could resist his air of helpless innocence. He never seemed to catch cold or suffer from the epidemics that sometimes closed the school. In the winter, coatless and with only a muffler round his throat, he would race through the streets with a mongrel for company, whistling some ballad, his face rain-washed and glowing with health. Had he had his way, he would have been off to sea as a cabin boy. The idea had obsessed him after an unforgettable day's outing to Ramsgate, sponsored by the Rothschilds, who had provided the entire class with bread and sausage, a bag of sweets and an apple apiece. Only the fear of breaking his mother's sentimental Jewish heart had prevented him from slipping away to the docks next morning. He consoled himself by buying a parrot from a sailor in The King of Prussia, the nearby tavern kept by his sister's husband, Joel Joel.

He celebrated his Barmitzvah or confirmation as a fully-fledged Son of the Covenant, by reading from the sacred Scrolls at the little synagogue in Aldgate. Henceforth he would wear phylacteries on his left arm and forehead while reciting morning prayers, but otherwise his religious observance was casual and limited to the

Holy Days. His spiritual and temporal horizon was dominated by an awesome trinity: the Almighty, who had a special regard for Jews even if He seemed at times to make them pay rather painfully for the privilege; Queen Victoria, who enjoyed semi-divine status because prayers were regularly offered in the synagogue to remind the Lord of her family's health and happiness; and, finally, the frock-coated Rothschilds whose carriages, country estates and banks were solid proof that virtue and industry could still be richly rewarded even in a Gentile world.

The Rothschilds inevitably grew into figures of fantasy in a ghetto where the cruel night bugs nipped one's flesh during suffocating summer nights. Isaac Isaacs might dream of a glittering world far beyond Aldgate Pump, but only a miracle could release him from the relentless struggle to provide for his family. He had worked at cap-making before setting up as a dealer in second-hand clothing. His big donkey iron was always hissing away in the shop which smelled chronically of naphthaline, musty fur or sour urine left by the stray cats which Barney habitually smuggled into the yard.

Before the three daughters were married off, they had scraped together most of their dowries by sewing, stitching and making buttonholes far into the night. The boys were not sorry to see them depart. Now at last they could move up to the room next to their parents.

The family was reasonably prosperous by neighbourhood standards. They did not have to queue outside the Jews' Soup Kitchen in Fashion Street and were too proud to appeal, even in bad times, to the Board of Guardians who assisted needier members of the community with loans, medical care and apprenticeships for orphan boys. None of the Isaacs children ever went barefoot or short of a meal. On Friday nights the festoon of fly-papers would be taken down and a sparkling white cloth spread over the table. Two tall wax candles were ceremoniously lit in the heavy silver sticks, a wedding gift to Leah Isaacs and pawned only *in extremis*. The Sabbath plaited loaves, sprinkled with poppy seed, would appear with the ritual flask of wine and silver goblet. Fried fish, the flesh succulent and firm and the skin golden-brown, was served cold in the Jewish fashion, and as a special treat *gefüllte* fish, boneless and spicily stuffed, preceded by soup with *lockshen*, that local apotheosis of vermicelli. For an hour or two, even when the banquet was reduced to only bread and fried sprats, the light of Sinai shed a Sabbath radiance over the squalor of Cobb's Court.

As soon as they left school, the brothers automatically helped their father in the shop. They also made themselves useful by trundling a barrow to Exchange Buildings in Houndsditch in search of old clothes and odd lengths of cloth ('remnants', the trade called them) which could be resold to bespoke tailors and dressmakers. They earned extra coppers by carrying panes for the local glaziers or a sofa that someone wanted upholstered. Barney usually did well selling penny canes which he swished like a Squeers or used for some fancy juggling to amuse his customers.

His supreme asset was an invincible cheerfulness tinctured with Jewish-cockney wit. When business was slow in the shop he would load a tray with laces, collar-studs and pieces of elastic and walk to Hatton Garden, then the centre of jewellers, workers in precious metals, gold refiners and clockmakers, as well as a few pioneer traders in cut diamonds. He bustled round the coffee-houses where men drank endless glasses of lemon tea and played cards or dominoes. Few bought his rubbish but he was liked for his merry smile and the funny way he moved, walking lightly on the balls of his feet while he thrust his tray under their noses and rattled off jokes. A man named H. M. Codd, who had a glassworks show-room, used to give him sixpence regularly each week even if he bought nothing, and an occasional half-crown at Christmas. Barney never forgot his kindness.

Sometimes he invested in a five-shilling basket of lemons in Duke's Place, near the synagogue, and sold them at two a penny to net a profit of 100%. Goulston Street came alive before the festivals with the cackle and clucking of poultry, and it was easy enough then to pick up some cash and perhaps a juicy pickled cucumber by plucking chickens. But Sundays in Petticoat Lane offered the fattest dividends. The brothers wheeled out their barrow, piled with old clothes from the shop, together with a few sidelines for themselves like insecticides, birdseed, bootlaces and a 'miraculous' headache powder. Barney, mounted on an orange box, acted as spieler and used a non-stop patter of gibberish and slang that kept bargain-hunters in good humour. Harry handed out goods and nimbly collected the cash. Both were adroit salesmen who sometimes applied the doctrine of *caveat emptor* with a briskness that would have dismayed the Master of the Rolls.

Neither was tempted to follow the earnest example of David Harris who took a course at a commercial college and went to work as an office boy and junior ledger clerk for a City export firm. His sharp nose was always pecking at Macaulay, Gibbon and Shakespeare while his cousins preferred the boxing and racing news or played billiards for threepenny side stakes at the Black Lion in Middlesex Street. Harry finally went to work in the evenings as a barman in The King of Prussia where his sister, Kate, made sure that he had a hot meal. It was a dingy spit-and-sawdust gin palace frequented by Irish labourers, dockers, whores and a number of seedy actors from the new Cambridge Music Hall in Commercial Street. Harry's skilful kidney-punching was handy, and his young brother would help out as 'bouncer' on Saturday nights. Barney soon began to go there most evenings, making himself useful as a tapster and heaving barrels up from the cellar. Here he first acquired his lifelong taste for nourishing nips. The theatrical folk took to him and sometimes handed out free passes or allowed him to watch from the wings. He also acted occasionally as an unpaid scene-shifter and went out for their beer and sandwiches. In exchange they showed him their make-up tricks and taught him to juggle and do soft falls.

On warm Saturday nights Barney and his friends would stroll along Aldgate High Street to ogle the girls. It was not too rewarding: he was small for his age and unprepossessing by local standards; and he rarely had the price of a drink, still less a restaurant snack, much preferring to invest in a game of billiards if he could be fairly sure of a profit. He found the Jewish maidens too protected by taboos and their own shrewdness to dispense favours for anything short of betrothal. Anyway, he was more attracted by buxom women of Viking colouring and stature and long nursed acute sexual fantasies over a coloured picture of Boadicea which he had cut out from one of his school books.

He had quickly become something of a pet with the ample and good-natured actresses of the neighbourhood halls. They laughed when he threw his voice or walked about on his hands after discovering that this was one of the famous Edmund Kean's accomplishments. Nobody took him seriously when he declaimed 'To be or not to be' and confessed his ambition to become a dramatic actor. The *Hamlet* soliloquy was so unintentionally comical that he was encouraged to repeat it while walking on his hands. It became one of his party tricks, together with balancing glasses on his head, although Harry was easily his superior at sleight-of-hand.

His physique was astonishing for his size, and he needed no persuasion to take off his shirt and ripple muscles like small walnuts. In later years when he was the talk of London, an old-time actress recalled how he had once slipped into her dressing-room while she was changing for her act. 'He looked just like a choir boy with that yellow hair like silk, and those tin-framed glasses on his funny brussels sprout of a nose. He just stood there watching me get into me corset, and I felt like offering him a bit of toffee or something. Then he gave me a wink and I knew he wasn't after toffee. No, he was no choir boy, that Barney!'

He found a cash market for his theatre passes and soon noted that people would leave a music-hall at the interval, either throwing away their tickets or ready to hand them over for a couple of pence. It was easy enough to resell them at a profit for the second half of the show. By mistake he was once handed two shillings instead of tuppence. 'What did you do?' he was asked when he mentioned this windfall years afterwards. 'Do? Do? Why, I never stopped running until I'd put eight streets between me and the theatre.'

He could not always resist using the half tickets himself. He loved the music halls but preferred robust melodramas at the old Grecian Theatre, particularly *Sweeney Todd*, and never missed a chance of seeing his idol, Henry Irving, as Bill Sykes at the Queen's in Long Acre. When Irving first electrified London in November 1871 as Matthias in *The Bells*, Barney would spend his last coppers to sit in the gallery. He found a second-hand copy of the play and painfully memorized the whole part. He was determined to become a tragedian, having already made himself word perfect in the rôle of Othello, but the managers took one look at the squat little Cockney with the yellow hair and roared their heads off. He would return to Cobb's Court with the tears misting his glasses, but soon he was marching up and down the shop again, spouting Shakespeare while Harry practised his juggling.

'They'll never get a living at this rubbish,' Mrs Isaacs told her husband privately. 'Harry might make a little bit at it, but Barney, never.'

Harry, rigged out as a dandy from his father's stock, developed a mock-tipsy juggling act which badly needed a foil. His brother had only to dab a little more red on his cheeks and put on a false moustache and a pair of baggy pantaloons to transform himself into an acrobatic clown. His juggling was amateurish and clumsy, mainly because he could not wear his glasses on stage, but the audience seemed to enjoy the comic effect and specially appreciated his double somersaults. Although they played only the halls in the Commercial Road and Leman Street, the stage-struck couple began to spend far more time rehearsing their act than taking out the barrow.

Harry regarded himself as the main draw and habitually took the bow, until a kindly stage manager signalled one night to the wings and called out, 'And Barney, too!' On the way back to The King of Prussia for a drink, Harry repeated thoughtfully, 'And Barney, too'. It gave him the idea that 'Barnato' sounded far more professional than 'Isaacs' for a juggling comedy act. Within a few weeks 'Barnato Brothers' began to appear in small print on music hall bills, although bookings were dismally scarce.

One evening early in 1871, they were at home practising routines for an act which must surely make their fortune, when a very dapper David Harris walked in, twirling a new umbrella with a silver handle. He carried a sheaf of yellowing newspapers and an atlas under his arm. 'I'm going to South Africa,' he announced dramatically. 'For the diamonds.' Almost hysterical with excitement, he unrolled his atlas. 'Look, boys, here's the British in the Cape Colony and Natal. Up there above the Orange River are the Boers.' He made some crosses on the Vaal. 'And here are diamonds. *Millions* of 'em!'

He had booked passage by Royal Mail steamer and said farewell after pledging himself to report progress. The brothers could not sleep that night. They had ridiculed their cousin at first but felt less sure after hearing that their very cautious aunt had given him the whole of her savings, £150. 'Who knows?' Harry kept repeating. 'Even if there are no diamonds, one could always fiddle a living. What's the name of that funny place he kept talking about? Dutoitspan?' Next morning he hurried over to the old school to borrow a map.

2

IN APRIL 1867 the children of a Boer farmer had picked up an unusually pretty pebble on the banks of the Orange River. It was sent to Dr Guybon Atherstone, a leading mineralogist in Grahamstown, who confirmed it to be a fine diamond of over twenty carats. Two years later, a much larger stone was found near the Vaal by a shepherd boy and bought by a sharp-eyed farmer for a few cattle. He sold it rough to the Lilienfeld brothers of Hopetown who in turn disposed of it to the Earl of Dudley. It was the celebrated 'Star of South Africa' which Sir Richard Southey, the Colonial Secretary, prophesied would become 'the rock on which the future success of South Africa will be built'.

Several thousand prospectors were soon scouring the river banks and shredding mounds of soil through primitive sieves. Finds were satisfactory but far less valuable than those made further inland, the so-called 'dry diggings' on land owned by Boers. In 1860 the De Beer brothers had bought their farm, Vooruitzigt, from the Orange Free State Government for only £50. A Port Elizabeth firm paid them £6,000 for the property which had been pegged by November 1871 to produce £50,000 in diamonds a month. Somewhat precipitately they had sold out to the Cape Government two years later for £100,000.

Two minefields on this rich property were to be public diggings, comprising the original De Beer Mine round the farm-house and another near by on the Colesberg 'kopje' (hillock), which was called De Beer's 'New Rush' but would become better known as the Kimberley Mine. The neighbouring Dutoitspan and Bultfontein farms, also of enormous potential value, were bought by the German-Jewish brothers, Mosenthal, owners of the South

African Exploration Company. They had moved very profitably into diamonds from exporting wool, hides and ostrich feathers. For little over £4,500 they purchased land on which hundreds of claims could be let to diggers at 30s. a month. (The Mosenthals retained this remarkably lucrative investment until 1900 when the De Beers Company took it over for £1,625,000.)

David Harris was only one of many who had joined the frenzied scramble for wealth. Before the end of 1871 over ten thousand diggers swarmed over the fields. Old-time prospectors arrived from Australia, New Zealand and America, soon to be joined by a very mixed bag of Fenians, German speculators, rabbis, ex-convicts, professional gamblers, boxers, actors, cashiered soldiers and the inevitable camp followers, white, black and yellow. The De Beer farm was 650 miles from Cape Town and nearly five hundred from Port Elizabeth, until then content to export wool. The privately-owned railway from Cape Town only ran to Wellington, fifty-seven miles to the north. From there or Port Elizabeth the only way to Golconda was by coach for those who could afford it or mule cart and ox-wagon for nearly everyone else.

Seamen deserted their ships, and one mariner who called himself 'Champagne Charlie' could not wait to get out of his bell-bottoms to make the long trek from Durban. He salted his first claim with a broken glass bottle-stopper. Tradesmen put up their shutters in many townships to pitch their tents in the treeless camps of mud and dust with not a blade of grass visible for miles. Younger sons of the British nobility donned corduroys, dirty checked woollen shirts and sombreros; like all the others they soon had their manicured hands infected and scarred with lime-encrusted sand from the diggings. Nobody was safe from the deadly virus of diamond fever. The cathedral at Grahamstown lost its organist and most of the choir, and John Xavier Merriman, son of the Bishop, was among the first to try his luck in the fields.

Some arrived with only a blanket and a billy-can, scrabbling in a yellow hole with a native to do the cooking and help ransack the dirt through a cradle sieve. Barefoot natives deserted their kraals to sleep in the open at below-zero temperatures, broiling by day in the blinding red dust or lashed by storms and pitiless rain which often flooded the pits and drowned them like rats. Others were buried under avalanches of shale. They cheerfully accepted such risks for the white man's gun or 'gas pipe', a bottle of fiery liquid and, above all, the opportunity to steal some of the pretty stones for their Chiefs.

Only one in five prospectors made his daily expenses, many abandoning their claims because they could hardly cover their licence fees. Yet the output from De Beer's 'Old Rush' and the Colesberg Kopje had shot up from 100,000 carats in 1870 to over a million within two years. Some struck it rich. A man mined three stones, one of fifty carats, before his native boy had even finished cooking breakfast. A single small claim, sold originally for £20, soared to £4,000. Others, bought for a few pounds, would be split up to fetch as much as £900 for seven foot by four.

Even the big strikers had to pay the price of dirt, disease and often death. Dysentery or camp fever claimed victims who had no hope of proper nursing. Only the very rich could afford an extravagant soda-water bath at 5s. a bottle. A cabbage cost 30s. during the drought, a half-crown onion was a luxury and sugar remained scarce at 2s. 6d. a pound. There was no building timber, and the lucky ones were glad enough to share a double tent. Many a hut was crudely fashioned from a packing case with only a tin lining nailed over it to keep out the torrential rains. Every pound of stores had to come by cart from the Cape or was hauled in by opportunist Boer farmers who found it more profitable to sell potatoes at 4s. a pound than to tend their flocks.

They had good reason to feel both cynical and bitter towards the diggers who had descended on their lands. One could still hate these godless and greedy invaders even if a single bullock-wagon, hauled through the sand belt with a load of fuel and vegetables, often brought more money than a week's sievings from the gravel. But wealth alone, after years of struggle on the lonely veld, could not heal wounds that were far deeper than the holes dug by the intruders, for these men had corrupted the coloured farm hands with the devil's bounty of liquor and guns.

The principal diamond claims had been pegged in the territory known as Griqualand West, peopled by a race of mixed white, Bantu and Hottentot blood ruled by Chief Waterboer. They were

feared and despised by the neighbouring Boers in the Orange Free
State and the Transvaal Republics, descendants of the pioneer
Voortrekkers who had first gone north in their tented ox-wagons
in 1836. They had risked torture and massacre at the hands of
tribesmen, as well as the horrors of drought and rinderpest, rather
than remain in the mockingly-named Cape of Good Hope under
hated British rule. Among those who had reached the promised
land across the Vaal River was a ten-year-old boy, Paul Kruger.

Chief Waterboer had been deftly won over by Cape officials
who wanted his rich diamond lands and could not risk being
blocked permanently from Central Africa by hostile Afrikaners.
He agreed to be incorporated into the British dominions after an
'impartial' referee, the Governor of Natal, had conveniently
defined the disputed territorial limits of Griqualand West in his
favour. Thus a new Crown Colony of immense potential wealth
was born. The Free State was indemnified with £90,000 which
they used to found a National Bank, but President Pretorius of the
Transvaal would not soon forgive them for selling their birthright,
or the Cape for robbing his burghers of their share of the diamond
fields.

The Transvaal never forgot the lesson of Griqualand West, as
the gold miners of the Rand would most painfully discover when
they later came to reckon with Kruger instead of a docile Chief
Waterboer.

David Harris had no thought of power politics or the deep resentments breeding like crocodiles on the banks of the Vaal as his ship
nosed into sunshine south of the equator. He felt far less assured
than fellow-passengers like Julius Wernher, a tall blond man with
deep-set blue eyes and the stiff bearing of an Uhlan officer. Wernher
was the son of a general from Darmstadt and had lately served in
the Franco-Prussian War. Surprisingly, he had then entered the
firm of Jules Porges, a leading diamond merchant in Paris. After a
spell of banking and brokerage in London and Frankfurt-am-Main,
he was going to Griqualand as a buyer for Porges who held the
view that his own countrymen were far too emotional to handle
diamonds. Wernher would be among the first of many Germans

to show a cool aptitude for the competitive thrust of Kimberley.

Among others making their way to the diggings was Cecil John Rhodes who had travelled the four hundred miles from Natal by ox-cart. His destiny would soon be linked with both Wernher and the nervous Jewish youth from London who had not exchanged a word or so much as a nod during the long voyage. Too delicate to be sent to Eton or Winchester, like two of his brothers, Rhodes had had to content himself with the local grammar school but dreamed of one day going up to Oxford to become 'a gentleman' and prepare for a career as either barrister or clergyman. His brother, Frank, had left Eton for the First Dragoons, while Herbert was growing cotton in Natal. Rhodes had to shelve all thoughts of the University when he contracted a lung infection and was warned that a warmer climate offered his only chance of recovery. In June 1870, then barely seventeen but with £2,000 lent him by an aunt, he sailed for Durban. He did not stay more than a few months as Herbert had quickly joined the diamond rush. By October of the following year, Rhodes followed him to Colesberg Kopje. He remained behind to dig their three claims when Herbert again became restless and decided to return to his plantation.

Rhodes was then a rather dreamy and ungainly youth with a shock of tousled auburnish hair. He usually wore faded flannel trousers with a shrunken school blazer from which his wrists shot out. He was often to be seen sitting on an upturned bucket, sorting his diamonds or reading a copy of Virgil. After the little packets were made up on trestle tables at sundown, he would ride across the moonlit veld on his rusty pony, with an odd tailless dog trotting peacefully by his side. He drank alone rather than with the noisy diggers who thought him a cold fish and laughed at his squeaky voice and beak of a nose, but few dug harder or sieved with more patience. His gangs of naked workers, perched on their ramps, hacked and scraped unceasingly at 'the big Stilton cheese', as he described the reef in a letter to his mother. He was fortunate in escaping the fall-ins of several neighbouring mines but broke the little finger of his right hand while carrying a heavy bucket. It did not set properly and left him with a permanently limp handshake which suited his abrupt and withdrawn manner.

Among the other diggers, Rhodes found Merriman well-read and congenial, but drew closest of all to Charles Rudd, a former champion hurdler at Harrow and Cambridge Blue who had also come out to Africa for his health. They formed an excellent partnership. Rudd, the senior by nine years, was the son of a shipping magnate and Norfolk landowner. He had the right background and temperament to stabilize the younger man, but Rhodes in fact carried them through most of the ups and downs of their first years together. His was the initiative to buy a six horse-power steam-engine pump in Port Elizabeth, the earliest to appear in the fields. They used it at first to manufacture ice cream and later pumped out another digger's flooded claim for a fee of £1,000. They found no large stones but steadily began to average £100 a week.

David Harris was less fortunate and found it difficult to fit into the rough mining camp. He could not match the sharp-witted 'Peruvians', as the scourings of the world's ghettoes were being called. They had a reputation for tricky deals, cheating Boer and Native alike, and many were in the market for stolen diamonds. Harris avoided them and rented a claim for 10s. a month. He failed to find any diamonds and once had to sell his tools to pay the native help. He did better as a 'kopje-walloper', joining other itinerant brokers who toured the diggings to buy up the small parcels of diamonds which the miners laid out on their sorting tables. He developed such a good eye for a stone that a dealer agreed to finance him on a commission basis which earned him over £400 in three bumper months.

He saved his money in the hope of buying a good claim and some machinery, but it was a lonely existence in Kimberley, that ugly sprawl of shacks, tents and pitted roadways littered with kerosene tins. He was too finicky to join the drinkers and often thought wistfully of the pretty young Jewess whom he had met on board ship with her uncle and aunt. Women were scarce in the camp, and the few prostitutes who ventured from the Cape or the kraals were in strenuous demand. Kimberley folk-lore will long cherish the plump saffron-coloured octoroon who put herself up for auction. She stood on a champagne case in Graybittel's Canteen and cheerfully invited bidders. The prize was won by one

John Swaebe (later Barney's leading broker) who carried her off for £25 and three cases of champagne. His unlucky rivals promptly uprooted his tent and ended the short honeymoon.

Harris's spell of prosperity was equally brief. Although himself a man of integrity, his commissions dwindled as the diggers grew warier of 'kopje-wallopers' who paid notoriously low prices and often used faked scales. Many preferred to take their day's siftings into Kimberley and deal with Wernher and other respectable merchants on Main Street.

Harris had written home enthusiastically during his flush period. He assured his cousins that diamonds were only part of the bonanza. The 'Peruvians' made money out of ribbons, tooth-combs and all manner of rubbish. He thought that Harry and Barney could more than hold their own and, alternatively, they might please camp audiences with a music hall act. Nevertheless, he was a little dismayed when Harry Barnato arrived within a few weeks after barely scraping together enough money for his passage out. Equipped with his stage wardrobe, props and make-up kit, he soon announced himself as 'Signor Barnato, the Great Wizard from London'. His tipsy dandy act had novelty appeal. Audiences liked his patter in cockney, Yiddish and pidgin French but soon turned to more robust, knockabout entertainment. His broad and topical asides, so popular in the Shoreditch music halls, were either incomprehensible to polyglot audiences or rather too sophisticated for their taste. They would no doubt have preferred Barney's acrobatics and comic juggling or even his soliloquies from Shakespeare. Harry refused to change his style. Instead he earned himself a few shillings a night by giving sparring exhibitions with Fred Abrahams, a burly ex-policeman from Natal. However, he was rather too careful not to spoil his hands to shine as a booth attraction in the Market Square. He then bought himself a pair of scales and some pliers and wandered hopefully among the mounds. But knowing next to nothing about diamonds and without capital, he had little attraction for Harris whom he continually importuned to form a business association.

Harry had to move out of his hotel room. His funds and morale dwindled together. He used to crawl into his tent at night and count the hours until he could earn or borrow his return fare to

England. In the catch-as-catch-can of the mining camps he could not compete with the more energetic Jewish hucksters whose donkey carts were laden with the right kind of merchandise for a quick turnover in the claims and back-veld farms. His cousin finally came to his rescue by finding him a berth behind the counter of a diamond dealer in Dutoitspan named Van Praagh. It was not very exalted but stimulated him enough to write home exuberant letters urging his brother to join him.

Barney did not become excited until David Harris made a dazzling reappearance in London. When his luck had all but run out and it seemed hopeless to stay in the diggings, he had ventured one night into Dodd's Bar where the free whisky, snacks and cigars attracted him to an upstairs room. He had drifted to the roulette table and in a single incredible hour scooped £1,400. He took the very next boat to England where he spent three slightly hysterical weeks on holiday. He returned his mother's £150, but she could not persuade him to stay. He planned to set up in Kimberley as a diamond merchant and perhaps seek out the girl who had travelled on to Cape Town but had never left his thoughts.

Barney grew restless when his cousin left again for South Africa. He had replaced Harry as a part-time barman in The King of Prussia but found it hard to secure anything except one-night bookings at the Cambridge, despite billing himself as 'The Great Barnato'. For the next few months he took the barrow out on his own and did any kind of odd job. He saved every penny, even giving up cigarettes, until by the summer of 1873 he had enough for his passage out and even a few pounds over.

His old schoolfellows and some of the regulars at the tavern subscribed 25s. for a second-hand nickel watch as a farewell gift, while his brother-in-law, Joel, generously contributed a silver chain. Joel had a last-minute inspiration. Having learned from Harris that luxury goods were in short supply, he pressed Barney to take forty boxes of cigars with him to sell on a fifty-fifty basis, with the thrilling possibility of building up an export business. The origin and pedigree of these 'Finest Quality Coronas' remained mysterious, but hard-up dockers and thirsty sailors habitually brought such treasures to The King of Prussia.

Barney was plied with drinks and good wishes. He kissed his sister, Kate, and her three boys, Jack, Woolf and Solly, before making the rounds of the halls to take sentimental leave of old friends. He took his Indian clubs and packed his phylacteries in a blue velvet bag, rashly promising his father never to miss morning prayers, wherever he might be. His mother also insisted on buying him a set of long flannel underwear which he thought absurd for Africa.

Life seemed full of bright omens as the sparkling white *Anglian* steamed out of Southampton on her maiden voyage. It coincided with his twenty-first birthday. Steerage was not too uncomfortable and he made himself popular with the children by juggling or swallowing lighted cigarettes. The berths and saloon were cramped, but he was not sea-sick and kept going up on deck to gulp lungfuls of air and joke with the crew. A gala atmosphere had spread over the vessel when it became certain that she would break the record for the run and might even reach the Cape in twenty-seven days. Everyone had hurried on deck to wave to another ship steaming towards Southampton. On board was Cecil Rhodes who loftily declined to rush to the rail or lay aside his copy of Marcus Aurelius. He was sailing for his first term at Oriel, Oxford, where he would study intermittently until he graduated eight years later. (He did not keep his second term until 1876.) He had gone aboard so bemused by visions of dreaming spires that he failed to notice that his one pair of threadbare trousers was falling apart. They had to be patched with canvas by the ship's sailmaker. He travelled first-class but looked more like a stowaway than a man who was temporarily leaving claims already worth the better part of £5,000.

Barney went ashore at Cape Town with close on £30 and his brother-in-law's stock of cigars. He registered grandly at the Masonic Hotel and refused to be patronized by the desk clerk whose glance rested superciliously on the immigrant's flashy stove-pipe trousers, shiny blue jacket, natty bowler and cane. Barney gave him a broad wink and loudly directed a porter to take his shabby kitbag upstairs. He bounced boisterously on the

springy mattress before composing himself for a long and untroubled night's sleep. Wishing to surprise his brother, he had not
informed him before sailing. It was just as well. Harry might have
warned him of the blight that had settled on the once-fecund
gravel of Colesberg Kopje, recently named Kimberley in honour
of the British Colonial Secretary.

After yielding over £2m the diggings appeared to be exhausted.
Worse, the price of diamonds had slumped alarmingly through
dumping on a market suddenly afflicted by a crisis on the world's
stock exchanges. The effect was catastrophic for Kimberley in that
summer of 1873. As the price of diamonds fell, Porges and the rest
were naturally unwilling to add to their already unsaleable stocks.
Many diggers panicked and sold out, while the natives returned by
the thousand to their kraals or implored the Boer farmers to take
them back. But for a slight heart attack and his preoccupation with
Oxford, Rhodes would surely have overruled Charles Rudd who
stubbornly refused to sink all their reserves into claims, even at
bargain prices. 'We could have bought up practically the whole of
De Beers for only £6,000,' Rhodes used to recall sadly.

Barney unconcernedly smoked a cigarette on the stoep outside
his hotel the morning after his arrival in Cape Town. His first hint
of trouble came from a massive brick-faced man in a white stetson
who stopped to pass the time of day. He had made a glittering
entrance with his diamond waistcoat buttons, cufflinks and a huge
stone in his silk cravat. Barney confided genially that he was 'off to
the Fields' where his brother happened to be one of the magnates
in Dutoitspan and 'a partner' in the leading firm of Van Praagh.

'Too late, boy, too late,' the other boomed sympathetically.
'Nothing left. I struck it rich, but the sands are dry now. Best take
the next boat back.'

Some fifteen years later, according to Barney, he met the very
same man in Johannesburg. The stranger did not apparently recall
their first meeting and remarked, 'I hear you're boss of the diamond
fields. How did you do it?'

'By not taking your advice,' was Barney's alleged reply. It was
the kind of embellishment he could never resist making for
dramatic effect.

He was less concerned with the stranger's discouragement,

which he thought suspicious, than the £40 demanded by the
Transport Company for the thirty-five-day coach journey up
country. Unless he sold his cigars it was quite beyond his means.
He moved out of the hotel and into cheap lodgings while looking
around. Within a week he arranged for an ox-wagon to take him
'to the diamonds' for £5. He piled his luggage on top and walked
beside the four oxen, after promising to sleep under the wagon at
night.

They headed north in slow stages and took two months to
cover the six hundred miles. They crossed the Great Karroo and
hauled themselves up steep passes and over scorched plateaux in
the tracks of the first Voortrekkers. In the flooded mud-brown
rivers they had to avoid numerous upturned wagons. The surly
driver cursed and lashed his four oxen, often needing Barney's
strong shoulders when the wheels stuck in the mud. At times he
was too exhausted to take another step and had to get up on the
wagon which was like riding a camel. He tossed in his soaking
clothes during the star-frosted nights, chilled to the skin and
tormented by blistered feet. But hope always returned in the
drowsy sweep of golden veld when they rested in the shade to eat
their mealie porridge or sun-dried biltong steaks. On the firmer
ground they passed wagon teams driven by bearded slow-moving
men in shovel hats who solemnly returned Barney's greeting when
he waved his bowler.

He had begun to feel light-hearted and curiously exalted as they
pitched and rolled over this tranquil land. It was exactly as he had
always imagined Palestine from his school picture books. The
illusion was reinforced when a farmer with the head of an Old
Testament prophet invited them to share his mutton, black bread
and coffee. Afterwards he read from a huge Bible with a deep-
voiced gravity that recalled Isaac Isaacs back in far-off Cobb's
Court.

'It was just like *seder* (Passover) night,' Barney later told his
brother. To his delight he managed to pick out a few words of the
Dutch dialect which had some echoes of Yiddish. However, he
made the mistake of offering to sing for his supper. The racy
cockney ballad was incomprehensible to the worthy Boer and his
family but his crude gestures seemed to scandalize them. After a

dreamless sleep in the barn he tried to make his peace next morning by opening his first box of cigars.

His mood of exhilaration quickly vanished as scores of dispirited miners and storekeepers rode south from the diggings. He failed to sell them any of his 'Havanas' but recovered his spirits when they came at last to the Orange where a friendly gang of natives chanced to be on hand to ferry their baggage across the swollen river by canoe.

He was shocked by his first view of Dutoitspan which had flickered in his mind's eye as a smaller edition of gracious Cape Town. It seemed only a dusty flyblown mass of pits between mounds of gravel, ringed by rough shacks and saloons far more primitive than the beloved King of Prussia. Stumbling among the pot-holes, he passed a few derelict-looking claims with names and licence numbers still nailed to scraps of torn canvas. A native boy pointed out Harry's tent. In bed, unshaven and looking sick from fever, he blinked at the half-familiar face now tanned to a deep amber. 'My God, Barney!' he croaked. 'You're really here.'

That night he devoured his first solid hotel meal in weeks and introduced his young brother to everyone in the canteens. Long after midnight a shivering Barney peeled off his clothes, still reeking of dung and sweat, and curled up in a blanket with his bedroll for a pillow, grateful for the long underwear which his mother had so wisely forced him to pack.

'Remember what Shakespeare used to say?' he chuckled suddenly in the darkness. ' "To be or not to be . . . ?" ' Warmed by excitement, the rich food and several reunion tots, he had little doubt of the answer.

The Great Barnato had arrived in Kimberley.

3

———

BARNEY'S FIRST WEEKS were soured by disappointment, although he showed a smiling face in the saloons where he recognized quite a number of slippery customers from London's East End. These young *momzers* (Yiddish: bastards) relished his company at cards or billiards, but did not welcome business competition. Shrimplike little men, agile and rapacious, they screwed up their eyes when he offered to peddle their bead necklaces, printed calicoes, combs and pen-knives among the diggers and Dutch farmers. He soon gave up going to the evening auctions at Nutzom's Hotel in Dutoitspan where the 'Peruvians' would rub their blue-black jowls and rig bids for the junk that arrived in loads from the Cape. Newcomers like himself were quickly edged out.

The world's stock exchanges had recovered and diamond prices were rising, but there was little chance of entering this market with his meagre capital. He did not know a diamond from a glass eye, as David Harris informed him very bluntly when Barney offered his services. Harris's shipboard romance had developed as soon as the girl reappeared unexpectedly in Kimberley. That November they were married in the newly-built synagogue at the end of Currey Street. Harris continued to prosper as a broker. He retained a soft spot for Barney, and his wife always laid a plate for him on Friday nights, but they privately agreed that his taste for low company could damage their reputation. Harry, himself none too secure with Van Praagh, was equally unhelpful.

Prospects looked bleak all round. Barney soon discovered that his brother-in-law's cigars were unlikely to make his fortune. He sold one box to a digger who swore they were made of gunpowder and demanded his money back. Barney argued that they might have suffered superficially on the sea voyage and bribed him with a free box on condition that he spread the word among his pals that the Barnato 'Havanas' were the finest smokes in the whole of Africa. He did better with the Boers who hired him to unload sacks in the Market Square and make deliveries. A crowd of potential customers always gathered when he clowned around and juggled with eggs. Many farmers stopped to shake hands and greeted him with a cheery 'Good day, Barney,' but he lacked cash to invest in the merchandise they wished to take back to their farms. At best he could make a small grudged commission by handling goods in short supply for the fly members of the Nutzom ring. They gave up trying to cheat him when he knocked two of them unconscious after a dispute over his commission.

He literally punched his way into his first job when Payne's Travelling Circus pitched tents in Kimberley. One of the main attractions was a gigantic booth boxer, billed as the Champion of Angola. He offered to take on all comers for a gold medal plus the return of their shilling entrance fee. Barney badly wanted that medal and climbed into the ring, bowler hat, wire glasses and all, while the crowd jeered and waited for the execution. The challenger barely reached the navel of this big-moustached Portuguese but he was lighter on his feet and kept feinting, weaving and prodding away, repeatedly making the 'champion' miss. A hard blow to the solar plexus finally stretched him on the canvas. Barney acknowledged the storm of applause by juggling with his bowler, three beer bottles and some sponges from his corner. As an encore he gave them 'To be or not to be' while standing on his head.

He received the promised shilling but the gold medal was made of solid cardboard. However, Payne was so impressed by his performance that he fired the Portuguese and engaged him instead as boxer-cum-clown for five shillings a day and his keep. His engagement lasted only five days. 'The Greatest Conjurer in the World' had to return to peddling but soon found a novelty attraction. His ventriloquism helped him to create a 'talking' hen which he was lucky enough to exchange for several pairs of elastic braces. He bartered them in turn for some writing pads and pencils, a much better selling line than Mr Joel's deplorable cigars. He also wandered about the claims, humping tools like a menial or running errands for any digger who would give him a chance to resift the gravel after he had done with it. The gleanings were naturally meagre, but occasionally he found a few small stones which his kindly cousin bought from him at above-market prices.

Only a man of stout heart with an elephantine hide could have survived. He sold off several boxes of cigars for what they would fetch and parted at last with his silver chain. The works of his nickel watch went to a jeweller for five shillings, but he kept the case which might be useful for holding diamonds. It became his good-luck mascot. Every spare penny was invested in cheap trinkets, shaving brushes and practically anything else that could be quickly turned over.

Sharp competition honed his bargaining instinct, but he was also blessed with a natural jollity which bubbled within him and brimmed over. The Dutch farmers, the diggers and even his fellow-hucksters all reacted to this sparkle. He was never short of an audience to enjoy his jokes or join him in many a convivial evening at Ashwell's, a gaming room on the top floor of Dodd's Hotel in Stockdale Street. He would sometimes recite 'Dick Turpin's Ride from York' and other items from his repertoire for a hot meal, but could rarely afford the card games. One of his early friends was Ikey Sonnenberg who looked rather like a Jewish Abe Lincoln. He boasted of having fought in the Civil War and arrived in Kimberley with a white stetson and a German-American accent. He started by selling water at a shilling a bucket from a well outside his tent in Dutoitspan, but made far more running a faro table. He appreciated Barney's sense of humour and could also take a joke against himself. A man once owed him a large gambling debt and offered a regular supply of provisions in exchange for his I.O.U. Week after week he kept sending a leg of pork until Ikey agreed to cancel the debt.

'I want to be fed, not converted,' he objected.

Sonnenberg's huge feet seemed to be planted in every local enterprise. He sometimes placed a small deal Barney's way and hinted that he might make a good faro dealer, but nothing else tempted him once he had sifted and washed his first loads of earth, even when the stones rarely fetched more than a couple of pounds.

Barney teamed up finally with a hard-bitten diamond buyer of his own age. He was Louis Cohen from Liverpool who claimed to have had two years' schooling in Brussels and peppered his talk with fancy French words. Barney was even more impressed after Cohen confided that he was also interested in acting and had written part of a play. One night Barney formally proposed a partnership. He would go round the claims and look for diamonds which his more knowledgeable friend might profitably sell. Cohen agreed to put up £60 against Barney's £30 and the remainder of his cigars. The joint capital was deposited in the name of Cohen who trusted nobody.

Barney found a suitable base in Maloney's on the road to Dutoitspan where thirsty diggers used to stop for a dram. He talked the Irishman into erecting a nine foot by six lean-to corrugated shed adjoining his bar for the exorbitant rental of one guinea a day. 'Too much,' objected Cohen, but Barney overruled him. 'What does paying a guinea matter,' he argued, 'if you get back thirty shillings?' They set up a trestle table complete with scales, pliers and a magnifying glass, borrowing two stools which had to be returned to the bar every night. They slept together on a straw mattress under a single green blanket belonging to Cohen who regularly pulled it away. Barney, too much in awe of his senior partner to protest, always woke up frozen.

Mealies were cooked outside the hut, usually a little curry varied now and then with a few scraps of meat. For a rare Saturday night treat they might indulge in a sixpenny bowl of thick flyblown soup at one of the Indian eating houses. They undressed by the light of a candle stuck in a beer bottle, and Barney always saved fares by walking into town or out to the diggings. He trudged the claims, often ankle-deep in red sand and mud, but somehow remained immune from camp fever. His glasses protected him from the glare and dust storms until a smallish break in the skin round one eye finally resulted in dermatitis. He took some medicine which weakened him, but recklessly got up too soon to fight a big digger who had quarrelled with Cohen over some deal. He was soundly thrashed and put out of action for three days, after which he had to drag himself from his bed and resume operations.

Powdered with red dust from head to foot, he made his rounds from dawn onwards with a blanket round his shoulders, a black satchel for his scales and lens, and precious little cash in his wallet or 'poverty bag'. He had to compete with many other 'kopje-wallopers' who swarmed about the sorting tables, eager to examine the stones and snatch bargains from claim-holders often in need of cash to pay their labourers. To give himself more time for decisions, he took to polishing his glasses very slowly and rattled off jokes while looking for flaws. He was a tough bargainer and temperamentally suited to the bazaar-like haggling, but it became known that his scales were balanced fairly, and the diggers used to look forward to sharing his bottle of raw 'Cape Smoke' brandy together with the cigar that now ritually celebrated any deal with him.

For months on end he toiled harder than any native worker in the heat, glare and scorching wind, often gnawing a mealie-cob with a swig from his bottle to keep himself going until nightfall. He might return to the hut half a dozen times in a day to empty his satchel and impatiently chew cigarettes while Cohen rushed off to sell a stone and replenish their working capital. The guineas for Maloney were not easy to find. Money became even tighter when Cohen started to complain of insomnia and insisted on taking a hotel room. Irritable if the luck were not running for them, he also lacked the nerve to stand out for the right price even when a good stone chanced to come their way. He had by far the easier time sitting in the shady hut, but still resented every penny Barney spent on drink, partly because he had a poor head himself for spirits. They would rarely celebrate together and never again after one episode which almost wrecked their partnership.

Barney was at home in the canteens and 'spielers' but still thought wistfully of the backstage warmth of the East End halls. The few available women who came to Kimberley regulated their tariff by the law of supply and demand. Two prostitutes from Cape Town, a coloured girl and her white but less voluptuous comrade in arms, had established themselves in a couple of candle-lit rooms near the synagogue. Geographically this inhibited Barney who was greatly attracted to the splendid full-bosomed mulatto but hesitated to risk being spotted by Cousin Dave or some other respectable member of the congregation. However, he found the prospect impossible to resist and at last persuaded Cohen to join him in a stealthy expedition.

The ladies each demanded a fee of five pounds which the thrifty Cohen considered outrageous. Barney, however, thought it very fair and reasonable.

'Wait outside for me, Lou,' he called out cheerfully. 'Shan't be long.'

'Let's see the colour of your money, man,' the brown girl said briskly. Barney at once crackled his five pound note and Cohen departed angrily to station himself in the doorway of the synagogue a few yards along the street.

Soon afterwards he was astounded to see Barney leap nimbly from the window and come running towards him.

'Keep going,' he panted, 'until we get right away from here.' Cohen soon had to stop for breath. 'That wasn't worth it,' he protested. 'Not a fiver for ten minutes!'

'Fiver, *schmeiver*,' laughed Barney. 'I only showed her the note. I'd got a bit of tissue paper in me other 'and and gave her that instead when the candle went out.'

He could rarely induce Cohen to take risks. When competition grew too fierce in the nearby claims, it seemed to him that useful pickings might be found in the smaller remote diggings where few rivals ever ventured. But transport was a problem and it took weeks to win the confidence of these diggers, many of them suspicious Boers. He solved both difficulties in one enterprising stroke.

His sharp eyes had noted that a drunken buyer named Jack Saunders used to arrive almost asleep at Maloney's in a cart drawn by a yellow half-lame pony. But this was no ordinary animal. He knew his way about the claims and stopped at each one on his round without any prompting from Saunders who usually ended up too tipsy to hold the reins. When Barney heard that he was planning a trip to see his relatives in England, he offered to buy the pony and bridle for a mythical Boer friend who seemed 'interested'. He agreed to pay £27 10s. after a long and painful interview with Cohen who saw the point of the transaction but still considered it too speculative. Barney had his way in the end, and the ugly little animal not only saved his legs but, as anticipated, brought most of Saunders' goodwill and connection with him. Business improved but not fast enough to save the partnership. The pony had to be sold to pay their hotel bill and Maloney's rent. They split up finally with only £100 and the bare office 'equipment' to share after a year's work.

Barney refused to be discouraged. His stock-in-trade of experience would be valuable. He was one of the first men in Kimberley to use a watchmaker's glass, partly to help his poor sight, and could soon detect flaws almost as skilfully as buyers from the important houses of Paris and Amsterdam. He could now distinguish a pure white Bultfontein stone from the yellow ones of Dutoitspan and had learned to recognize the smoky, water-worn diamonds from the river diggings as easily as the oily markings on stones mined in De Beer's Old Rush. Within a few months his tweezers were automatically separating the good stones which he would hold up to the sun and squint at professionally like anyone who had served an apprenticeship with Porges or behind a Hatton Garden counter. Yet such knowledge was inevitably superficial. He still lacked the confident sense of market values which could only follow a long training under experts.

He already felt self-reliant enough to invest in a few small parcels but prudently hung about Cousin Dave's tent to watch him conduct his business. This resulted in the opportunity of a lifetime. Harris had left him one afternoon to look after things while he went off to see another broker. A digger strolled in with a diamond which he offered to sell for £150. Barney took out his glass and was certain of its high quality, but he had only a few pounds with him and had never bought on his cousin's behalf. He therefore played for time, chattering desperately and silently praying that Harris would arrive to rescue him. The digger became so impatient that Barney took alarm and feared he might go elsewhere. After some argument he offered £120 with a pounding heart, remarking that his 'partner' had the key of the safe containing the cheque-book.

'No cheque. I want cash,' growled the man, holding out a hand for his diamond.

'All right,' laughed Barney while he groped for a bottle under the counter. 'Let's have a drink on it. You come back at six for your money. I'll have to go to the bank.'

He sweated out the next few hours before Harris returned. If he approved, all would be well; otherwise, he might have to make himself scarce and rely on his cousin to repudiate the deal. Luckily, Harris confirmed that the diamond was worth at least £16 a carat. He gladly paid the digger the agreed price and sold the stone within a few days for £300, generously splitting the profit with his cousin.

The richer by £90 and delighted to have his own judgment so spectacularly confirmed, Barney now saw himself as a broker, although warned by Harris that similar deals might not be quite so easy without capital. Meantime he decided to celebrate his coup with a little of the high life which his good fortune surely deserved. A local hotel had started weekly dances for mining officials and the more prominent merchants with their ladies. To keep out the rougher elements, evening dress was made obligatory, but there was no difficulty in raiding Harry's props for a tail coat and trousers, complete with a concertina opera hat. The coat had been made for a narrower torso, and his brother's legs were longer than his own, but his experience of selling old clothes to unwary customers in Petticoat Lane was very handy. He pinned and tacked with a dexterity that would have gladdened his father's heart.

With his hair freshly pomaded and parted down the middle like the stage door johnnies he remembered so well, he entered the ballroom and greeted all and sundry with his usual bonhomie, although suffering grievously from the sheet of armour across his broad chest. Within an hour he strode into the London Hotel where Harry was helping out behind the bar. He climbed on a stool and ripped his boiled shirt open in disgust. 'Them geezers wouldn't have nothing to do with me after I'd 'ad a couple of goes round the floor,' he complained.

'Well, you can't dance, can you?' his brother reminded him.

'No, but I was learning, wasn't I?' Barney said bitterly.

He moved into the shack which Harry had bought cheaply during the slump. In the backyard they put up a small annexe for Barney to sleep in and soon decided to go into business together. Harry had limited prospects with Van Praagh, and his buying experience would be an asset. By pooling his savings with Barney's windfall their combined capital totted up to little over £200. Early in 1875 they proudly nailed a sign over the door to announce that 'Barnato Brothers, Dealers in Diamonds and Brokers in Mining Property' were open for business.

People smiled at the pretentiousness of this insignificant 'kopje-walloper' and his ex-conjurer brother, but Barney was convinced that more profits could be made from digging a claim of their own or acting as middlemen than by handling the few stones that came their way. Trade was stagnant at first on all fronts. The German and French buyers could offer better prices and spot cash to the diggers who queued outside their grilled windows in Commissioner Street. Many had formed syndicates when it was made legal for any individual company to own up to ten claims. The whole financial structure had changed dramatically since the first days when no one was allowed more than a single claim of thirty-one square feet, 'ten times the size of your grave', as the diggers used to say. Mining Boards, originally formed to stop claim-jumping, were now busily dealing with damage from rock falls and the frequent flooding of adjacent, badly-operated diggings. Many hard-up owners were going down too fast or too deeply for safety.

If the single claim-owner was doomed, the prospects of the small 'kopje-walloper' looked no brighter. A very different class of brokers took their supercilious ease in the newly-opened Kimberley Club. Some wore velvet jackets and white buckskin breeches with spurs on their highly-polished riding boots. They had fine leather courier bags dangling from the saddle when they rode out to their claims or occasionally condescended to buy at the sorting tables. Several were building themselves wood frame houses and even thinking of bricks. Trees were being planted and the pot-holes filled at the insistence of storekeepers who now displayed imported luxury goods.

A new élite of wealth and influence, including men of breeding like Rhodes, Rudd and their friends, formed a social nucleus with no use for the 'Whitechapel' pedlars and gamblers. The German colony was equally exclusive. They had their own Mess and were all excellent linguists with a reputation for clinical efficiency. They seemed to live only for business and sauerkraut. Apart from Wernher, whose shrewd buying more than justified the faith of Jules Porges, there were pioneer mine-owners like the Lilienfelds and Mosenthals, while Hermann Eckstein, a fastidious connoisseur of stones, skilfully managed a group of claims at Bultfontein.

Alfred Beit, another German Jew, arrived in 1875 as buyer for his cousins, the Daniel Lippert firm of Amsterdam and Port Elizabeth. He was then twenty-two, a week younger than Rhodes, but with a sound apprenticeship behind him. A plumpish man, even smaller than Barney, he looked unimpressive with his walrus eyes and abnormally large head, but nobody on Main Street had a keener diamond sense. He soon discovered that the 'kopje-wallopers' and most town brokers tended to cheat the diggers either through cupidity or plain ignorance. By accurately assessing a stone and allowing a reasonable margin of profit, he could still offer very fair prices. Consequently, he won the finest stones and the diggers' goodwill. They would make a practice of drawing silver from him in exchange for notes to pay their hired help. For this purpose Beit kept a large bag of silver on his counter, inviting customers to help themselves and leave the change if he happened to be out.

Such trust seemed like quixotic folly to Joseph B. Robinson, a quite different stamp of pioneer. Born in the Karoo, he had nursed an almost pathological hatred for coloureds ever since a mob had attacked his family home. He was no more friendly towards any white man or woman who stood in his path. Deaf, cantankerous and grasping, he was known as 'The Buccaneer' in the diggings because of his complete lack of scruple in business. 'He has a tombstone on his soul,' declared one hard-pressed miner who had pleaded for a little latitude. Lionel Phillips echoed that view when he went to work for him as a diamond sorter. The son of a City of London merchant, Phillips was a Jew who, like David Harris, proved that integrity was possible even in the Fields, but Robinson was a hard master. Sour and yellow-faced, he used to stand outside his office and leer at every girl who passed, rarely missing a chance to profit by anyone's misfortune whether man, woman or child. He never entered a bar without first making sure he would not have to play host. He liked to sit by himself, silent and glowering, nursing his glass while his suspicious frosty eyes watched every movement under a pith helmet.

As J. G. Lockhart, Rhodes's biographer, has pointed out, 'men might distrust Barnato, but at least they laughed at him and drank with him.' He would cut corners at times, but the diggers felt more at ease with him than Robinson or the high-stooled and impersonal German clerks on Commissioner Street. Barnato was one of them, free alike with his fists and his drinks; rough-tongued undoubtedly, but nobody genuinely down on his luck ever had to ask twice. This was not always easy since Harry kept an iron grasp on the exchequer and constantly reminded his brother to save farthings if they were ever to buy a claim of their own. He was growing so niggardly that Barney was forced to pay for his drinks and cigarettes by playing billiards. Even this became difficult as Harry often stood by to collect any winnings.

Nothing would ever give Barney more delight than the very first cheque made out to Barnato Brothers for a sizeable stone which he had bought at Bultfontein. In sheer ecstasy he snatched it from Harry's hand and ran up and down the street, waving it in triumph. 'We've got a checker,' he yelled. 'A real checker.'

Saturday became their best day of business as the banks closed early and they could then pay for stones by cheque, sell them in the afternoon and cover the outlay by the time the banks reopened on Monday morning. This did not make them too popular with some of their more devout co-religionists who shut their offices on the Sabbath, but many in early Kimberley were capable of far worse.

To celebrate the merry festival of Chanukah, traditionally marked by the kindling of lights to commemorate the victories of Judas Maccabeus over the Syrians, David Harris and his wife once gave an elaborate dinner party. All their best cutlery was on display and Barney happened to see one of the guests slip a heavy silver spoon into his boot. He said nothing but volunteered to do some conjuring when the company adjourned for a sing-song after dinner. He picked up a soup spoon and, with Harry's assistance, made it disappear. He then ordered a servant to 'examine the boot of that gentleman in the corner'. The 'sleight of hand' brought loud applause when the spoon miraculously reappeared. Barney warned the culprit off with some private, well-chosen words but charitably withheld the truth from David Harris to spare his feelings.

Barnato Brothers had a difficult first year which synchronized with yet another slump in world trade and a crippling effect on the price per carat. Although Kimberley was digging out £50,000 a week in diamonds, many of the smaller claims scarcely paid their way. Working costs rose as the yellow earth slowly exhausted itself. Deeper digging involved expensive machinery, but the banks were unsympathetic towards the diggers on whom 'kopje-wallopers' like Harry and Barney mainly depended. They also refused overdrafts to the smaller brokers, some of whom were thrown out of hotels when they could not pay their bills. Others, like Louis Cohen, closed their offices and went off north to prospect for gold newly-discovered outside Lydenburg in the Transvaal.

Local bankers were far more accommodating to the syndicates which had mushroomed when the ten-claim limit was abolished. Multiple ownership soon led to the formation of Joint Stock Companies, particularly if backed by European diamond houses. Men like F. S. Philipson-Stow had arrived from England to set up the leading legal practice in Kimberley. He bought several useful claims for his well-breeched clients and himself.

Barney became aware of more engineers and geologists poking around the claims. A mining expert named Gardner F. Williams arrived from Michigan to make surveys for magnates like the Rothschilds, who had recently financed Britain's purchase of Suez Canal shares with their £4m loan and were taking a livelier interest in Africa's mineral potential. Hans Sauer, a big jovial man whom Rhodes called 'my genial ruffian', combined a medical practice with mineralogy, while Dr Atherstone from Grahamstown was actively confirming his theory that the diamonds were the product of extinct volcanoes formed under tremendous pressure on the ocean bed. If this was so, more and richer diamondiferous deposits must surely be found in the schist beneath the yellow ground.

The early crude cradles and buckets were slowly being supplemented by steam-powered pumps from England which the less rich diggers had to hire at high prices. The old mules and cars were replaced by a vast cobweb of steel ropes for lowering and raising the buckets by windlasses from chasms in which the miners tried to blast the rocklike blue ground and often broke their picks. The wires made a whining devil's symphony punctuated by the roar of buckets tipping their contents at the surface in a cloud of smouldering dust. Huge pits, looking rather like great waffle-irons, were now being shored by timber, but accidents from drowning or cave-ins were still frequent. More of the smaller claim-owners were selling out, unable to afford the shafts and tunnels needed for deeper digging.

Barnato Brothers not only held fast during this first crisis year but even managed to add to their capital. The diggers who grimly hung on preferred to deal with them rather than the standoffish Germans behind their grilles. Barney did not wait for the miners to come into town. Instead, working his way round the claims, he often picked up bargains. Moreover, he developed an up-to-date, almost hour by hour, intelligence service about the output in each sector until he knew every turn and twist of the reef like his own hand. He was quite convinced that Atherstone was right about those former volcanoes. The obstinate schist was not bedrock and might be immeasurably richer in diamonds than the alluvial yellow top soil which was only an oxidized form of the blue ground. It seemed to him that the obvious course was to buy the best potential claims at a reasonable price, but that demanded capital which 'kopje-walloping' alone could not provide.

With Harry's grip on their savings, Barney forced himself to economize. He also supplemented his earnings from the claims by dealing in any and every kind of merchandise. In later years he could justly boast that 'there is nothing this country produces I have not traded in, from diamonds and gold, right away through wool, feathers and mealies, to garden vegetables. I have always found that I was as good a hand at buying and selling as most people I came across, and my experiences with the *slimme* (Cape Dutch: sharpish) farmers in the Kimberley market were sometimes very queer; but they soon found that any man who tried on a game with me, or whose goods were not up to sample, had a bad day sooner or later.'

His constitution helped to keep him miraculously free of illness. At first light every morning he would be seen swinging his Indian clubs outside the wooden shack. He never missed his exercises even when the temperature fell below zero and baboons used to creep into town for shelter. After cracking the ice in a frozen bucket he would pour the contents over his head and begin a vigorous session of shadow-boxing. Nicknamed 'Pug', he was soon acclaimed unofficial champion of the diggings and took on all comers for a stake of a pound or two in Grussendorf's Canteen or the London Hotel in Stockdale Street in which Harry had bought an interest. The so-called hotel was no luxury establishment but its bar was a popular rendezvous for diggers and small brokers as well as many less reputable characters.

In the early months of 1876, Harry overheard a whisper that two brothers named Kerr were anxious to sell their four adjoining claims in the Kimberley ('New Rush') sector. After much haggling they agreed to accept £3,000 which all but emptied the Barnato coffers, but Barney had absolutely no doubt that this location, sited almost in the middle or 'tube' of the mine, must be rich in diamonds if Atherstone's theory about the funnel vents of old volcanoes proved sound.

While others hesitated or made tentative moves, he convinced Harry that the blue ground held the key. Their one hope was to turn it before the richer syndicates moved in, but only immediate results would justify the gamble. After buying out the Kerrs their remaining capital was so ludicrously small that even a minor cave-in could wipe them out overnight. There would be no margin for costly pumping gear or the faintest chance of bank loans if they failed to pay their workers or meet the heavy charges imposed by the Mining Board for water and repairs.

'The little prancer,' as Rhodes contemptuously called Barney years before they met, had staked everything on a rapid turnover. His workers penetrated the igneous blue rock but at first found only a few stones of insignificant value. He drove himself and his crews still harder, encouraging or sometimes bribing them to take risks, and always ready to take off his own coat and wield a pick beside them. If a wagon wheel stuck in the mud, he helped to jack it up, joking, cursing and generating an excitement which made his men work twice as hard as anyone else's.

Whenever Harry reported despondently on their sortings or seemed fairly satisfied with a small haul of stones, he refused to compromise. 'Since I was certain that the diamonds came from below, it followed that there must be more lower down,' he said afterwards. 'If not in the blue, then on the other side of it. I determined to go on until it broke me. And I was right; it didn't break me. We soon found that the blue itself was the true home of the diamond. We found in it, as I expected, more and better diamonds than all the yellow contained . . .'

The loads began to disclose stones of ten, fifteen and twenty-five carats. In one single bumper week they actually recovered the whole of their original investment. Barney would boast that he had picked up thirty good stones in the very first hour's digging and sold them for a round £10,000—'about half their real worth, as I found out later.' The claims were soon yielding £2,000 a week, altogether some £90,000 of diamonds by the end of their first year, and still without sign that this Aladdin's Cave was anywhere near exhaustion. Several syndicates naturally waved cheque-books to buy them out or offered to take shares. Harry was tempted to sell for what seemed a fortune to him, but Barney overruled him. He was equally firm against forming any partnership with the German and Dutch brokers who now offered to send their output to Europe. They would mine *and* sell their own diamonds, he insisted, while building up capital reserves to buy more claims in the blue earth that had so emphatically fulfilled its promise.

Rhodes had not been idle. Like Barnato he was convinced that the blue rather than the yellow ground would prove lastingly diamondiferous. He also believed that by buying up whole blocks of adjoining claims he would be able to cut costs, reduce working risks and boost output. As a guiding line it was sound and clear-cut, but Rhodes's major miscalculation, partly due to Rudd's super-cautiousness, was to buy extensively into the old De Beer mine rather than the higher-priced Kimberley sites. In electing for what turned out to be quantity rather than quality, he was already exhibiting a power complex that had begun to blind him to routine practicalities. Barnato was sifting a crop of diamonds from an area no larger than a house, and he stuck to his theory that well-sited mines, like the best vineyards, could not be judged by size alone. Rhodes's half-formed dreams of expansion led him to covet the infinitely more alluring fourteen acres of neighbouring De Beers.

Rhodes's grail, painted vividly in red, white and blue, had already beckoned him clear across the Dark Continent to the sparkling waters of the Mediterranean. But it would be prudent to make money quickly and try to gain control of South Africa's most valuable export. In September 1877, as soon as he had made his first substantial purchases in the De Beers sector, he drew up a Will appointing the Colonial Secretary as one of his executors. His estate would help establish a Secret Society, 'the true aim and object whereof shall be the extension of British rule throughout the world ... and especially the occupation by British settlers of the entire Continent of Africa.' That same year, Sir Theophilus Shepstone, Secretary for Native Affairs in Natal, rode into Pretoria with a few policemen and Civil Servants (including Rider Haggard) and calmly annexed the Transvaal despite the Queen's earlier most solemn proclamation pledging its sovereignty.

President Burgers had no heart to fight but failed to convince his more militant countrymen. Their spokesman was Kruger, now senior member for Rustenburg, who reminded him bitterly of the twenty-sixth chapter of Leviticus: '*Ye shall sow your seed in vain, for your enemies shall eat it.*' Meantime he thoughtfully sucked his maimed thumb, the top of which he had cut off with his own knife after his rifle accidentally exploded during a rhino hunt.

A rough shrewd man, Kruger typified rugged obstinacy from his grizzled mane to a massive nose that split his tiny, pouched and inflamed eyes. He had gorilla arms and puffed morosely on a long-stemmed pipe while his elbow rested on the fat Dutch Bible which he invoked to denounce his enemies in and out of the beleaguered Republic. He always spoke Afrikaans except at prayer when he favoured the Almighty with his confidences in High Dutch. He brooded constantly on the avarice of the British and their cynical, indeed criminal, folly in selling arms to the natives, but his more immediate target was to take over from Burgers.

When gold was found at Pilgrim's Rest, Kruger and his fellow-deputies in the Volkstaad became intoxicated with visions of a rich harvest from licences. But the 'Uitlanders' (foreigners or, more literally and offensively, outsiders) were soon discouraged by the government ban on gold exports and other tiresome restrictions. As soon as the seams started to give out, only a minority could afford to replace old machinery or prospect elsewhere. Most of them moved off, cursing their own stupidity in selling diamond claims for the lure of fool's gold.

The Barnatos had eagerly bought shares in Pilgrim's Rest but did not lament their losses. Barney used often to joke that it had turned out one of his finest investments because the Kerrs were among the many claim-owners who had hastily abandoned Kimberley to go panning for gold up in the Transvaal. He failed completely to see the widening gulf between British and Afrikaner. With money at last jingling in his pocket, he was further insulated by his indifference to history. He saw nothing but goodwill and prosperity in his Boer neighbours and could not identify them with the frustrated burghers of Pretoria in the north.

When he rode out across the veld to the Afrikaner villages, he saw only a happy and dreamlike land basking in Kimberley's good fortune. The men came to market with wagons crammed to the tilt and easily sold all they grew. They had remained his friends from the first days, and now he was able to repay many past kindnesses. He would fill his saddle-bag with sweets for the children and trinkets for their mothers. Blond, blue-eyed and sturdy of shoulder, he could almost pass for one of them. They welcomed his crackling good humour and gave him no suspicion of muttering among themselves at the double-tongued Cape politicians who had bought off the Free State and broken faith with the Transvaal. Barney knew nothing of this as he danced merrily with their blushing, half-protesting wives and daughters and bear-hugged any of the big-built youths who clumsily tried to wrestle him to the ground. He sat back in their orchards, eating a peach or going out to admire a matching span of red long-horned oxen.

He hated to miss a birth or a wedding party in the hospitable farmhouses, relishing their sweet Mossel wine with the rich cakes and thick steaming coffee. Once he had impulsively invited a Dopper pastor and his lady to be his guests at the forthcoming Barmitzvah of a friend's son in Dutoitspan. The good *vrou* declined with a shudder. 'No, no, I couldn't bear to see it. It's too cruel.'

His former landlord, Maloney, was also a trifle hazy about Jewish observances. They met one evening as Barney was hurrying into the synagogue in Currey Street. 'What's all that wailing about?' asked the Irishman. 'It's the Yom Kippur service,' Barney explained. 'Holy Jaysus, what a waste of toime! Nobody up there will understand a word at all, at all.'

Even when his claims were bringing in a steady £2,000 a week or more, Barney still boxed at the back of canteens with anyone ready to go three rounds, greeting all his digger pals with the ritual, 'What yer goin' to 'ave, guv?' He always had a sovereign or two for somebody down on his luck, especially those who had seen him through the lean times.

He had left his little cabin in Harry's backyard to move into the hardly more luxurious shack of his friend, Leo Lowenthal, a Scottish Jew who had also prospered as a diamond merchant and shared his sporty tastes. They sparred together every morning, but horse-racing was their great passion. Together they formed a Turf Club for twice-weekly racing, with Barney often putting up the prize money. Before his pink smiling face had become part of the Kimberley scene, three genial strangers who 'happened' to have a pack of cards casually invited him to make a fourth in the rough racecourse bar. To kill an hour before the first race, he agreed to play and duly separated them from all their cash. He then handed, each of them a sovereign. 'Take this for a drink, boys,' he said cheerfully, 'but don't ever mark Barney Barnato down for a mug again.'

Later that afternoon he refreshed himself from a lemonade stall and asked the woman what she expected to make in a day. 'Ten pounds, if I'm lucky,' she told him. 'I'll give you twenty for the stock and a fiver for yourself,' Barney said promptly, unable to resist a chance of practising his old Petticoat Lane patter once more. It went down so well that he had sold out within half an hour.

But it was far more difficult to back winners. Punters had to contend with doping, 'ringers', crooked jockeys and heavily-rigged odds on horses that were sometimes led a couple of hundred miles across country in those pre-railway days. Barney became so irritated by his own repeated losses that he once snatched up a pair of binoculars, borrowed a satchel and turned bookmaker. That day he cleared nearly £400. A week later he reappeared in a loud checked suit with a florid buttonhole and put up a board proclaiming himself 'The Leviathan'.

'You ought to be ashamed of yourself,' Lowenthal reproached him. 'Why?' shrugged Barney. 'D'ye think I'm going on punting just to lose my *gelt* (Yiddish: money), like all the other steamers?' He only gave up when rival bookies complained that nearly all the diggers were rushing to place their bets with him.

Although his claims were spawning more diamonds than mealies on a cob, he still enjoyed gambling for small stakes. His card sense was impeccable even when he had drunk everyone else under the table. With a napoleonic gift for being able to catnap, he would get up fully refreshed after an hour or so. He could also sleep on a hard floor for fifteen hours at a stretch, snoring loudly and completely oblivious to all noise around him.

Billed to play Fagin in a sketch at the Lanyon Theatre near the Central Hotel for a benefit smoking concert, he disappeared until just before curtain-rise when he was found in a deep drunken slumber with an old sack for a pillow. As there was no understudy someone proposed cancelling the sketch, but Barney would not hear of it. He plunged his head in a bucket and then downed a pint of rum and hot water, after which he went straight on stage without missing a cue. It was such an excellent performance that some of the synagogue elders objected afterwards that his wheedling interpretation was too realistic and might arouse anti-Semitism. He never appeared again in that rôle and soon eliminated all other Jewish caricatures from his repertoire.

He had become a leading figure in the local dramatic society within a few months of his arrival in Kimberley. He helped Lou Cohen and other volunteers to knock up a rough stage in a hostelry at Dutoitspan, shifting scenery and doubling as carpenter and wardrobe master when there was no part for him. During his years as a 'kopje-walloper' and market porter he had little time to rehearse, and opportunities for acting became rarer still when professional companies began to arrive.

His new-found wealth gave him both the leisure and the funds to realize ambitions which had never left him. Audiences here were less critical and welcomed full-blooded performances by a popular local figure who did not expect payment and even bought the whole house for gala benefits. He would implore touring managers to give him a small part, rightly assuring them that all his digger friends and many of the Boer community would pay to see him.

For a performance in aid of the Kimberley Hospital he ambitiously attempted *Othello*, promising to double the house takings from his own pocket. With his short legs and Whitechapel jauntiness it was hardly ideal casting for the noble Moor, and the audience did not help much. When he declaimed, 'Unhappy that I am black,' someone called out, 'Then go and wash your face, Barney.' In the second row sat Benny Hart, a diamond-broker member of the dramatic society, who suffered from professional jealousy. He could not resist guying him during a tense scene with Iago. Half-way through his speech, Barney stopped abruptly and advanced to the footlights. 'Wait until I'm through with this lot, Benny, and I'll make you laugh the other side of your big *pisk* (Yiddish: mouth).' When Hart refused to take the warning seriously, he vaulted into the stalls, gave him a heavy blow on the jaw and calmly resumed. He drew rounds of sympathetic applause but his florid style was far happier in Lyceum melodrama. His portrayal of Matthias in *The Bells* was a splendid essay in eye-rolling bravura, although some purists might have objected to his recital of lines like ' 'Ow the dawgs 'owl.'

His technique was better suited to smoking concerts in the Red Light saloon where he rendered 'Dick Turpin's Ride from York' in a raucous baritone but with ample 'expression'. The pianist, a cadaverous individual with a chronic thirst, thumped hard but Barney's bellowing usually won. He became such a favourite that producers began to find him rather a problem. When a charity show was being arranged for synagogue funds, he offered to give a couple of songs but the promoters feared the audience might join in all the choruses, demand encores and wreck the whole programme. He agreed reluctantly to act as an usher instead, but insisted on wearing his new dress clothes, the very first suit he had had made to measure.

A digger staggered in rather late after a tour of the saloons. Barney knew him well from his 'kopje-walloping' days but the man failed to recognize him in his finery. To prevent a disturbance, Barney steered him firmly into the back row of the pit.

'I've got a sheat in L,' protested the drunk.

'Sorry, all seats to hell taken,' Barney said soothingly.

The man took off his coat and bunched his fists, but Barney held him off. 'Don't you know me?' he laughed. 'It's your old mate.'

A glazed light began to dawn, but suspicion lingered. 'Whash ye doin' 'ere?'

'I'm an usher now,' explained Barney.

'Poor bugger,' said the digger with deep feeling. 'Here's a quid for ye. I'm sho shorry, sho shorry.' He then fell into his seat and snored rhythmically until 'God Save the Queen'.

Barney continued to support the local dramatic society and soon became aware of an attractive young actress, Fanny Bees, who performed in her spare time when she was not working as a barmaid. She was a striking brunette with a flawless olive skin and jet-black hair. She stood a head taller than Barney and was six years younger. Her family was of Huguenot descent and hailed from Simonstown, the naval base, where the father had struggled along as a tailor before deciding to try his luck in the dry diggings in the late 'sixties. He packed his wife and eight young children into three lumbering ox-wagons which took some months to reach Dutoitspan. They had to live rough, eating their daily meal round a camp fire. Their first home in Bultfontein was a canvas double tent.

John Bees failed to make his fortune but he was a God-fearing man of missionary stock and thought little of this hard-drinking and perky young Jew as a suitor for his daughter. The acquaintance had ripened while Fanny acted as prompter at rehearsals. She would tease Barney about his accent and dropped aitches but he could make her laugh and cry when he talked about life in Cobb's Court and his early disappointments on the East End halls. She used to recall afterwards that his kindness, particularly towards children, captivated her as much as his bubbling sense of fun. (After his death she once remarked to Tennyson Cole, the portrait painter, 'People thought my husband ugly, but to me he always seemed a very handsome man with a smile that lit up the darkest room.')

Barney often used to declare that they went through a civil ceremony in 1877 but kept it secret from his parents until Fanny had been solemnly converted to his faith. Harry Raymond, Barney's first biographer, accepted it without question and others have followed suit. It is more likely that the union was blessed by a rabbi who may not have gone too deeply into the civil formalities. At that time in South Africa, marriages between Jews and Gentiles were sternly discouraged by the authorities who prohibited any public announcement for two years at least.

The position was only regularized several years later. At their registry office marriage solemnized in London in November 1892, the bride was described as 'Fanny Bees, Spinster' and Barney as a bachelor.

4

HAVING SET UP HOUSE with Fanny in the mid-seventies, Barney did all possible to persuade his parents to leave Spitalfields for a comfortable villa in Cape Town. He and Harry had sent them ample funds on which to retire but they discovered all kinds of ingenious excuses to remain in the East End. Barney found it almost as difficult to convince his sister, Kate Joel, that Kimberley offered splendid prospects to her three sons whom he promised to take into his business and treat as his own. She argued that Jack, her first-born, was needed by her ailing husband to help in The King of Prussia, while Solly, the youngest, was scarcely past Barmitzvah age. She agreed instead to send out her fifteen-year-old, Woolf, who was rather frail and might benefit from the South African sunshine. Had she known about the occasional epidemics of smallpox or the still-high incidence of camp fever, she might not have been tempted by all the diamonds in 'The Big Hole'.

Woolf Joel thrived almost from his first day in the firm of Barnato Brothers. He lived in his uncle's cramped wooden bungalow of three rooms and kitchen with a small yard fenced in by corrugated iron. Fanny mothered him and made sure that he did not drift to the saloons with Barney, although he never missed an opening night at the theatre. He was a quiet and well-mannered youth with a good head for figures. After leaving board school, he had soon shown initiative by opening a small tobacconist shop off the Whitechapel Road, but his partner, an older boy, was lazy and the booth had closed down for lack of capital. There was cash in plenty in his uncles' firm and limitless opportunities for expansion, as Barney was steadily buying up more claims adjacent to his original four.

He made Woolf learn all about diamonds, from gravel sifting to the final marketing, and encouraged him to study the geologists' reports which he rarely had the patience to read for himself. Now that Harry was spending more time in his hotel and kept threatening to go back to Europe and enjoy his money in London or, preferably, on the Riviera, Woolf soon began to act as Barney's deputy. He took naturally to office routine, answered letters promptly and held the fort when Barney failed to keep appointments. Only eleven years separated him from his uncle, and they were soon on almost brotherly terms of affection although completely antithetic in temperament.

Woolf revelled in paper work which Barney respected but found irksome. He collected and read books, especially history, while his uncle rarely opened a newspaper or glanced at anything in print except to memorize a dramatic part. When Barney flew into rages or became over-exuberant, his nephew remained impassive, but he was so quick, clever and ready with his columns of figures that many a hasty step was avoided. Soon his working life had fallen into a pattern which it was to maintain for the rest of his career. Barney was the thrusting, huckstering raider, almost a one-man guerrilla force, but Woolf knew when and how to bring up the cash reserves. He developed an acute perception of high finance, while Barney was still in the abacus stage and over-inclined to rely on his memory.

Woolf's letters home brimmed with confidence. Uncle Barney was paying him the truly immense salary of £50 a week, plus some generous slices of commission when deals turned out well. His one extravagance was clothes which were exquisitely cut from the finest imported English cloth. Slenderly graceful, with dark curly hair set off by his ivory skin, he constantly stroked a small silky moustache. Women found his Byronic looks attractive, but the languid manner was no pose. He was subject to bouts of melancholia and spent many evenings alone in his room with a book. However, he circulated gracefully enough at Fanny's occasional dinner-parties. These bored Barney unless he could talk shop across the table or persuade his guests to adjourn for a sing-song while Fanny tinkled the piano keys. Barney liked to conduct his social and business affairs in his office over a bottle or, even more congenially, in the backroom of some saloon where proceedings would usually be rounded off by an all-night game of poker.

He had maintained his habit of rising at dawn, vigorously swinging his clubs before riding out to the claims to see that everything was shipshape. Fanny soon reconciled herself to supervising breakfast for half a dozen engineers and diamond buyers over whom Barney presided or, rather, catapulted. He could never stay long in his chair and whizzed about the room, picking up bits of food as he went, mumbling asides to Woolf who tried to compose cohesive notes from the gabbled telegraphese.

Fanny stoically accepted his gambling, the snatched meals at odd hours and his preoccupation with diamonds seven days a week. On the rare evenings he spent at home, he would often lie on a sofa for hours on end, staring into space while he brooded on his schemes. She forgave much for the gentleness he reserved for her alone; above all, his solicitude for her brothers and sisters whom he helped to start in life. One sister who showed a talent for the stage was sent to England at his expense to study music and drama with the best teachers. She became well known as an operatic singer and had a successful career as a performer of comic opera in Europe and the United States under her stage name, Alice Holbrook. During her early days while she was still playing small parts, Barney made her a regular allowance.

Fanny ran her household with brisk efficiency and rarely emerged except to go to the theatre or visit the poor with hampers of food and clothing. She read much and played the piano but her real preoccupation was a hoard of trinkets to which she added constantly. Only Barney and her closest friends were privileged to see the jewels, charms, lockets and tiny watches in her collection. In spite of her soft voice and calm self-effacement, she could be stubborn. To wean Barney from his absorption in money, she persuaded him to stand for the municipal council although he protested lack of time and his dislike of making speeches. Fanny guessed that he was more troubled by his inner sense of inferiority and a terror of making himself ridiculous among men who had book learning and could express themselves fluently. With much patience she and Woolf helped him write his letters and corrected the spelling. Too restless to read anything himself, he would listen attentively when Woolf quoted some interesting passage from a book. His actor's ear picked up phrases and expressions which gradually helped him to formulate complete sentences instead of the staccato bursts that normally passed for conversation. Fanny could not, however, have won her point without appealing to his genuine concern for the welfare of the diggers and small tradesmen. It was mainly through his drive and contempt for red tape that he was able to persuade Sir Charles Warren, Administrator of Griqualand West, to begin constructing the long-overdue water-works.

His election to the Council was hotly opposed by the German set who had always resented his competitive sales methods. One of them, probably Martin Lilienfeld, sniggered that 'if a pretty girl came to Kimberley, Robinson would try to shear her, Beit would float her, and Barnato would have her gold teeth'. But even his enemies had to admit that, once he had given his word, Barney always kept it. He was almost ludicrously finicky in demanding that the smallest business detail should be written down (so long as he did not have to do it himself!). Still only half-literate, his simple-minded reverence for contracts produced a gem long before it was added apocryphally to the Goldwyn collection. 'A verbal agreement,' he once assured Woolf Joel, 'is not worth the paper it's written on.'

He adopted a wary business neutrality towards the influential Germans but could not resist baiting the snobbish Kimberley clubmen or Rhodes's bachelor disciples who looked down their noses at him. He was always sure of an audience in the saloons when, with a few drinks under his belt, he reproduced Rhodes's jerky movements and recited a Latin-Yiddish mishmash in falsetto. But Alfred Beit was easily his star turn. With a bowler hat crammed down over his ears, he waltzed around an imaginary tall partner, trying to keep in step and finally falling over his own feet. The diggers roared, but the British set greeted this buffoonery with frozen smiles.

Barney underrated them at first. He dismissed Rhodes as an

effeminate dilettante from Oxford who had only eme~~rged from~~
obscurity by pumping out other men's flooded claims. ~~He was~~
nonetheless happy to buy diamonds from the De Beers Company
and in time became one of their best customers. Their dealings
were always correct but rarely without a jarring personal note on
both sides. Barney soon preferred to leave this side of the business
to Woolf. His firm's holdings in the Kimberley Mine had prospered to a degree which made these snobbish Englishmen seem to
him quite insignificant, despite the airs they gave themselves.

Barnato Brothers had extracted over £200,000 in diamonds
from the Kerr diggings and these were still far from exhausted.
Barney was now rich and had long taken over the driving seat
from Harry who did not appear to resent being referred to as
'Barney Barnato's brother'. Both, however, were linked by rumour
with Illicit Diamond Buying or peddling stones smuggled out of
the mines. Less fortunate diggers envied the Barnatos and whispered that their output was too phenomenal to be entirely legiti-
mate. It was hinted that they had bought their first claims from
the proceeds of 'I.D.B.' and were merely using them as a cover for
continued operations. The very fact that they sold all their own
diamonds, usually of far-above average size and quality, was
another ground for suspicion.

It was reinforced when Harry took over the London Hotel, one
of several rendezvous favoured by receivers of 'illicits'. No charge
was ever laid against him although detectives or informers
constantly prowled the bars and card-rooms. However, the
rumours revived after the brothers bought a claim for £10,000
from a Polish Jew who was subsequently picked up for receiving
stolen diamonds and sent to the Breakwater for five years. There
was no evidence that he had maintained any connection with the
Barnatos, but the episode was seized upon by their enemies.
Neighbours hinted that half-tipsy Basutos in dingy blankets
appeared at Barney's house at dead of night, whispering '*mooi klip
baas*' ('fine stone, master') and departing with bottles of Cape
Smoke.

Since this smear campaign was never pursued in the open, the
brothers were powerless to defend themselves. They were not of
sensitive fibre, but the creeping vilification hurt them. 'How many

times in the years from '76,' Barney confessed later, 'was I inclined, almost determined, to quit Kimberley and South Africa for ever! I was making a pile and gathering power but no one knew, or ever can know, how hard I worked for it all. If I have made millions I have worked for them as few men ever can have worked. But I have been blackguarded by men who could neither gain nor work!'

His brother, like practically every other hotel and saloon-keeper in town, resigned himself to police raids. It was impossible to stop diamonds being passed across tables or examined at the bar when diggers needed spot cash. One broker in Madame Delatée's French Café hastily dropped a stone into his tankard just as 'Baas' Fox, the chief diamond detective, burst in. Fox was a bandy-legged individual with a ginger moustache and ferrety green eyes that could make even an innocent man feel uncomfortable. He became Kimberley's implacable 'Javert' and had a notoriously sadistic streak. His amiable custom was to handcuff two or three prisoners and parade them slowly past the veranda of the Kimberley Club as a warning to members that he had his eye on them all and was not taken in by their cigars or aristocratic manners. He would have shown Harry and Barney no mercy had he been able to bring charges against them. He did most of his social drinking in the London Hotel, although Harry was never quite sure whether or not this was intended as a tribute to his honesty. It was certainly no help to trade, as Fox could thin out a bar almost as quickly as 'The Buccaneer', Robinson.

'The Buccaneer' was, from the first, a violent campaigner for stiffer penalties against the I.D.B.s. It became his main election pledge when he stood for membership of the Cape Assembly early in 1881. He was at once chosen by the diggers to represent them for Griqualand West, but it seemed that he would have to withdraw when an important deal at the Cape threatened to keep him away on nomination day. The diggers then approached Barney who agreed to stand in place of Robinson. The latter did not like him—or indeed any other trade rival—but despite Barney's alleged I.D.B. dealings, raised no objection. At the last minute, however, Robinson cancelled his previous engagement and was duly elected.

Had Barney been returned, he would have found himself in the Cape Assembly with Rhodes who had at last taken his degree at Oxford and seized his chance, as Member for Barkly West, to show his contempt for both the vacillating Imperial Government and the extremists in Pretoria. When Rhodes took his seat in March 1881, wearing his English tweeds like a uniform, the Assembly was in gloomy mood after a recent indignity at the hands of the Boers.

Early in the New Year a Boer commando, mainly bearing German-made weapons, had invaded Natal and routed a British force at Majuba, leaving hundreds of dead redcoats among the sugar-loaf hills. The Transvaal Republic was reborn, although nominally still under the suzerainty of the Crown. Paul Kruger, now the coming man and a clear successor to President Burgers, gave tongue to his hopes for the future: 'Then shall it be, from the Zambesi to Simon's Bay, Africa for the Afrikaners.' There would be no place for the British or any traitors of his own race who plotted for an Anglo-Dutch Bond.

Rhodes made an instantly favourable impression on an Assembly still smarting from the humiliation at Majuba. He was not yet skilled in debate or so eloquent an orator as Merriman who had preceded him at the Cape, but he cultivated influential friends like the new High Commissioner without losing sight of his main objective. Kimberley alone offered his one chance to acquire the wealth needed to realize his dreams without dependence on Whitehall.

In the diggings he lived monastically in his shack opposite the Club, sleeping on an iron bedstead with a gladstone bag as bolster. One entire wall was covered by a map of Africa, sprinkled with tiny Union Jacks. He had his Greek lexicon, and a copy of Marcus Aurelius and never seemed to tire of studying the lives of The Roman Emperors. His quarters were later shared with Neville Pickering, whom he appointed Secretary of De Beers and to whom he left all his 'worldly wealth' in his second Will.

With his suspect lungs and leaking heart valve, he also needed a doctor he could trust. He chose Leander Starr Jameson, a man of his own age who had come out to Africa for health reasons. A first-class surgeon and almost equally able physician, he soon established the best practice in Kimberley. His surgery was opposite the London Hotel where he often patched up the drunks Harry bounced out, as well as a crop of Saturday night casualties. He attended Woolf Joel for anaemia although Barney did not approve. He and Jameson had disliked each other on sight.

The stocky little doctor had mild-looking spaniel eyes which belied what a friend described as the stance of 'a Scottish terrier about to pounce'. He was impatient for daring physical action and had hero-worshipped Clive from his schooldays. Rhodes now wrapped the mantle of Empire around his private dreams of glory. As soon as he escaped from his patients, Jameson would hurry off to the British Mess which was locally known as 'The Twelve Apostles'. Rhodes, Rudd, Pickering and a few kindred souls would meet in a tin hut to gossip, drink, play cards and smoke Boer tobacco. Sooner or later, someone would launch Rhodes on a tirade against weak-kneed Whitehall until he grew so red-faced that Jameson would have to place a warning hand on his shoulder.

Alfred Beit, another of his patients, seemed an unlikely recruit to Empire-building but the timid German would become Rhodes's ideal Chancellor of the Exchequer. He had left the Lipperts to start on his own. Apart from buying shrewdly and selling to the best markets in Europe, he now bought up good sites in the fast-growing township of Kimberley to net himself £1,800 a month in rents alone from shanty offices.

In 1880 he went into partnership with Julius Wernher and Porges to form the biggest local organization for buying and selling diamonds. That same year they also invested heavily in the newly-floated Compagnie Française des Mines de Diamant du Cap (popularly known as 'the French Company') whose property was sited in the Kimberley Mine.

The Joint Stock Company was the logical outcome of deeper and costlier digging and the growth of larger syndicates. More and more capital was needed to buy the best machinery and brains and few single claim-owners could now hope to meet the heavy charges imposed by the Mining Board. The French Company showed the way by issuing scrip for purchasing claims instead of cash. Within a few months some sixty flotations were on the market, not all concerned with diamonds. Almost every kind of venture was frenziedly promoted, including new stores, hotels and even laundries.

Barnato Brothers held back from this scramble. They had only four important claims which were still producing many thousand pounds' worth of diamonds each year. They did not lack capital for new plant and saw no need to bring in investors. Barney, the individualist, had a special horror of giving up the firm's complete ownership of its hard-won property, whatever the inducements. He was highly suspicious of the fortunes made overnight by diggers who parted with their land to drink champagne and wave sheaves of coupons.

Having always dealt in cash or kind, he preferred diamonds, gold sovereigns and banknotes—wealth he could physically see and touch—to the crisp pieces of paper that were called 'shares' and kept changing in value even while one was still reading the complicated rigmarole written over them. He understood nothing of company techniques and found most of the prospectuses too intricate to follow or, in several cases, downright misleading. They usually ended up in his waste-paper basket or as cigar spills.

Woolf had a clearer picture of what was going on but saw his uncle's point of view. It more or less fitted in with his own immediate plans. Barney had decided to open an office at 106 Hatton Garden under the title of 'Barnato Brothers, Diamond Dealers and Financiers'. It would market the firm's diamonds more efficiently than through a number of brokers and might compete better with some of the old-established houses in Paris and Amsterdam who handled the output of Beit and others in Kimberley. He promised a partnership to his nephew whom he planned to put in charge of the London office. Woolf was delighted by the prospect of going home after over two years and agreed to try and persuade his brothers to come out as replacements.

Barney sat back to watch others burning their fingers over a bonfire of worthless share certificates. He was startled but still unconvinced when the Rhodes-Rudd partnership pooled its holdings with those of Philipson-Stow and other claim-owners in the 'Old Rush' to form the De Beers Mining Company Ltd on 1 April 1880. 'April Fool's Day,' Barney chuckled, noting that the new company's capital of £200,000 amounted to far less than his own private fortune. It amused him to hear that Rhodes, the Secretary, had needed to draw a cheque for £5 as an advance on his salary because all his own spare cash had gone into the company, without, however, giving him anything like a majority holding. Although De Beers shares started to boom, like all the others on the market, Barney still held back until the new London office was safely off the ground.

Woolf made something of a sensation when he drove out to The King of Prussia in a hansom. At seventeen he had already several thousands in his bank account and had sailed home as a first-class passenger. His elegant clothes, the high glossy collar, silk cravat and lavender gloves advertised his success, although his mother was shocked to see him looking so pale and scraggy. It made her hesitate to send out her other two boys who were naturally quite overwhelmed by Woolf's prosperity. He scattered ten-pound notes like confetti and slipped a diamond necklace round his mother's neck. After seeing a few shows and spending some weeks in Hatton Garden, he quickly tired of London and convinced his uncles without too much trouble that he would be more useful in Kimberley.

Barney sailed for England soon afterwards, still bristling over the rumours that associated him with I.D.B. He thought of buying a house, perhaps in the Bayswater area, which was adjacent to the Park and fairly convenient for Hatton Garden. He could now comfortably afford his own carriage and servants and might even buy a few racehorses, but the nostalgic vision of London, so golden to an exile, quickly faded. He mooned about his hotel and took a bus to the East End almost every day. However, once the excitement of emotional reunions was over, he was horrified and depressed by Whitechapel. Thousands had swarmed into the ghetto as refugees from Tsarist pogroms. He wept over the rickety, tubercular children and looked away from the pinched faces in the synagogue where men coughed into their prayer shawls after long hours in the tailors' steamy cellars. He gave liberally to the soup kitchens and Board of Guardians, offering to assist any who needed passage money to South Africa or the United States.

He could not, however, persuade his parents to leave Cobb's

Court. Although they now took life more easily, it was still difficult to make them accept any luxuries, but he was a proud man when he walked to the Great Synagogue in Duke's Place on the Sabbath morning with his mother who looked elegant in her new silk dress with a fashionable bustle, the six-buttoned gloves and a splendid ostrich feather in her hat. Strolling down Bond Street one shivering afternoon, he noticed a sable-lined overcoat which, he thought, would make a splendid farewell present for his father. It had a price tag of £150. Not wishing to be accused of wicked extravagance, he assured his father that he had bought it cheap, 'a real bargain', for £30. Mr Isaacs announced gleefully a week later that he had sold it for £75.

'Easiest *gelt* I ever made!' he crowed, returning the 'original' £30. 'You may have a diamond head, but you can't tell *me* what a coat like this is worth.' Barney kept a straight face and promptly invested the £30 and a tidy bit more on another overcoat which his father had to swear not to re-sell.

He looked up several old friends whom he helped to start up in business, but took special pleasure in shaking the hand of his former teacher at the Jews' Free School. 'You remember giving me that new penny? Well, it brought me luck. I'm repaying it with compound interest. Take it, just to please your little Barney.' It was a cheque for £100.

On his very first visit to Hatton Garden, he also called on the kindly man who had so often slipped him a welcome sixpence for a pair of bootlaces. 'This is for your wife,' he said cheerfully. 'Just a little present from Kimberley.' The diamond was later set in a ring which is still treasured by the Codd family.

The only lasting satisfaction from this disappointing London trip was to persuade Woolf's brothers to come out to Kimberley. Jack, then eighteen and rather solemn for his age, was plainly unsuited to the rough and tumble of The King of Prussia, but sixteen-year-old Solly was a laughing, quick-witted youngster. 'They're no more alike than champagne and port,' Barney confided to his wife. Solly already showed the kind of resourcefulness that reminded his uncle of his own early days. He once talked his brother into buying some homing pigeons which turned out to be a good investment while it lasted. They sold them over and over again to bird-fanciers who did not enjoy them for long as they were trained to return to the Joels' loft on the tavern roof. Such talents would not be wasted in Kimberley, thought Barney.

By the time he arrived back at the end of 1880, share mania was at delirium point. Woolf and Harry were now frothing with enthusiasm and had counted the hours until his return. Everyone in Kimberley seemed to be so prosperous that he finally decided to join the mainstream. He was fascinated by his proposed title of 'Chairman of the Board', particularly when his lawyers assured him that he would remain the largest shareholder and in full control of the new Barnato Diamond Mining Company. He placed a capital value of £100,000 on the four claims, plus a further £15,000 for installing new plant. It was a cautious valuation by contemporary standards and almost an innocent virginal ingénue compared with some of the brassy and highly temperamental prima donnas whom Barney would launch in later years, but he was still a novice in company matters and sensitive to any accusations of sharp dealing.

The response was almost apocalyptic. The capital was subscribed twice over within an hour. Next day the shares stood at a premium, and his own holdings trebled inside a few weeks. He bought more claims, all in the Kimberley Mine, but spread the risks by also investing quietly in De Beers and the Oriental Mine. He kept the bulk of his own company's stock for Harry and himself in order to safeguard their control over policy, but allocated a generous quota to his nephews.

He compensated for a lack of piety by extreme clannishness, largely manning his offices in both London and Kimberley with Jews, including several who claimed the vaguest family kinship. Others were chosen, irrespective of race, for their knowledge of mining techniques or other specialized fields. Wages and salaries were high, but Jew and Gentile alike would be shown no mercy for dishonesty or inefficiency. There was, however, a broadminded tolerance for opportunists who kept to the rules reasonably well. 'You have no right to spoil another man's game as long as he plays it cleverly,' Barney once cynically reminded Woolf. 'He will expose himself soon enough when he ceases to be clever at it.'

Few now mentioned I.D.B. even behind his back, and his share-holders were calling him 'The Great Barnato' without the slightest irony. He seemed to grow in stature with each rise in his invest-ments. Company promotion appealed to the two dominant elements in his personality. It gratified his gambling instinct to play tipster, punter and bookmaker simultaneously, while the actor in him savoured the delights of chairmanship. Speech-making lost all its terrors when audiences laughed so readily at his jokes. They made him feel almost like Irving as he sat down to roars of applause.

His ego began to blossom. Bankers who had never looked twice at him now called by appointment and were kept waiting. Lawyers, engineers and a fair number of continental speculators seemed flattered to be asked to his business breakfasts. They gladly over-looked his coarse manners in the hope of sharing his good fortune, but he was far more comfortable with his saloon cronies who did not sponge on him or try to wheedle hot tips.

He celebrated his twenty-ninth birthday with a memorable Jewish meal cooked by one of the Polish refugees whom Fanny had taken under her wing. Woolf proposed the toast after which Barney embraced each of his nephews in turn. It was an emotional moment for them all. The Joel boys had announced their wish to adopt 'Barnato' as their middle name, a gesture which had made Barney shed tears of simple-hearted pleasure. As Fanny was childless, his name would live through them.

They talked, drank and laughed until well past midnight. Fanny played the piano and Barney led a dozen choruses. The Polish cook was given a glass and coaxed to forget her troubles; the other servants were brought in, and soon half the neighbourhood seemed to be drinking Barney's health. As more bottles appeared and dis-appeared, the talk became gayer and wildly exuberant. Everyone seemed to be a millionaire or at least heading that way.

But the share bubble had to burst. Over-inflated values led to collapse, precipitated by the banks who called in loans even faster than they had granted them. Companies committed to costly installations were suddenly abandoned. The frenzy of investment had led to such feverish digging that the 'Big Hole' became a disaster area for scores of companies which died like ants when their claims were flooded or collapsed. The Mining Board itself dissolved under the strain. The situation reached crisis point when yet another world trade slump hit the vulnerable diamond.

From the autumn of 1881 onwards, most companies were flying some very motheaten banners. It was a time for nerve and cool thinking. Woolf was directed to buy any of the group's shares that were being thrown on the market, while Solly and Jack kept their eyes open for diggings that had been hastily abandoned and could be cheaply snapped up. Instead of retrenching, Barney poured more cash into his claims and built galleries to enable his labour force to work more safely and efficiently. He also had horizontal tunnels running from the shafts towards the 'column' of blue earth almost two years before any of his competitors. The result was increased output and a 36% dividend to shareholders.

Investors were, however, slow in coming back, thanks to glum warnings from newspapers like *The Times* which assured its readers that 'reports from South Africa are wicked inventions of adventurers circulated for the purpose of rigging the market'. The De Beers Company, too under-capitalized to develop new methods, came under special pressure. The original shares soon stood at half their nominal value which gave Rhodes, now Chairman, many sleepless nights. On the one hand, he saw a permanent world demand for diamonds ('Four million engagement rings a year and each worth at least £1 a carat,' he once remarked excitedly); on the other, an uncontrolled output which played havoc with prices whenever supply exceeded demand and caused under-cutting. There could be no permanent salvation for Kimberley while diamonds were sometimes sold for as little as 10s. a carat and production costs were rising to 15s. and over.

He was at a disadvantage with Barney who had more working capital and, in any case, produced better-quality stones in his claims. Rhodes countered boldly by starting the Compound System. Natives signed on for six-monthly periods and were confined in De Beers for the term of their contracts. Work improved dramatically as soon as they were cut off from bad liquor and provided with decent food and housing. I.D.B. losses were also reduced, thanks to barbed-wire fences patrolled at night by guards, alsatians and bull mastiffs. The firm's stores sold goods at cost or a little over. Profits were earmarked for better amenities within the compound or new schools and hospitals for the community at large. The Kimberley shopkeepers, however, supported by Barney and other councillors, opposed what they considered a dangerous trading monopoly. The Chamber of Commerce finally forced De Beers to charge full retail prices in their stores. Even so, Rhodes would never be wholly forgiven.

By March 1885, he enjoyed an income of some £50,000 a year, but this was still quite inadequate to finance the territorial expansion which he thought desperately urgent in view of Germany's obvious designs on West and Central Africa. He therefore looked with increasing envy at Barney who was about to pull off another spectacular coup which would make his company by far the richest in the Kimberley Mine.

Even before the diamond slump was over, these two men had emerged as the most dynamic figures in Kimberley. Surprisingly, they had not met formally throughout the whole previous decade. Rhodes continued to think of his competitor as a lucky but unprincipled huckster and thoroughly endorsed Beit's verdict on him as 'an impossible person'. Barney told his nephews with a laugh, 'Rhodes looks down on me because I came out here with a few quid and your dad's boxes of cigars to peddle—and he had his Greek dictionary.' He could afford to shrug it off. All the cards seemed to be in his hand; a strong constitution, flourishing claims and a heart-warming tribal loyalty. Unlike Rhodes, he could direct his full energies to expanding his business, untroubled by imperial pipe-dreams or the enmity of men like Paul Kruger who had at last become President of his little pastoral Republic.

5

———

WOOLF'S DECISION to stay in Kimberley gratified his uncle who could ill afford to spare him, but it meant a readjustment on the executive side. Harry was more than willing to go to London where he would soon be joined by Jack Joel, although Solly had the keener flair for diamonds and might have been more useful in Hatton Garden. Solly was a spry, genial lad who regularly accompanied Barney to the races or plays and enjoyed taking a hand at cards, but diamonds became his absorbing passion.

Unlike his uncle and brothers who thought of carats in strictly practical terms, Solly would fondle stones with an almost sensual excitement. He took a similar aesthetic delight in collecting objets d'art and used to haunt Kimberley's better shops for snuff-boxes, watches and any tasteful bric à brac that was being imported from France or Italy. He startled the diggers with his well-cut breeches and polished riding boots and took to dabbing himself with eau-de-cologne before dressing for dinner or the theatre. He liked to wear silk next to his skin and carried fine linen handkerchiefs that made Barney feel a trifle self-conscious about his own gaudy bandanna. To keep up with Solly, Barney began to sport a moustache carefully waxed at the ends, but his attempts to smarten himself up for board meetings or dinner parties were rarely successful. A new suit soon looked crumpled on him since he never troubled to retain the crease in his trousers and usually carried a layer of cigarette ash on lapels studded with cigarette burns. He now wore bow ties but was either too impatient or too clumsy to knot them properly and used to compromise with clip-ons which often went awry or became unhooked.

Jack was far more serious than his younger brother and dedicated himself to a very thorough all-round apprenticeship. Barney thought he had the makings of a sound man of business, although possibly too deliberate and withdrawn for the tempo of noisy Kimberley. He was meticulously punctual, wrote everything down in fine copperplate and seemed unlikely either to make mistakes or initiate anything startling. When he later returned to London he tuned in excellently with the Hatton Garden office which was not expected at that time to do much more than sell parcels of diamonds and keep Barney updated on market trends and prices. There was as yet no European dealing in diamond shares, but Harry was quick to follow Ludwig Lippert who, by the mid-eighties, had started a rudimentary share mart on the kerbside between Hatton Garden and Holborn Viaduct. Harry and his nephew were also useful when Barney suddenly needed a London syndicate to back his amalgamation of several claims on which he had taken an option for £100,000. It was swiftly and efficiently carried through at both ends, ultimately yielding the firm a clear profit of nearly £250,000.

But Barney's major coup was the purchase, in 1884, of six new claims adjacent to the original four acquired from the Kerr brothers and located even nearer to the dead centre of the Kimberley 'funnel' which had abundantly justified his confidence. They were owned by a digger named Stewart who had long withstood all attempts to buy him out. A steady crop of diamonds enabled him to survive the worst of the slump and still meet the working costs that had ruined other individual diggers. Barney judged precisely the right moment to flourish an offer of £180,000, cash on the barrel head. No mining ground of that size had hitherto commanded anything approaching such a stupendous price, and Stewart gave in.

Barney soon took the logical step of linking all his claims with those held by Kimberley Central, easily the largest group in that Mine. The Chairman was Francis Baring-Gould, a well-bred Englishman on the friendliest personal terms with respected figures like Philipson-Stow and Charles Rudd. Barney showed unaccustomed self-restraint in not attempting to unseat him. He saw the wisdom for once of staying in the background to pull the strings. Everyone who counted knew that he and his family held most of the shares, but even those who still considered him suspect felt reassured by Baring-Gould's City background and connections. But the vast majority of rank-and-file investors helped most, in the long term, to foster the fast-growing legend of Barney's magic touch.

By the time Woolf celebrated his coming-of-age in November 1884, his share holdings plus a partnership interest in the separate family firm of diamond merchants had made him a millionaire. Barney's own income was by then approaching £200,000 a year. He made sure that Jack and Solly, who had arrived on the scene when their brother was already on the way to a comfortable fortune, did not nurse any sense of grievance. They started at the same salary of £50 a week, sweetened by commissions and shares allocated to them at par as each new company was floated. All three were allowed to draw advances almost at will, in the same way as Barney and Harry. They could, therefore, speculate within reason for themselves. As a result, they inherited shares in a flourishing business without the enmity, prejudice and malicious gossip which would always pursue their uncles. This made it easier to rub off traces of the ghetto in a remarkably short time.

Barney remained the firm's driving force but the newcomers wisely based their style on their brother. While still in his teens, Woolf could already more than hold his own with Beit and other leading merchants who looked askance when Barney blew his nose through his fingers or clowned about the saloons. They still suspected his every business move and became acutely apprehensive when he first began dabbling in De Beers shares.

Barney's main purpose was to keep in touch with what was going on in 'that nice little mine' but he had no confidence in Rhodes who made him squirm whenever he heard that high-pitched voice arrogantly asserting the right to speak on Kimberley's problems at every local meeting. He continued to despise him as an absentee Chairman who, when he was not holding forth at the Cape on Anglo-Dutch federation, kept charging up to the north on wild expeditions. Barney found it difficult to understand how these very remote territories, mainly peopled by native herdsmen, could possibly concern the future of either De Beers or the Kimberley Mine.

Kruger did not understand diamonds and believed to the end of his days that the earth was flat, but he had a sixth sense about people. He saw Rhodes for the first time early in 1885. Their meeting at Fourteen Springs on the Vaal was scarcely auspicious for future good relations. A few months earlier, Kruger had extracted almost complete independence for his Republic by signing the London Convention with Gladstone. His delegation had been fêted in Berlin where Bismarck was then celebrating his new protectorate to the south of Portuguese Angola. This coup had encouraged the Transvaal Boers to annex two small territories adjacent to their own Bechuanaland frontier.

The dangers of a German-Boer wedge athwart the trade routes to the north became plainer to Downing Street after Gladstone's departure. Rhodes was therefore warmly supported when he revived his dream of establishing a Protectorate over Bechuanaland, but he was soon put in his place over the ways and means. The Colonial Office was determined to run the new Protectorate from Whitehall and not the Cape. It did not console Kruger. Confronted by a show of force and hastily abandoned by the Germans and his own impoverished burghers, he had to give way. Nor was the pill sweetened by Rhodes's ambiguous double-talk about an Anglo-Boer Bond.

Kruger did not make Barney Barnato's mistake of judging Rhodes by the shabby coat, soiled flannels and tennis shoes which made him so conspicuous among the clanking British dragoons. 'I have learned one thing: to distinguish friends from foes,' he growled at General Joubert, his deputy and rival for the Presidency. 'This young man will cause trouble if he does not leave politics alone and turn to something else.'

Instead, Rhodes made more speeches forecasting government 'by the people of South Africa with the Imperial flag for defence.' That plainly meant brotherhood with the Cape Dutch whom Kruger considered traitors for adopting English ways and even giving their daughters to them in marriage. He despised them bitterly for sacrificing the God of their fathers to Mammon but still chose to regard the discovery of gold in the eastern Transvaal as a heaven-sent rod with which to smite his enemies!

In the summer of 1884, when two brothers named Barber found large deposits of gold-bearing quartz, Kruger saw the seven lean years after Majuba ending in a glorious dawn. The sun shone on 'Barberton' as hopeful diggers poured in with pick, shovel and pan to make a fortune for themselves and his Republic. Shops and hotels sprang up; banks stayed open twelve hours a day; and three newspapers advertised house property and share prices. By the end of 1886, stock was at dizzy levels. Promoters grew richer by the hour and mines were being merrily 'salted' to convince those who still hung back.

Only a small number justified the fantastic share issues. One of the genuine companies was Sheba Gold Mining in which a Russian-born immigrant, Sammy Marks, held a major interest. He later arranged several loans for Kruger with whom he was on the most cordial terms. Sheba survived, but Barberton became almost a ghost town overnight after Gardner Williams, the American mining expert, made an adverse report. He was soon afterwards engaged by De Beers as Chief Engineer and later became its General Manager.

Neither Barnato nor Rhodes had been tempted to join in the gold rush. Barney still remembered losing money at Pilgrim's Rest, while Rhodes was too busy checkmating Kruger's north-ward thrust into Matabeleland, then ruled by a crafty chieftain, Lobengula.

On 17 August 1887, Rhodes lunched with Charles Rudd in a private room at the Kimberley Club to discuss his expedition to the royal kraal in the hope of squeezing mineral concessions from 'Old Lob'. After lunch Rudd quietly withdrew £5,000 from his bank and concealed it in a wagon drawn up at the back of the Central Hotel. It would buy supplies, but far more funds would be required to bribe the rapacious chief with the cash and guns he coveted. Rhodes explained his hopes in the broadest outline to his triumvirate, Rudd, Beit and Jameson. Beyond Lobengula's kingdom lay Mashonaland which, once seized, would carry the British flag to the very banks of the Zambesi, thus effectively cutting off the Transvaal Boers and all other would-be colonists, leaving the way clear for the final thrust to Cairo itself.

He would need capital far beyond his present resources to build railways and buy weapons to subdue tribesmen and any foreign freebooters who might stand in his path. He therefore proposed to seek Whitehall's approval for a Chartered body, somewhat on the lines of the old East India Company, to infiltrate and develop Central Africa. This would appeal to jingoists at home, he felt sure, but only if he could also guarantee a cash return on their investment. He summed it all up with a cynical smile: 'Patriotism plus five per cent.'

It would stand or fall by his chances of rapidly securing concessions from Lobengula. Matabeleland and what lay beyond was the prospectus he planned to offer his Chartered investors. By the spring of 1887 he had brought almost the whole of the De Beers Mine into his company, usually paying claim-owners in stock. With increased share capital he felt equipped to move forward but still lacked the resources to finance adventures in Matabeleland. That would be impossible unless and until he had captured the whole Kimberley Mine, by now the largest single diamond-producing area in the world.

It was already clear that Barney Barnato would be the main stumbling block. So far he had shown no taste for amalgamation and would be most unlikely to give Rhodes the supreme direction of policy even if he could be induced to agree in bare principle. He could withstand any price-cutting and it would be impossibly costly to force him out of his dominance of Kimberley Central. The obvious course was therefore to weaken his position by infiltrating into other sectors of that mine.

Barney was shrewd enough to guess that an attack might come through the French Company in which he held one-fifth of the shares. He had himself vaguely contemplated buying out its claims which intersected those of the Central Company and caused him inconvenience when both were working underground simultaneously. A merger would no doubt have resulted in greater efficiency and lower costs, but Barney had not pressed too hard.

Although the French Company was paying small dividends, its directors—Porges and others in Paris—would demand a very high price, he surmised, even if they could be induced to sell out to him. Kimberley Central was strong enough, he decided, to do without the French Company, and he could use his own voting shares to block any other interested party, including De Beers.

Had he suspected what Rhodes was about, he might well have followed his father's old boxing injunction to ''it 'im first'. Instead, he showed an understandable complacency. He was by far the wealthiest man in the diamond industry, while the Central Company, of which Woolf was also a co-director as well as Chairman of the Mining Board, now owned the largest and most productive group of claims in the Kimberley Mine. Moreover, the family firm ranked among the world's leading diamond merchants and had become a force to be reckoned with long before South African mining shares were brought to the European markets.

Barney's word counted so heavily in Kimberley that any whisper associated with his name was enough to start a wave of buying. When he arrived on his annual visits to London, he was made much of in Hatton Garden. Now that Cobb's Court and its squalid environs had been demolished—including the old King of Prussia—to make room for the widening of Middlesex Street, his parents and the Joels had at last left the East End. They became neighbours in comfortable houses near Marble Arch and worshipped at the fashionable synagogue in St John's Wood. Barney's father liked his elegant new carriage but never dared to drive across London in it to the East End. He and his wife went by bus to Whitechapel at least twice a week to see old friends and sample the fried fish at Polly Nathan's. But in winter the Isaacses and Joels would spend a month or more at Harry's villa in Nice.

Barney was now leaving much of the London office end to Jack Joel, while Solly continued to sparkle both socially and in business in Kimberley. Fanny busied herself in welfare committees and played hostess to Barney's cosmopolitan and bohemian friends. Her great delight was to sail with him on his trips to Europe. On board he relaxed from all business worries and made everyone enjoy themselves, particularly the children, whose deck games he usually organized. No ship's concert ever went flat if his name appeared on the passenger list. He needed little persuasion to act as M.C. or give one of his recitations.

During their visit to London in 1887, when they made gay shopping expeditions through streets bedecked for the Golden Jubilee celebrations, Barney first heard a story in Hatton Garden which confirmed the many whispers he had so far ignored. It seemed that Beit was trying to interest a Paris syndicate in buying the French Company. He made little headway, and Barney was delighted when Rhodes himself came to London to be snubbed in turn by City financiers. There was little support until Beit was inspired to suggest an overture to the House of Rothschild.

Rhodes reacted with enthusiasm. New Court, their London headquarters, had become super-eminent in banking. Even Queen Victoria, who had long denied the English branch a peerage because of its wealth derived 'solely from money contracts', acknowledged its prestige by granting a barony to 'Natty' Rothschild.

Rhodes sensed that his proposed purchase of the French Company might not be unreservedly welcomed by New Court. It would be no routine affair of risk-taking and profit-making for these bankers. A prickly hedge of mistrust still separated the Cape from Whitehall, and this always vigilant clan might be nervous of becoming involved with a politician who had shown himself so critical of 'the Imperial Factor' over Bechuanaland. Rhodes therefore made what was, for him, a gingerly approach. Invited to come to London in July 1887, he reassured Lord Rothschild by talking sensibly about De Beers and the French Company in the general context of unification. And he wisely refrained from making any emotional appeals to colonialism.

'Natty' Rothschild, although gruff in manner, listened courteously and nodded approval when Rhodes spoke hopefully of reconciling Boer and British in an era of prosperity which would surely follow the 'rationalization' of South Africa's leading export. He sat impassively in his high-backed chair and stroked his beard while the experts on both sides raked over the details. 'How much will be needed?' he suddenly asked Rhodes. One million pounds sterling, he was told; the rest, if required, would be raised by De Beers, Beit and some others. 'He would sometimes become a puzzled and anxious ally,' Rhodes used to recall later with a mischievous smile, but 'Natty' seemed happy enough at this stage. Nevertheless, he made Rhodes sweat a little and gave him only a friendly promise to do what he could to arrange the loan. He was barely out of the building before Lord Rothschild beckoned an intermediary with a smile. 'You may tell Mr Rhodes,' he said casually, 'that if he can buy the French Company, I think I can raise the million.'

Softened up by Jules Porges, the French Company directors agreed to recommend acceptance of an offer of £1,400,000 by their shareholders. Half would come from the Rothschilds and the balance in De Beers shares issued to a syndicate organized by Beit and Wernher. Rhodes was so confident that the deal would go through after being rubber-stamped by his own fellow-directors, that he was already planning the next move while sailing back to Cape Town. He would fuse the French Company with Kimberley Central whose Chairman, Baring-Gould, had already been gently sounded out. It seemed that he had himself long had this scheme in mind. Besides, it would give him a splendid chance to score off Barnato, whom he feared and disliked, while cementing his friendship with the far more socially congenial members of the other camp.

Barney had, however, taken lightning action as soon as reports of the Rothschild-Rhodes coalition were confirmed. By the time Rhodes arrived back in Kimberley at the end of September, the French Company was already slipping from him. The Barnato group was buying up blocks of shares through nominees. As the market price rose on this wave of buying and reports of a take-over, stockholders soon asked themselves whether an offer of £1,400,000 was high enough. Barney's agents in London, Paris and Kimberley lobbied against acceptance of the syndicate's bid which was about to come up before a meeting of shareholders. He made it known that he had their interests at heart and moreover was ready to prove it with hard cash. He promised that Kimberley Central might go £300,000 better than the first offer which had been engineered behind their backs.

Rhodes could see his grand design crumbling before his eyes. Lord Rothschild, unaccustomed to failure, plainly disliked having his name bandied about in this unseemly scramble for shares which was 'seriously prejudicing our prospects of a settlement'. If the Rothschilds withdrew, the syndicate would dissolve, tossing the French Company plum to the Barnatos. That might well end all Rhodes's hopes of Lobengula's concessions at the very moment when Rudd was fitting out his expedition to Matabeleland. If that were held up, the whole plan for a Chartered Company would be doomed.

In this agony of frustration Rhodes saw his dreams being wrecked by a tiresome cockney adventurer who, it seemed to him, was plainly manoeuvring for easy pickings by bulling the market. Blinkered by prejudice, he was quite unable to credit Barney with anything but the basest motives. He ignored Barney's work on the Mining Board where he had made himself unpopular by consistently advocating shorter hours and more humane conditions all round for diggers working hundreds of feet underground in foul air. He preferred to echo Jameson who said bluntly, 'I can't stand the sight of that scoundrel.'

The time had come to put a ring through that blobby nose. Rhodes, however, mistook his man by summoning him to De Beers for a talk. Barney retaliated by suggesting he might be available in *his* office if some mutually convenient time could be arranged. He seemed in less hurry than Rhodes who had to climb down. He was, therefore, far from affable when he arrived. At the last minute he slipped a cheque book into his breast pocket.

The confrontation was a disaster for Rhodes. He tried to overcome his repugnance for this fidgety little man whose innocent-looking blue eyes gleamed behind those owlish pincenez. Barney kept blowing his nose vigorously with a big handkerchief to interrupt his visitor's arguments for an amicable settlement. Knowing that Rhodes liked a mixture of stout and champagne, Bismarck's favourite tipple, he poured out hospitable tumblers while both chain-smoked furiously. The drink did not mellow Rhodes who began to wriggle in exasperation while Barney sat back with an amused look on his face, stroking his waxed moustache-tips after each sip of the 'Black Velvet'. With his loudly-checked suit, the sprouting flower in his lapel and the outsize polka-dot bow, he struck Rhodes as vulgarity incarnate.

He began to talk far less guardedly than he had dared to do in

New Court. Forgetting that he had primarily come to buy off Barney, he spoke passionately, almost hysterically, of his plans for 'unification' of the diamond industry which would herald a millennium of peace and plenty for a united Africa. Once or twice he was so carried away that he squeaked Latin quotations. ('When he talked *Greek* at me,' Barney later confided to Woolf, 'I knew he was dotty. He thinks he's Kimberley's bloody messiah.')

Rhodes made no progress. Each argument was countered by Barney's bland assurance that he was not thinking of himself but the French Company shareholders who were entitled to a better offer than £1,400,000 for their shares. He was only the honest broker chosen to speak up for them. This was minimally true; the rest was play-acting, and both knew it. Rhodes saw only one way to make him withdraw his nuisance bid. He pulled out his cheque-book and grabbed a pen.

'I'll cover you for all you think you will lose by allowing my offer to pass,' he announced with a cold chisel smile.

That was his second and far more serious mistake. Barney had never doubted that the syndicate could be forced to improve on their opening bid; failing that, he would go ahead as planned and buy the French Company for Kimberley Central or even raise the cash himself if Baring-Gould's supporters took alarm. This clumsy, almost contemptuous, bribe incensed him, but he managed to keep his temper while Rhodes was plainly losing control. His face reddened as Barney repeated with pious gravity that he owed his shareholders a duty far above self-interest.

After parting with a bare touch of fingertips, Barney exploded. Woolf found him stamping round his office, tossing back one brandy after another, while he babbled insults at Rhodes, Beit, Baring-Gould and the rest. He would show Rothschild himself that not even a million could buy off Barney Barnato!

'Rhodes looks down on me,' he snorted, 'because I've never been to college like 'im. If I'd had his education, there would have been no Cecil Rhodes.'

Allowing for his irritation and the resentments that had accumulated inside him since his 'kopje-walloping' days, the remark typified a dangerous capacity for self-deception. Barnato might move with breathtaking speed but his values had remained static. Rhodes had emerged from his dreamy youth as both man of action and visionary. When he turned to finance, money became no more to him than an instrument of power for discharging his ambitions. Kimberley's diamonds had simply transformed Barney from an East End barrow-boy into a huckster with a protean flair for speculation. As soon as he escaped from poverty, he needed only to gratify his gambling urge by constantly increasing the stakes.

This fundamental conflict of personality might have been partially resolved by more goodwill and understanding on both sides. But neither was ready to give an inch. Barney, hurt in his pride yet too shrewd to overplay his hand, could afford to wait for the next move. Rhodes, when he had cooled down, appreciated that he might have erred through impatience and a lack of finesse. To break the deadlock, he would regretfully have to change his tactics. 'The little blighter means business,' he told Beit. 'He'll be a hard nut to crack.' The cheque book would still be needed, he felt certain, but more subtlety was now essential. Helped by Beit, he carefully prepared some additional bait which even Barnato might find it hard to resist.

6

———

'IF YOU CANNOT MANAGE a thing one way, try another,' Rhodes
was fond of saying. He put this maxim to effective use when
resuming negotiations with Barney a few days after that
stormy first meeting. In the interim, fanned by rumour, the
French Company's shares crackled brightly. Many were now eager
to seize quick gains. Beit's syndicate or their nominees were thus
able to pick up blocks of stock which Barney was forced to try
and buy back at inflated prices.

Rhodes felt more confident but was careful not to show it when
he revisited the Barnato offices. Both men remained coldly polite
and wary, but Rhodes now produced his arguments in a crisp
businesslike way that impressed his opponent far more than his
previous air of disdain. 'Your leading shareholders are patting you
on the back, but selling out round the corner all the time,' he
pointed out, stroking his chin with his right forefinger, a gesture
which his associates always recognized as a danger signal. He went
on calmly, 'You can go on bidding *ad infinitum* for the French
shareholders because we shall have it in the end.' Before Barney
could take offence, he quickly put forward a proposition that took
some of the sting out of the threat; 'I am prepared to unite the
purchased interest in the French Company with the Kimberley
Central.' De Beers would buy the French Company claims for the
£1,400,000 previously agreed and re-sell it to the Kimberley
Company for £300,000 in cash, plus a block of deferred shares.

Barney had his suspicions of this change of front, but Woolf and
Solly argued there was everything to gain by the takeover. It
would give De Beers approximately one-fifth of Central, but the
Barnatos' holdings would still remain far more substantial. Barney

could at last see himself as virtual owner of the whole Kimberley Mine, 'the richest hole on earth' and big enough to swallow St Paul's Cathedral. He seemed totally unaware that De Beers' acquisition of an interest in Kimberley Central might be a classic wooden horse move into his fortress. Rhodes did not appreciate, however, that he had an invisible ally in the background. The little East Ender would never quite forget his fruit and bag of sweets on that school outing to Ramsgate or remain insensitive to the mystical glamour attached to the Rothschild name. It still worked a powerful alchemy which misled him into believing that his own worth was at last being recognized in New Court. The famed dynasty now had an interest in Kimberley Central, *his* Company.

He was understandably cock-a-hoop when addressing shareholders at the general meeting on 3 November 1887. He preened himself on having originally offered 70,000 Central shares for the French Company and now had it for about half, 'a saving of a million of money'. Before the applause had subsided, Beit got up to observe acidly that, 'Mr Barnato is only mistaken by about half a million.' Barney joined in the laughter at this dry aside and, quite unabashed, murmured to A. A. Rothschild, 'If I had Beit's reputation for honesty, I would be worth millions.' He left arm-in-arm with Woolf, both well satisfied. Beit slipped thoughtfully away to Ebden Street to plan the next moves with Rhodes, and Mr Rothschild pocketed a £100,000 commission for his firm.

Barney's position in Kimberley Central, already strong with the rank and file, appeared to be impregnable when Baring-Gould's health—and possibly his morale—forced him to take a long leave in England. In spite of Philipson-Stow's staunchness, he could not hope to survive between opportunists as ruthless as Rhodes and Barnato. Investors had no time for tears. The Company's £10 shares had jumped to over £40 before the end of that year and looked like going even higher. While Woolf in Kimberley was watching these stock developments, Harry Barnato and Jack Joel kept an accurate eye on Throgmorton Street. They reported that the Stock Exchange was at last showing a lively interest in the booming diamond shares, particularly those of The Great Barnato.

Barney began seriously to examine the prospects of floating the

Kimberley Mine in London as a public company. A Stock
Exchange quotation would not only give him immense personal
prestige—who would dare to sneer about I.D.B. after *that*?—but
might funnel enormous cash into Kimberley for further development. He knew that Philipson-Stow, Rhodes's proxy in London,
was having frequent meetings with the Rothschilds to arrange for
amalgamations of the Dutoitspan and Bultfontein mines, probably
with De Beers, but this did not alarm him. He was now pouring
colossal quantities of diamonds on to the market. With a huge
turnover he could afford to operate on a smaller profit margin and
was steadily undercutting all competitors, including De Beers, who
began to take serious losses.

N. M. Rothschild & Sons, through Philipson-Stow, were
showing a deep concern. They urged Rhodes to take counter-
action before Barnato could bring the Kimberley Mine to market.
Once that happened, all hope of unification would obviously be
lost. With Rudd and his party heading for Lobengula's kraal,
Rhodes could not discount this threat to his future plans. He set
out to convince Barney that it would be suicidal for them both to
flood the diamond market with stones at an uneconomic 18*s.* a
carat.

A kind of 'gamesmanship' now opened in which Rhodes tried
to prove that the De Beers production, backed by the Rothschilds
and other powerful financiers, could be stepped up to withstand
any undercutting. Barnato, he argued, would ruin himself in the
end by trying to go it alone. Barney went on smiling. At one of
their meetings he displayed several parcels of diamonds arranged
on a side-table in his office. 'Just a small part of our reserve stock,'
he remarked airily. Not long afterwards the De Beers workers
brought in a large haul of stones, gathered 'like mushrooms in a
field' after a week of heavy rain. When they had been cleaned and
the best neatly parcelled, Rhodes took them along to Barney's
office. 'Twelve thousand carats,' he said grandly, adding with slight
inaccuracy, 'and only one day's workings.'

He showed more subtlety over the 'bucketful of diamonds'
episode which is now part of South African diamond lore and has
inevitably gathered picturesque moss over the years. It has been so
often distorted in the re-telling that the facts may be worth

recalling in their proper context. After De Beers had acquired a small mine in their sector, they found themselves with several months' supply which could upset an already top-heavy market. It was not only surplus to their normal requirements but would further depress prices if sold in bulk. At the same time Rhodes desperately needed capital to buy more Kimberley Central shares, apart from footing the bill for Rudd's life-or-death expedition to the north. He therefore invited Barnato and other leading merchants to his Board Room to inspect the enormous collection of some 220,000 carats. His main object was to raise cash, but he had quickly noted the gleam in Barney's blue eyes as he surveyed this truly dazzling evidence of De Beers power. The stones were laid out on tissue paper in 160 piles and graded according to size, shape and quality. They rested on a long trough running down one entire side of the room.

Barney decided to rely, as usual, on the more expert judgment of Solly and David Harris, the latter being empowered to bid on behalf of the firm. Rhodes had been assured by his valuers that the stones were worth about half a million but deliberately set the high price of £700,000 on the whole collection. He advised his visitors to decide among themselves exactly what proportion each would take and resisted every argument to lower his price or sell smaller lots to individual dealers. He then withdrew, leaving an angry but excited 'jury' to argue out their verdict.

David Harris was unanimously elected 'foreman'. After much haggling they agreed with reluctance to meet Rhodes's price. As expected, Barnato Brothers would take the largest share. Rhodes received the decision with nonchalance but urged them all not to re-sell too quickly and thus unbalance the market. He guessed, however, that the smaller dealers would not be able to hold on, despite any 'gentleman's agreement', while he knew Barney too well to doubt that he would use this new haul to undercut De Beers if it suited his book. Then, to everyone's astonishment, Rhodes calmly raised one end of the trough and tipped all the stones helter-skelter into a bucket concealed at the base.

'I have always wanted to see a bucketful of diamonds,' he explained genially to Barney. 'Now let's walk down to your office with it and make the people stare.' It would also, as Barney knew, proclaim to the world that they were on the best of terms and might help to put the noses of Robinson and some of his other relentless enemies out of joint. Above all, his sense of the theatrical could not resist walking along Ebden Street with Rhodes, each with a hand on that bucket of diamonds.

Nevertheless, as soon as the stones began to cascade down the trough, Barney had guessed what was behind it all. This was no whim on Rhodes's part nor some quixotic gesture of unity. Re-sorting the vast quantity of diamonds would take at least six weeks during which they could be kept off the market. De Beers would therefore enjoy valuable breathing-space for maintaining their own prices.

It was a superb bit of *chutzpah* (Yiddish: cheek) which Barney appreciated rather more than his fellow-merchants. Indeed it gave him a new respect for a man whom he had too long despised as a priggish amateur in business. This was worthy of any 'Peruvian', and Barney long enjoyed telling the story against himself. 'Rhodes only beat me once,' he used to laugh. 'Over those diamonds in that bucket of his. But I didn't mind—it pleased him. Just a bit of sugar for the birds.' In the end, the buyers had reason to thank Rhodes for his stratagem. Their diamonds fetched better prices after the market had settled down.

The Rhodes-Barnato relationship had thawed a little but Barney still seemed maddeningly indifferent to the perils of unrestricted production, taking comfort in a share boom which persisted despite the downward spiral in diamond prices. With the whole Kimberley Mine steadily entering his control, it might soon be possible to absorb Bultfontein, Dutoitspan and finally even De Beers itself. That would be time enough, he decided, to limit production and control prices.

Rhodes called his emergency council of war in a private room at Poole's Club in Cape Town in February 1888. To forestall Barnato, he told Beit and Philipson-Stow that they would need to buy enough shares in Kimberley Central for a majority holding. This was the obvious prerequisite to any sound amalgamation formula. It would cost at least £2m (in the end, it was nearer £3m) at current inflationary share prices, but Beit was sanguine about raising the money. He quickly offered a loan of £250,000 from his own pocket without asking a single penny in commission or interest. The Rothschilds and others would also be canvassed to provide further capital to expand De Beers' one-fifth interest in Kimberley Central into the three-quarters needed for full control.

Rhodes was the Bismarck in this campaign, with Beit as his Moltke. It would be short and sharp, lasting less than six weeks. Central stock was bought discreetly, mainly in small lots through nominees. Barney at once started to hit back, snapping up as many £10 shares as he could even when they went as high as £50. 'He fought me tooth and nail,' Rhodes afterwards admitted, but he himself had one supreme advantage. Barney could inspire affection but not complete loyalty except among his own clan. Many of his shareholders and even some of his fellow-directors were tempted to sell out for big profits while the rival consortium held grimly on to every scrap of acquired stock. Before long they were only fractionally short of the vital three-quarter mark.

Barney had lost control of the Kimberley Mine but still straddled the gap and could yet block any attempt by the opposition to enforce amalgamation. 'I'll tell you what you will find out presently,' Rhodes warned him when his share battle was almost won. 'You'll be left alone in the Central Company.' Barney laughed but had to acknowledge to himself that he had spent huge sums to buy what was still only a minority holding.

Rhodes now decided to break the deadlock. His choice of venue was masterly. He knew it would be tactless to summon Barney to De Beers, nor could he risk calling again at the Barnato offices which might be interpreted as weakness. He showed inspiration and perhaps a touch of machiavellianism by proposing lunch at the Kimberley Club where Barney had long been regarded as a social leper. He was impressed by the invitation but affected to be amused. Barney had suffered too much in the past, however, not to seize his chance to scandalize the members. He behaved quite outrageously, talking in a voice as loud as his sporty suit and helping himself to liberal pinches of snuff to make his sneezes heard. From his jacket pocket dangled a bandanna handkerchief on which he blew reveille whenever the room grew quiet.

Rhodes was not deceived by this buffoonery and guessed what

lay behind it. It simply reinforced his view that money alone would not carry the day. He took to asking Barney so frequently to the Club that the Committee angrily proposed a new rule prohibiting non-members from lunching there more than once a month. This was plainly directed at Barney, but Rhodes chose to regard it as critical of himself and vetoed the resolution. 'They can't ostracize me,' Barney laughingly assured him. 'Too late. It was done years ago. I'll show 'em if they like.' Rhodes chuckled, 'I'll make a gentleman of you yet.' He offered to propose Barney for membership which was perhaps rather less of a crude bribe than has often been suggested. Undoubtedly he wished to put the Committee in their place by challenging them to blackball his nominee, but he would also unmistakably demonstrate his own standing and prestige to Barnato at this critical stage in their talks. Barney himself had no interest in this ugly corrugated shack in which glazed members staggered from dining-room to library or sat like mummies at the card table. He would use the place far less often than his favourite saloons, but Rhodes had guessed right. Barney was still flattered by the invitation and decided to join precisely because the Committee did not want him.

Meantime Barney was being steadily won over to the idea of exchanging his shares in Kimberley Central for those in De Beers at their current high market price. He had also accepted in principle the formation of the new company, De Beers Consolidated Mines, in which his holdings would make him easily the largest single shareholder. 'Rhodes is a very able man,' he told Woolf after one of these lunches. 'I think he means well. He has big ideas and will not allow a million to stand in his way. He is offering us a high price, but not more than others, and his generosity will make all interests join up. It's a mighty scheme, and Rhodes is the only man to pull the thing through.'

They now met almost as equals, Rhodes talking earnestly while Barney behaved with more propriety at the Club as soon as he was put up for membership. He stopped calling Rhodes, 'Mr', although he would never dare to address him by his Christian name or refer to him as such even in his cups. To Rhodes he was always 'Barney' when they were alone and 'Mr Barnato' at other times.

When the talk drifted to politics, Barney felt distinctly less comfortable. He regarded the Amalgamation simply as a mammoth deal of reconstruction which could lead to increased output, efficiency and revenue. He was confused by talk of 'tracts of country to be acquired by the company in Africa or elsewhere' and failed to be reassured by the promise that he and Woolf would become directors with a full share in all policy decisions. Rhodes, however, was subtle enough to inject tranquillizing doses of flattery as soon as Barney became restive. He dropped the hint that he would personally nominate him for membership of the Cape Parliament at the forthcoming election, arguing that it would be to the advantage of the diggers to have someone with their interests deeply at heart, as well as helpful to the new company. He also reminded him confidentially of their enemies at the Cape. Men like Robinson and his hirelings had opposed amalgamation for their own selfish ends, he pointed out, and Barney could help him to present a united front in the Assembly.

Rhodes showed a very different face when he came away from these luncheons. 'Barney wants to be a Member of Parliament as well as a member of the Kimberley Club,' he told Beit and Jameson with a shrug. 'God knows why! But if he wants it, let him have it. It is surely a small thing compared with the success of amalgamation.' This was characteristically disingenuous since he had himself offered precisely these baits, but he needed to justify his actions in advance to friends who openly detested the little Cockney. He was likewise ready for trouble from Philipson-Stow who had already written to warn him that 'the day that man comes on the Board, I go off; and there will be others with me.'

Barnato and Rhodes had reached full agreement by mid-March, subject to hammering out details, especially over the Trust Deed which gave the new company almost unlimited powers of territorial annexation and development, including the authority 'to treat with Rulers or Governments of any country'. Barney thought this could mean raising an army or even making war. He said so bluntly when they met in a private room at the Kimberley Club. The argument had started in Dr Jameson's iron-roofed bungalow, which Rhodes was then sharing, and continued when they adjourned to the Club opposite for lunch. They were joined afterwards by Woolf and Beit who sat with them rather like junior counsel, equipped with documents and lists of figures.

They were still locked in argument at midnight. Every financial clause had been minutely examined and agreed, but after so many hours they had reached an impasse on the question of the Trust Deed which would clearly involve the whole future management of the Company. They walked across to Jameson's bungalow and had drinks and sandwiches on the veranda before resuming their discussion in the untidy sitting-room which soon grew thick with tobacco smoke. Rhodes looked flushed with heat and drink while he talked feverishly about railways and the potentialities of Central Africa. The halo of iron grey hair now spiked angrily in the lamp-light as he unfurled his maps and stabbed out routes to the great lakes of the north, snapping one pencil after another in his impatience.

'Aren't these just dreams?' Woolf protested. 'Dreams don't pay *dividends*.' He stressed the last word mainly for the benefit of his uncle who was dozing off.

'Dreams!' squeaked Rhodes. 'No, my young friend, they're not dreams, but *plans*. That's the difference.' Out came still more maps which Beit held down with his thumbs, while Woolf played for time by trimming the wick in the oil lamp. 'It was tiresome and monotonous,' he later recalled, 'but I would have sat up for a week if necessary.'

Rhodes could no longer control his exasperation. He curtly reminded Barney and his nephew that amalgamation had no value for him without the powers set forth in the Deed of Trust. Scenting victory, he kept repeating and with added emphasis that diamonds alone could never satisfy him. Barney was nearing exhaustion point. A cat-nap of even a quarter of an hour might have revived him and possibly hardened his opposition, but Rhodes permitted no let-up. He talked on while Barney sipped his rum and hot milk, puffing continuously at cigarettes until his jacket front was white with ash. Woolf nudged him back to attention when he closed his eyes. He then jumped abruptly to his feet and began pacing back and forth, polishing his glasses. By some miracle he had tapped reserves of nervous energy and suddenly seemed the freshest-looking man in the room.

At thirty-five he was the oldest of the four, but his pink cheeks showed no trace of stubble, unlike the others. He poured himself a drink with a remarkably steady hand and took Woolf aside. 'After all, every man has got a fad,' he murmured. 'This is his fad. If it will please him, we'll let him have it.' He then crossed the room and smilingly touched Rhodes on the arm. 'Some people have a fancy for one thing, some for another,' he said in a voice rough from smoking. 'You want the means to go north, and I think we must give it to you.'

But it was not yet complete surrender. Behind half-closed eyes Barney had quietly thought out the full implications of going on the new Board. Directors could be dismissed almost as easily as they were appointed. Once Rhodes had his way, there would be no security of tenure under his chairmanship. Barney, therefore, proposed a super-body of Life Governors in addition to the ordinary Board—'just to guard against the adoption of any unwise policy,' he explained, cocking an eyebrow. Rhodes looked across at Beit who nodded wearily and seemed close to one of his fainting fits. The details were agreed before they parted at 4 a.m. The Life Governors would be Rhodes, Barnato, Beit and Philipson-Stow, and each share in Kimberley Central would be exchanged for two in the new company plus a cash payment per share.

Barney woke Fanny to tell her the news. She prepared an early breakfast but her husband was too excited to eat and Woolf looked like yesterday's gardenia. Holding a mug of steaming black coffee laced with rum, Barney walked up and down his study, going over every inch of the ground they had covered in the past eighteen hours.

He shrugged off Woolf's doubts about Rhodes's intentions. 'Remarkable bloke,' he assured Fanny. 'He tied me up as he ties up everybody.' Never before had she known him to admit defeat over a transaction. Within a few hours, truer to form, he was claiming total victory, arguing that he had yielded only on minor points to achieve the bigger prize.

Rhodes and Beit had a painful meeting with Philipson-Stow who only agreed when Rhodes reminded him that the whole plan could collapse if he tried to blackball Barnato. Philipson-Stow gave in but expressed angry disapproval of the exclusion of Baring-Gould who, in his view, had helped to smooth De Beers' way into Kimberley Central and amply deserved a Life Governorship. Baring-Gould had to settle instead for a place on the Board, but Philipson-Stow never forgave Rhodes for what he considered shabby treatment, not far short of a breach of trust, towards his friend and ally. Rhodes, with his practical outlook, now had no more use for the former Chairman of Kimberley Central who had served his purpose and could be nothing but an irritation to Barnato whose continued co-operation was vital.

Barney, who of course knew about the confrontation with Philipson-Stow, was standing outside his office when Rhodes emerged with Beit. Both looked strained as they came down the street towards him. A nod from Rhodes was enough to inform him of the result, but he could not resist a little thrust of his own. 'I thought I must have been holding things up,' he remarked genially.

The new Company, De Beers Consolidated Mines, Ltd, was duly incorporated on 13 March 1888 with a nominal capital of £100,000 in £5 shares of which Barney held over 6,000 and his three fellow Life Governors some 4,000 each. It was agreed that, after distributing dividends, they should also split one-fourth of any remaining net profits.

Some dissident shareholders in Kimberley Central had expected better terms but camouflaged their profit motive by bringing a case in which they attacked the De Beers Deed of Trust as *ultra vires*. The hearing went up to the Supreme Court who ruled against the merger but hinted broadly that the company might be bought by other means. With their three-fourths holding, the Rhodes-Barnato group promptly placed the company into voluntary liquidation. It was then bought on tender by De Beers Consolidated for £5,338,650. The cheque is now framed in the De Beers boardroom in Kimberley, while a huge uncut diamond still adorns the mantelpiece of the Partners' Room in New Court to remind the Rothschilds of their own decisive part in the negotiations.

Barney, Harry and their nephews scooped the best part of £2m most of which was profitably reinvested in the new company as the price of diamonds quickly shot up. The original capital was increased to nearly £4m by the end of the first year, plus a big issue of debentures for which the Rothschilds acted as trustees and guarantors. Majority interests were soon acquired in neighbouring claims which, together with those now held in the De Beer and Kimberley Mines, gave the company a virtual monopoly of almost 95% of the world's diamond output.

7

RHODES HAD KEPT HIS PROMISE to nominate Barney for the
Cape Assembly but this had certain drawbacks. By openly
endorsing him, Rhodes had lent the prestige of his own name
but had simultaneously saddled him with the *persona* of a mining
overlord and a member of the Kimberley Club. Barney might well
have fared better without Rhodes who was himself so unpopular
at this time that his friends insisted on giving him police protection
for several weeks after the amalgamation.

Barney did not at first appreciate the full animosity of the
opposition. His showmanship rejoiced in the smoking concerts
and enthusiastic back-slapping which followed his endorsement by
the Miners' Union and the Licensed Victuallers' Association. He
spoke lucidly and without notes, making his points with a jovial
informality. Every speech was so warmly received by his supporters that he expected to be returned unopposed. Nevertheless,
he did not wish to deprive the diggers or himself of 'a bit of a
circus'. He ordered a coach from Cape Town and had it lavishly
decorated in gilt, with an elaborate 'B' monogrammed on the
panels. Fortified by still-fresh boyhood memories of the Lord
Mayor's Show in London, he then harnessed four matching grey
horses from nearby farms and hired two cockaded footmen and
half a dozen outriders in jockey caps. They were dressed in olive
green with masses of gold braid and lace. A local giant named
Charley, part-time drummer in the municipal band, was taught to
trumpet fanfares.

The candidate dressed the part. A Jewish tailor made him a
silver-grey morning coat with scarlet silk facings. He wore a
rakish grey topper with which he juggled to raise a laugh. When-

ever the coach appeared on the streets, it was surrounded by a laughing crowd who were regaled with drinks and a stream of jokes, while Charley handed out cigars described as 'La Flor de Barney Barnato'. The labels depicted the candidate against a background of the Kimberley Mine.

The carnival atmosphere faded as soon as the Citizens' Political Association went into action. They put up four opposition candidates and heckled him brutally at every meeting, several of which were held in bars and often led to rough-houses. Gangs of ruffians would suddenly throw bottles and start a free fight. Barney's supporters were heavily outnumbered at one meeting but Charley, who was more pugilistic than musical, did powerful execution with his knuckle-dusters. He was vigorously assisted by Barney's old friend, Leo Lowenthal. They cleared a path but he only escaped by jumping clean through a plate-glass window. He was howled down by a claque at another meeting and had to be restrained from taking off his coat and wading into the crowd. It took self-control and the presence of Rhodes's friend, Dr Rutherfoord Harris, on the platform to remind himself that he was now a parliamentary candidate and not a Saturday night bouncer in the old King of Prussia. Finally, he made himself heard. 'If you won't listen to me,' he bellowed, 'I'll recite instead.' He then gave renderings from *The Bells*, but the 'To be or not to be' soliloquy was too serious. He quickly reverted to his bawdier repertoire which at least kept the meeting from being wrecked.

This heckling and rowdyism worried him far less than the vigorous campaign which soon opened under the skilful command of Merriman who may have been influenced by his failure to secure an amalgamation of the diamond mines through lack of resources, but was probably motivated more by his disapproval of Barney and his business methods. He made a speech at Woodstock, in which he declared, 'Men are being put forward for election who, if returned, would be a disgrace to any society, and it is quite possible that we may see the spectacle of the dupe on the Breakwater and his employer in Parliament.'

It was an obvious reference to Barney, nailing him with the old I.D.B. slur. One newspaper editorial then stigmatized him as 'not a fit and proper person to represent this constituency. His wealth is divorced from honour.' He charged over like a billy-goat and became so threatening that the editor crumpled and even offered to sell him the paper!

Nevertheless, Barney's speeches grew more restrained. As election day drew nearer, he still drove furiously round the constituency, fanfared by Charley, but began to score his debating points with some dignity. For a man of such limited education he was developing into a most accomplished speaker. He was expected to be quick-witted with hecklers, but impressed Rutherfoord Harris and others by his ability to present facts in an energetic yet conversational style that exactly suited the audience. He memorized most of his speeches but had the knack of making them sound impromptu.

He gave more or less the same address in bar and hall. Stocky and muscle-packed, blatantly playing to the gallery, he spoke decisively of his hard work and self-made success. Pausing for dramatic effect, he kept asking, 'Is that wealth divorced from honour?' It became almost a drumbeat of contempt and defiance. He received his biggest ovation when, after recalling all the major transactions which had shot him from 'kopje-walloping' to a Life Governorship in De Beers, he challenged his opponents to stand up and justify a single charge of impropriety.

Rhodes's personal intervention was valuable if not completely disinterested. It gave him a welcome chance to answer his own critics, but Barney was nevertheless grateful for his eloquent support. Taking the chair at one meeting, he observed: 'Mr Barnato has been accused of being devoid of honour. If he is good enough to be a co-Director with me, he is good enough to represent us in Parliament. I shall stick by Mr Barnato until it is proved to the satisfaction of a British jury that he is not a fit and proper person to represent this community.' It was perhaps due to what would now be called 'a Freudian slip' that Rhodes inaccurately referred to the candidate's ownership of '*a tenth* of our industry'. Barney corrected him in his vote of thanks by affably recalling his *one-eighth* interest.

On election day, 13 November 1888, he gaily toured the fifteen polling stations while Charley trumpeted for support. By early evening, long before the country votes had arrived, it was obvious that Barney had topped the poll by an overwhelming majority. His supporters, wearing light blue rosettes, gathered in force outside Barnato Brothers' offices in the Diamond Market. His landau led a dozen other carriages and an excited crowd on foot to the Court House where he made a speech of thanks. Bonfires were lit on the Market Square, and 'Kimberley was swimming in whisky' that night to an accompaniment of fireworks. 'There was considerable animation, and a portion of the crowd were abnormally exuberant,' reported the still-hostile Press. 'The police made several arrests.' Barney saw to it that supporters and opponents alike had their fines paid.

He never forgot that election. Years later he confessed to an interviewer, Harry Raymond, that the vicious personal attacks had tempted him to withdraw altogether after one of the early meetings. 'But I stayed and faced it out, and fought that Kimberley election as no election had ever been fought in South Africa before and came in at the head of the poll. And then no dog barked. D'ye understand? D'ye follow me?'

Within a week of his triumph at the polls, he drove up to Johannesburg in the gilded coach with Solly at his side. He reluctantly left Charley and the outriders behind, but otherwise reverted to his old barnstorming. Young Neville Abrahams, who had been sent up to look after the local office, arranged for a brass band, a top-hatted welcoming committee and a curtseying girl to present Barney with a bouquet. Abrahams then called for three cheers which were given with genuine, if practical, enthusiasm.

Barney's arrival in Johannesburg, although later in the day than the financial dinosaurs from Kimberley who now stalked the Rand, had a tonic effect. The diggers were already feeling the crushing weight of taxes imposed by 'Oom Paul' Kruger who had seen his strip of veld transformed overnight into a City of Gold. Many real estate promoters and claim-owners, less happily placed than magnates like Beit, Eckstein and Joseph Robinson, soon found themselves desperately short of investment capital.

Barney's flair for profitable speculation was now so legendary that everyone, with the exception of competing financiers, prayed that his millions would start another share bonanza on a Kimberley scale.

'What are you going to buy, Mr Barnato?' a woman called from the crowd.

'The answer is everything, ducks,' he shouted back jovially. 'Everything, d'ye follow me?' He was carried shoulder-high to the nearest bar where he stood drinks to all comers. He wore an outsize sparkler in his silk cravat and plucked a white carnation from the bouquet to pin on his frock-coat. 'This town must have been born with a gold spoon in its mouth,' he remarked to Solly as they strolled along Commissioner Street whose new brightly-lit shops were doing a brisk trade well after midnight. The clerk at Height's Hotel deferentially handed him a sheaf of messages, including a card asking him to be guest of honour at a St Andrew's Night banquet in the Theatre Royal.

Up to now he had enjoyed the true gambler's anticipatory tingle of playing for high stakes, perhaps even higher than in Kimberley. This heart-warming, unsolicited invitation seemed almost to justify everything that had gone before: Cobb's Court, the heat and dust of the Big Hole, even the bottles and charges flung at him during the election.

He stretched luxuriously between crisp sheets and lit a last cigarette. It was barely fifteen years since the night he had humped his kitbag into Harry's leaky tent in Dutoitspan. Like a child he would always identify places with never-forgotten incidents. Cape Town was a fat old man in a white stetson assuring him that all the diamonds had gone. Kimberley became a few precious boxes of bad cigars and the grateful warmth of long underwear when Lou Cohen yanked his green blanket away. And roaring Johannesburg could never again be dissociated from a slip of pasteboard left by some Scottish miners who had not forgotten him when they rushed north to prospect for gold.

Part Two

JOHANNESBURG
and
PARK LANE

8

———

ARNATO AND RHODES had both arrived late on the Rand scene and for very similar reasons. Heavily involved in the skirmishes that preceded their merger, they had also been misled by experts who reported adversely on the early gold finds. Rhodes had other pressing distractions: apart from parliamentary affairs, he was busily planning his expansionist manoeuvres in the north. Barney was himself too preoccupied with consolidating his diamond interests and getting himself elected to the Assembly to pay much heed to excitable reports of gold strikes on the Witwatersrand ('White Waters Ridge'), some thirty miles to the south of Pretoria. With still raw memories of the costly nuggets found at Barberton and Pilgrim's Rest, he had remained sceptical when the brothers Struben hit pay dirt on a bare treeless plateau hitherto used by Boer farmers to pasture their cattle.

The Strubens had hardly begun to crush quartz with a primitive five-stamp battery when two ex-Kimberley diggers also found traces of ore in the rock outcrop on a farm at Langlaagte, a couple of miles away. They had struck what turned out to be the Main Reef. On 8 September 1886, the Rand was officially proclaimed a goldfield. By the end of the year, three thousand miners were working in public diggings on a thirty-mile wide, gold-bearing reef, with more arriving daily by stagecoach, wagon and even on foot.

It had seemed like Kimberley all over again. A market square was ringed by bullock wagons, tents, reed huts and camp fires. Vacant plots in the sun-cracked red earth were marked out by wooden pegs, and a few tin-shacked offices almost melting in the hot sun handled land plots and claims. By December plans were approved for an official township to be called Johannesburg. That month the first auction sale of building leases realized £13,000, prices ranging from a few shillings a plot to £200. The main thoroughfare, soon named Commissioner Street, separated it from the rival settlement of Marshall's Town.

There was neither sanitation nor public lighting. Covered by lakes and deluged by heavy rains, the plateau was 6,000 feet above sea level but often became a swamp in summer. Diggers also found the red-brown dust more trying than anything they had experienced in Kimberley. Many died from pneumonia in their first bitterly cold winter. All raw materials, wood, iron and provisions had to be brought by ox-wagon from the Cape hundreds of miles away. The Boer farmers now had less far to come with their produce, but a voracious demand sent prices rocketing to early Kimberley levels. Potatoes fetched 5s. a bucket, firewood 28s. a load, and a few pats of butter were eagerly bought for 3s. a small tin. The best hotel, the Grand, was of corrugated iron with bedrooms hastily erected in tiers out of tin and matchwood.

The traditional camp followers reappeared; prize-fighters, whores, touts, confidence men, gamblers and a horde of fortune-hunters of a dozen nationalities. A prospector found only two gold teeth in a mine he had bought at a high price. They turned out to be from the very denture stolen from him a few days earlier. The first Standard Bank branch was a mud-thatched hut without a strong room and only a few handy six-shooters to guard deposits.

Early Johannesburg had all the primitive zest and ugliness of a frontier town, but powerful financial and political factors marked it off from any similar mining camp in history. Kruger paid an official visit in February 1887, wearing his frock coat and blue-green sash, and made it clear that these Uitlander diggers would have to pay dearly in tariff charges, licences and every other kind of taxable revenue. He was also eager to hand out concessions and monopolies to the highest bidders, especially Germans, in his anxiety to make his Republic economically self-sufficient.

Surprisingly, even Kimberley's sharpest opportunists had been a little slow off the mark. Joseph B. Robinson was among the first to see his chance but lacked the cash to go it alone. Squeezed by the banks, he had had to swallow his pride to call on Beit who had also seen preliminary reports and a few promising samples. He agreed to guarantee The Buccaneer's overdraft at the Cape of Good Hope Bank and advanced him a further sum against a one-third share in the proceeds.

Robinson secured several options and bought claims, often by unscrupulous methods, on the Main Reef. Langlaagte was snapped up for only £6,000, Robinson bragging later that he had made up his mind to buy the farm after panning a few samples in his topee. He also purchased the large and valuable de Villiers property and called it the Robinson Gold Mine. Unhappily for him, he made a serious misjudgment in deciding that the Western Rand, in which Langlaagte was sited, had a richer potential than the East preferred by Beit. After some acrimony they decided to split up their quickly-won empire, Robinson keeping the properties in his favoured sector. He later sold a half-share in his mine for a mere £50,000 and was chagrined to see it rise in value to over £18m.

Beit's phenomenal success in gold mining led him and Wernher to back Eckstein & Co. who had set up their headquarters on a corner of Commissioner Street to handle Rand properties and a variety of other company business. Hermann Eckstein, one of the Kimberley veterans, became the Rand's first President of the Chamber of Mines, an office in which he was succeeded by Lionel Phillips who had joined the Company after leaving J. B. Robinson. 'The Corner House' developed into the most powerful force in Johannesburg until its supremacy was challenged by Barney Barnato.

Rhodes might have achieved his Rand millions much sooner had he linked up with Eckstein, Beit and the others in this group. 'Little Alfred' gave him every opportunity, even offering him half shares in his own holdings at cost, but Rhodes long had a blind spot about the Rand. In the end Wernher, Beit & Co. picked up several excellent claims—some for only £750—which Rhodes had declined.

Soon after the Langlaagte finds, Dr Hans Sauer had become so excited about the Rand that he drove south to Kimberley and even woke Rhodes from his sleep to show him his samples. Still apathetic about gold when he had a world monopoly in diamonds practically within his grasp, Rhodes reluctantly advanced him his expenses and promised him a share in any suitable properties he might spot. The Doornfontein farm on which Sauer had taken an option would become one of Johannesburg's best building sites. It was valued at £3m within only two years. An option on the Duplessis farm, which would produce several million pounds' worth of gold, had been secured for only a few hundred. While Rhodes was hesitating whether or not to exercise these rights, he learned that his most intimate friend, Neville Pickering, was dying. Despite Sauer's protests, he hurried back to Kimberley, leaving everything in mid-air. Pickering died in his arms whispering 'You have been father, mother, brother and sister to me.'

Barney attended the funeral and could not help 'sniffing and blubbering', according to Rhodes, who shook him by the hand and sighed, 'Ah, Barney, he will never sell you another parcel of diamonds.'

David Harris's moderate success as a diamond broker had also made him eager to follow up the Struben finds. Barney and Woolf were only mildly interested but finally agreed to back his reconnaissance. Travelling three days and nights by Gibson's twelve-horse coach, he covered the three hundred miles to the mining camp now so jammed that he had to sleep on a bagatelle table. Pasture farms, recently worth no more than £750, were already changing hands for up to £70,000.

He toured the area, pounding and panning the banket at least one hundred times in a fortnight. He made a careful note of the most likely sites, taking samples from each. The yield was so astonishing that he decided to wire the good news to Kimberley, urging his cousin to come out at once and see for himself. Since there was no telegraph office locally, he sat up front with the driver of a mailcart who was on his way to Pretoria. They covered the thirty-six miles through a blinding rainstorm, but Harris despatched his wire before even troubling to change his sodden clothing. That evening a discouraging reply came from Kimberley. Barney was too busy to leave and would send two of his experts instead to make an impartial report.

Heath and Marshall worked in his Oriental Company as overseers and consultants and he had a touching faith in their judgment, thanks to their previous years in the New Zealand goldfields. When Harris showed them around his carefully selected sites, they sneered, 'We could find more gold on the sea shores back home than all the gold here put together.' Harris then took them out to a claim on which he had purchased a small option in the near vicinity of the original Langlaagte farm. Even this failed to convince them. They panned, tested and exchanged looks of amusement. 'Enough gold here to salt the other claims,' scoffed Heath.

Barnato decided against further action. After seeing ambiguous prospectuses and hearing tales of salted mines, he suspected another Barberton. So many companies were formed to raise capital that, by June 1887, it was necessary to start a Stock Exchange whose members crowded into a single-storey building opposite the Corner House. Hundreds of brokers and touts spilled out into Simmonds Street part of which had to be closed to traffic so that dealers could hear the latest prices called out. A special section was needed to accommodate this overflow, particularly for after-hours dealings and on Saturdays or public holidays. Iron posts, linked by chains, were put up. 'Between the Chains' became not only a recognized place of business but one of the city's landmarks.

Dealings grew more and more feverish as claim-owners waited impatiently for machinery which was piling up at the railhead in Kimberley. Diggers had frenziedly bored the reef only to find that the best deposits lay in the deeper levels. Reacting to their mood of frustration and near-hysteria, shares began to change hands like playing cards as promoters became more desperate to attract investment capital.

Barney paid a brief visit early in 1888 to make a lightning tour of the claims. Viewing the higgledy-piggledy mounds of excavated gravel with distaste, he refused to invest a penny. Only after considerable hesitation would he agree to send up Neville Abrahams to hold a watching brief for Barnato Brothers.

In the next few months he was far too busy with his election campaign to give full attention to the optimistic reports which young Abrahams was sending back from the Rand. But he could no longer ignore the figures of increased gold loads or the capital which Robinson, Beit and now Rhodes were sinking into the reef. Others also reminded him that his New Zealand 'experts' had lost him valuable time. His old friend, Ikey Sonnenberg, was not the man to give two stands free of charge to erect the Rand Club without some hope of a return on his benevolence. Barney was even more impressed by reports that Sammy Marks was financing President Kruger and had established himself as head of an already thriving Jewish community.

Some ninety pioneers had arrived from Barberton in '87 to form the Witwatersrand Goldfields Jewish Association. They were joined by so many others, including Russian refugees and an influx of 'Peruvians' from Kimberley, that the government had made them the gift of a plot for a cemetery. Soon afterwards, Kruger provided four stands or plots for the erection of churches or chapels to the different Christian denominations, but only two for the synagogue which it was proposed to build on President Street. Marks protested at this discrimination but Kruger had countered with one of his rare jokes. 'Your people believe in only half the Bible,' he growled back 'The others believe in the whole of it. When you change, I'll give you the other two stands.'

When Barney drove up for his second visit in November 1888, he at once called on the rabbi and contributed generously to building the domed synagogue. Its formal opening by the President would provide him with a cherished anecdote for his after-dinner repertoire. Kruger, never the diplomat, stood bareheaded. He then made his speech in Afrikaans and was about to declare the building open 'in the name of Our Lord Jesus Christ' when he retrieved his error in mid-sentence with a timely fit of coughing.

9

———

BARNEY HAD A THUNDEROUS RECEPTION when he rose to speak at the St Andrew's Night banquet. He beamed on the crowd of diggers in the one-storeyed Theatre Royal in Market Street, glanced briefly at his notes and then tore them up, handing the scraps to a waiter. It was a *coup de théâtre* which he had often practised during his election campaign. The audience roared approval and his speech delighted them even more.

'I am proud, pleased and happy to find myself amongst you tonight; for, although I am a stranger in a certain sense, yet when I look round and see so many faces familiar to me, I realize that I am with old friends and acquaintances. I can assure you that when I arrived a few days ago, I felt simply paralysed at the sight of what had been done. I came for a visit but I shall stay for months, and I look forward to Johannesburg becoming *the financial Gibraltar of South Africa*.'

That last resounding phrase had more than an echo of Rhodes, but it was no mere piece of rhetoric. Barney wrote to his brother and Jack Joel in London informing them of his intention to invest heavily in the Rand. He quickly approved setting up more spacious offices in Draper's Gardens off Throgmorton Street to handle an expected flood of new business in gold-mining shares and real estate, as well as the heavy diamond trade. His letters to Woolf were so sanguine that his nephew drove up to Johannesburg to investigate a silly rumour that Barney was spending money like a drunken sailor. It was even being said that he planned to leave Kimberley for good and would confine all his future investments to the Rand. At a dinner arranged in his honour on New Year's Day, Woolf dropped his reserve and spoke with a jaunty assurance new to him. Like Barney and Solly he reacted to the heady atmosphere of Johannesburg and shared their amazement at the prosperity of the township whose white population already exceeded ten thousand.

There was another reason for his cheerfulness. He was now very happily married. His bride, Olive Desmond, was a charming soubrette who had played small parts at the Gaiety in London and became a favourite with South African audiences. Like Fanny she was not a Jewess and duly embraced the faith before Woolf plucked up enough courage to inform his parents. Olive and Fanny soon became the closest of friends which helped to reinforce Barney's strong affection for his nephew.

He and Solly had been feverishly busy in the month before Woolf arrived. Prospectuses and dozens of glittering proposals cascaded into their hotel. There was always a queue of hopeful speculators, engineers and entrepreneurs from early morning onwards. Everyone needed capital, and Barney sent hopes soaring by expressing himself ready and willing to buy up 'the whole of Johannesburg that is still for sale'. He was more than half serious. Profits looked certain on a rising market, despite the inflationary prices being asked. He had to be restrained by Solly who never tired of reminding him that their most pressing business was to buy the best mining sites and carefully allocate the enormous sums which would still be needed to exploit them. They spent a week together doing nothing but tour the reefs, carefully noting sites in the heaviest yield areas. A small corps of metallurgists and assayers then prepared detailed lists of gold returns, earmarking the claims that would benefit most from large-scale development and re-equipment.

Barney's reflexes were remarkably fast. He always made up his mind without hesitation once he had satisfied himself that reports and accounts were reliable; even so, he was fortunate in having Solly by his side during a buying spree that left even booming Johannesburg breathless. Solly had an accountant's tidy brain allied to his uncle's truffle-hound nose for a bargain. While Barney raced about from before breakfast until well past midnight, Solly patiently cross-examined mine managers and costing clerks. He did not limit himself to the Main Reef and bought a number of lots cheaply in the outlying districts which were not gold-bearing but might be developed into valuable residential estates. He also convinced his uncle that building sites in the town centre, as well as corner stands on the city's fringes, would soon be at a premium for stores and offices.

Barney agreed in principle but was far more excited by the mines. He invested the better part of £2m in only three months. In addition to the New Primrose, his first Rand flotation, he took controlling interests in other companies, including the New Croesus, the Roodeport and Glencairn Main Reef. He signed cheques for stupendous sums, ordering the latest pumps and refining equipment and approving plans to sink shafts. He also chartered convoys of transport wagons to ensure a steady flow of supplies from the Cape and Natal. Warehouses and modern buildings made from stone quickly replaced the ramshackle hutments or tin sheds.

Once a deal was arranged, he delegated without hesitation and jigged on to the next enterprise, but nothing was ever bought on hearsay. 'I must look into everything that concerns me for myself,' he bluntly informed a reporter. There was no haggling over prices, despite Solly's protests, but Barney was far from happy-go-lucky. He memorized the details of every transaction, whether a £100 option or the purchase of claims and building plots running into thousands. He once upset Solly by hastily buying a plot with only a few miserable tin shanties to the east of the Market Square. Solly thought the price excessive but his uncle's sharp eye had spotted clay which could be invaluable for brick-making.

His investments gushed so generously that it became ritual for stockbrokers to ask 'What's Barney buying?' before making up the day's starting prices. They formed an odd-looking miscellany; some wore deer-stalkers, helmets and even cricket caps, while a number of share-pushers, anxious to cut a figure, regularly appeared in riding boots and breeches. The élite were headed by Eckstein, Beit and their associates in the Corner House, then the only two-storeyed building in Johannesburg.

Barney was passing late one night with his old partner, Lou Cohen, when he pointed out a light burning on the first floor. 'Beit's up there, still counting his money,' he laughed. 'He don't like me here. Don't care, don't care. I know 'em all. I'll make you tons of money, tons of it, not for your sake, for your family's. Damn fool I am, come and have a drink. Only drink champagne, never mix it.' He snatched a cigarette from Cohen. 'Light, please, light.' He bustled into a saloon to order his champagne—'put it down to me'—and was soon engrossed in Johannesburg's favourite game of 'tempting the flies'. Gold sovereigns were placed on the bar counter and each covered with a lump of sugar. The pool was won by the player on whose sugar lump the first fly settled. As soon as he tired of that game, he played 'Yankee Grab' in which dice were thrown for handfuls of sovereigns.

He tore about like a whirlwind, making sudden entrances and even more abrupt exits, giving staccato orders and never without a complement of hangers-on to nourish his self-esteem. He had always generated his own adrenalin even in the darkest hours of crisis. The non-stop excitement of speculation now worked in his veins to start a roaring bonfire of explosive energy. The sweet crystalline air of Johannesburg enabled him to dispense with even more sleep than usual. The altitude added a champagne sparkle to his blood and gingered him up for an eighteen-hour working day while he drank and smoked almost continuously. Such dynamic activity, coupled with the ceaseless outflow of investment cash, concentrated popular attention on him to the exclusion of others like Rhodes, Beit and Robinson who were also sinking shafts and quietly thrusting tentacles into every corner of Rand finance. Barney, however, was buying huge blocks of shares with such panache that a one-man boomlet automatically started the moment he appeared 'between the Chains', pink-faced and smiling, with a straw hat or bowler perched on the back of his glossy head. 'Without doubt,' enthused the *Star*, 'the increased value of landed property is largely due to Mr Barnato.' It was true, but the flattering approval which greeted his every move also made him over-sensitive to criticism.

His manner, even more than the powers of mystical divination attributed to him by grateful shareholders, gave deep offence to many who did not approve of his style. Merriman, disgusted by the recent election and still critical of the De Beers amalgamation, wrote to a friend, 'I confess that I would sooner go to hell alone than arm-in-arm with Barney Barnato.' Others who had crossed swords with him in diamond deals were equally hostile to his spectacular coups on the Rand.

He had joined the Stock Exchange in mid-January 1889. Soon afterwards he walked into the crowded Exchange Hall with Lou Cohen who overheard an aside from Arthur Lilienfeld, one of the old German Mess in Kimberley, that 'the cheap little Yid' ought to go back to Whitechapel. Barney rushed over at once and hit him squarely on the jaw. The committee ordered them both to sign letters of regret, but Barney declined to apologize or resign. 'Resign?' he scoffed. 'How can I resign when I own the ruddy place?'

It was only a slight exaggeration. He had acquired a majority holding in the Johannesburg Estate and Chambers Company which owned the site, shrewdly deciding that the volume of business would soon demand larger premises. The affray with Lilienfeld stimulated him to push ahead faster. He planned to pull down the old house and replace it with Barnato Buildings, a spacious two-storey structure on Commissioner Street with room for a new Stock Exchange hall, a large block of one hundred office suites, and a covered market 350 feet in length on the street level with enough stalls to supply food, clothing and almost everything else required by a fast-growing and prosperous population.

Solly was sent to the Cape to hire architects for Barnato Buildings which would cost a minimum of £100,000 to put up. Although workmen were put on three eight-hour shifts, it would still not be completed before February 1890. By then hundreds of companies were being quoted on the official Exchange and far more on the street market. Business grew so brisk that brokers shouted prices outdoors 'between the Chains', while the old hall was being demolished.

Dealings were unorthodox, encouraged by bankers who were all too alert to discount promissory notes or advance large loans on any scrip. Street trading was so erratic that it was not uncommon for a share quoted at 30s. on Saturday night to double by Sunday noon, reach 90s. before tea, and slip back to the original figure when business opened on the Monday morning. Shares could be bought on 'time call' for settlement by noon on the following day.

This enabled sharks without cash to buy stock which they often resold at a profit within a couple of hours. If the shares dropped before noon, the gamblers simply pocketed their gains and left town in a hurry.

Gold scrip became almost a second currency, freely acceptable as payment for stores, drink and even women. Two hundred wagons a day disgorged their produce in the Market Square, and men gladly paid £60 a month in rent for houses which had cost less than £2,000 to build. But the richest gains came from issuing bearer certificates as soon as a reef was scraped deep enough to dress a company prospectus. In this field the small promoter could not hope to compete with the ex-Kimberley magnates who had the resources to make big capital issues. Barney, in particular, had the magic of his name as well as Woolf's quite exceptional flair for stocks and shares.

The turnover was so enormous in the first quarter of 1889 that a financial writer declared half-seriously, 'If there is anyone who does not own some scrip in a gold mine, he is considered not quite right in the head.' William St John Carr, a former clerk who became the first Mayor of Johannesburg, made £20,000 in a single day. £1 shares were sometimes run up to £25 on mines which still lacked machinery and had little more than gaudy prospectuses on their scales. The nominal value of gold shares rose to over £100m although impartial experts estimated that the Rand's entire output could not have yielded even 3% of that figure.

The market, volatile and over-inflated, needed only a spark to blow it sky-high. A rumour started that the gold was giving out, whereas the trouble was purely technical. Near the surface it had been easy enough to process the banket by amalgamating the crushed ore with mercury. But as the reef became more pyritic, too little gold was left on the plates, the rest passing away with the 'tailings' of sand or slime. Metallurgists were unable to promise mine-owners a quick solution of this problem which not only halted further investment but caused alarm among those who had overreached themselves during the boom.

A panic selling of shares began as soon as the banks drew in their horns. Some £1 shares were unloaded for as little as 3d. each. Overdrafts were hastily withdrawn, but this did not save the

Paarl, the Union and the Cape of Good Hope Banks from having to close their doors. The few who survived had to give small monthly allowances to former magnates with only worthless-looking blocks of scrip for security. Pianos and furniture were sold for next to nothing in the Market Square by diggers who hurried back to Kimberley, the Cape and Natal. One-third at least of the stores put up their shutters, while even those who stayed on hopefully now jeered at Barnato's boasted prophecy that Johannesburg would become 'the financial Gibraltar of South Africa'.

He refused to be daunted. Reports on the New Primrose and other mines had finally convinced him that the gold-bearing reefs of the Rand continued for hundreds of feet. It might cost money, millions perhaps, to deal with pyrites and work the reef to its full potential, but when that was done nothing on earth could stop every square foot of Johannesburg—land and shop sites, quite apart from the diggings—being worth its weight in solid gold.

That April, Fanny laid the foundation stone of Barnato Buildings against a frieze of long faces. Barney looked rather less jaunty than usual but dealt summarily with the jeremiahs. 'I tell you here and now,' he burst out, 'that I have never made any mistake in speculation or in the investment of money.' It sounded like share-pushing but they sat up when he continued, 'I only regret I didn't come here two years ago and put money in bricks and mortar; but you see I am making up for lost time by doing it today in the face of depression.'

It was a fighting speech which he would repeat with increasing emphasis whenever he addressed shareholders or gave his business breakfasts. 'The gold is there in the earth, beyond a doubt,' he maintained. 'Money and patience, money and patience, will over-come all difficulties here as they did in Kimberley.' He gobbled shares, housing sites and claims at give-away prices from the faint-hearted who chose to ignore his advice. When he went 'between the Chains' he often lost his temper with the gloomy brokers who still played 'Yankee Grab' but made the dice sound like a death rattle. 'You're losing money because you're afraid of losing it,' he snorted. 'I've never been frightened of losses, and that's how I got where I am today.'

But the township's low morale was only partly due to the share

slump and the scare about pyrites. Johannesburg was suffering
from a severe drought which soon resulted in a real danger of
famine as the provision wagons failed to come through. Oxen and
mules died by the hundred on the bone-dry veld, and food shops
were looted nightly as prices reached impossible heights. Five
pounds was being asked for a bag of mealie-meal, and sugar had
almost disappeared from the market. In the backyard of Barney's
house stood two large hogsheads for water which were supplied
three times a week on a strictly rationed basis at 8s. a bucket.
Hungry native mineworkers had already begun to trek back to
their kraals when Sammy Marks produced a stop-gap solution. He
persuaded the President to offer a bonus of £20 each for every
wagon that arrived in town with three tons of foodstuffs. The
outlying farmers responded while stocks lasted, but Barney had
little faith in them or Kruger's proclamation ordering a day of
prayer for rain. A full-scale water programme was clearly needed.

Sir James Sivewright, an electrical engineer with many financial
interests, headed a syndicate formed in 1887 to acquire several
hundred acres of land adjoining the township and supply water for
the diggings and the domestic needs of the population. Barnato
Brothers had put in a few pounds, 'more because we were asked to
subscribe than for any other reason,' said Barney. Many others took
shares in Johannesburg Waterworks Company after plans were
announced to construct a reservoir near the Doornfontein farm.
But there was insufficient working capital for the pipes and
machinery which had to come from Port Elizabeth or the distant
Cape. Plagued by drought, impatient shareholders and banks who
were pressuring for repayment of their loans, Sivewright was all
too literally in low water when he turned to Barnato Brothers.
Barney at once advanced £30,000 from his own pocket to pay off
pressing creditors, soon pouring in still more cash to give his firm a
controlling interest.

It was an act of faith in the future of Johannesburg but few of his
enterprises would earn him more personal unpopularity. His water
kept the town habitable and he did not charge profiteering rates,
but investors expected spectacular Kimberley-scale profits as soon
as he took over. They would never reconcile themselves to small
dividends and grumbled at the cost of installing miles of pipelines

to service a population which would soon grow to forty thousand.

His intervention had been public-spirited, but there were valuable fringe benefits. Without a fairly reliable water supply he could not have kept his mines going or maintained property values in which the firm already had a considerable stake. He and Solly were quick off the mark in developing building sites owned by the Waterworks Company at Doornfontein. Bought originally for only £12,500 they would be worth over £800,000 within three years when a residential estate mushroomed into what Barney proudly called 'the Belgravia of Johannesburg'.

His investment in the Waterworks Company was, of course, insignificant compared with other outgoings during those first critical months of 1889. Barnato Buildings was sponging up enormous capital for labour and materials, with as yet no takers for marked-off stands in the imposing red and black brick Market Hall. However, digging continued in the firm's half-dozen mines several of which averaged a higher output than their neighbours. The Barnato underground workings were on the Californian system, in blocks, and the latest pumping plant and stamp batteries had been installed. Nearly all the buildings were of solid stone, the ore being conveyed by tramways from shaft to battery, then an innovation.

One man alone could not arrest a share slump but his personality contributed almost as much to public morale as the scale of his investments. He kept a smiling face at smoking concerts and constantly rallied defeatist townsfolk. He was one of the earliest to subscribe for the site and pavilion which became the headquarters of the Wanderers Club. There he welcomed the first English cricket team to visit South Africa under the captaincy of C. Aubrey Smith who stayed on for a time as a stockbroker. The slump finally drove him out of business and into a most successful film career.

When the cricketers departed, Barney at once began rehearsing for the star part in *Ticket of Leave Man* with Lou Cohen in support. His performance at the Globe in aid of the new synagogue's building fund won him an ovation but the night air brought on a severe chill as he hurried out of the theatre to celebrate with the company. It affected his lungs but he ignored Woolf's advice to call in Jameson who specialized in pulmonary diseases. He preferred to send for his old friend, Dr Joseph Matthews, who had seen Kimberley through camp fever and a smallpox epidemic and was now establishing a good practice in Johannesburg. The genial Scotsman looked grave when he sounded Barney's chest and noted the brown spots on his hands indicating liver trouble. The excitements of the past few months, aggravated by heavy drinking, had lowered his resistance to a point which made his chances of recovery very doubtful. Matthews told Woolf privately that the next few hours would be critical and advised him to have the Rev. Mark Harris on call.

Barney, glistening with sweat, rallied miraculously. 'I'll be all right,' he assured Matthews. 'Anyway, what a devil of a fight there will be over the chips! But not yet, doc, not yet. They'll all have to wait a bit.' Since Woolf was a partner in the family firm about which there had never been a whisper of internal dissension, and Solly was treated with even more affection by his Uncle Barney, Matthews gave no second thought at the time to his patient's extraordinary remark. He put it down to delirium.

While still running a high temperature, Barney held what he called 'a Court Levy' in his bedroom, rattling off instructions to Woolf, Solly and a corps of mine managers. Within a fortnight he was presiding in his dressing-gown at one of the Sunday breakfasts which he customarily reserved for his family or cronies like Sivewright whose cherry-red nose paid tribute to an inseparable hip flask of Mountain Dew. He also spent many hours poring over the architect's plans for his new brick house and refused to stay in bed. He marched up and down, brushing up his favourite part of Matthias in *The Bells*. Ignoring doctor's orders, he kept his promise to perform at a benefit show on behalf of a local actress whom he greatly admired.

Although the stock market was still ebbing, there were faint signs of a recovery. Barney himself looked as frisky as a springbok, throwing off greetings and good-humoured insults like a fire-hose jet as he made his round of the saloons before departing with Fanny that May. A fellow-passenger on the Kimberley coach was Rudolph Kahn, the French banker, who had been staying with

Lionel Phillips while discussing long-term finance with the Corner House group. Kahn was pale-faced and plainly nervous about reports that highwaymen often held up coaches on the long cross-country run. 'Well, I'm not taking any valuables with me,' he observed to reassure himself. 'That's all right,' Barney said cheerfully. 'I understand they take cheques.'

He stayed only a few days in Kimberley before going on to Cape Town for his first parliamentary session which he faced with some nervousness. He would have welcomed moral support from Rhodes who was in London lobbying for his proposed new Chartered Company. Rudd had at last secured the Concession from Lobengula to exploit all mineral rights in his territories and dependencies for a cash payment of £100 sterling per month, plus 1,000 rifles and, at Rhodes's suggestion, an armed paddle-steamer to patrol the Zambesi for defensive purposes.

But their troubles were not over. 'Old Lob' was soon besieged by other concession-hunters, including Beit's cousin, Edward Lippert, who began to make a mockery of Rudd's 'complete and exclusive' rights by playing on Lobengula's justifiable fears that he had signed away his independence. Lippert's pointed ginger beard and lobster face became a familiar sight in the royal kraal and Rhodes guessed that he had German money and support from Pretoria behind him. For the time being, however, he brushed aside this undoubted menace and concentrated on dazzling the Colonial Office. He was asking for a Charter for his British South Africa Company which would not only empower him to exploit mineral wealth but extend the railway and telegraph northwards from Mafeking, establish a British Resident in Bulawayo, make treaties and maintain a police force. In short, he now had his blueprint to colonize an area three times the size of the United Kingdom.

While Rhodes was assembling a glittering prestige board for the Chartered Company, Barney took his seat in the Assembly. He was slightly overawed by the colonial wood and green leather upholstery, but could not resist playing the fool. He entered the Chamber with a cigarette in his mouth, pretending to have forgotten to put it out. As a joke it misfired, and henceforth he took care to treat the House with more respect. Not for two years, by which time he had found his feet, would he propose 'that the House of Assembly should adjourn in order that Members might attend the English football match.'

He made a popular gesture on his first appearance by waiving his salary which he asked the Speaker to dispose of to suitable charities. Two months went by before he ventured to make his maiden speech. He attended every day, listened to the debates with a patience foreign to his temperament and diligently studied parliamentary procedure. In private he took a few elocution lessons from a former schoolmaster who preserved his aitches without endowing him with a fake educated accent. He decided to speak in favour of the Ballot Act although aware that, as the nominee of Rhodes who supported the measure, he might get a very rough passage from the Opposition. He refused to wait until the Committee stage and spoke up with some force. 'The Ballot is more, much more, needed in the country than in the town districts,' he said earnestly.

He steeled himself not to glance at the opposite benches where some stretched their legs and feigned sleep while others ostentatiously took snuff and sneezed as loudly as Barney used to do at the Kimberley Club. He talked clearly in a slightly mandarin English and was inclined to over-gesticulate in the Irving manner, but it was a good maiden speech, nevertheless. Later that day he intervened on behalf of the ill-paid and under-manned police force in Kimberley and succeeded in having a Select Committee appointed to go into the question.

It would be some years before his speeches became less stilted. He was at his best when his wit and common sense penetrated the cottonwool. One such occasion was during the debate on the Cape Liquor Law which proposed to forbid the sale of alcohol on the Sabbath without a solid meal. He addressed his fellow-Members with an easy informality which made Merriman, himself a brilliant parliamentarian, break into a friendly smile.

'A few Sundays ago I walked some distance from Cape Town. Being busily engaged in mentally reviewing the course of business of the Honourable House, I went on much farther than I had intended without noticing the time. Being hot and thirsty, I went into a decent and most respectable hotel for refreshment. I only wanted to quench my thirst.' He paused for an expected laugh, and the Members did not disappoint him. 'Mine host set before me a bottle of beer and a leg of roast pork.' He raised his eyebrows in mock horror. 'He had no other eatables. What was I to do? If I ate the pork, I broke the Law of Moses. If I drank the beer without eating, I broke the law of the land. Between the Chief Rabbi and the Chief Justice, I stood in a very awkward position.'

When he returned to Kimberley in July 1889, after braving the Assembly, he felt more confident to preside at the first Annual General Meeting of De Beers Consolidated shareholders in place of Rhodes. His task was to give an account of the Amalgamation and attempt to reassure gloomy shareholders about the issue of debentures. He would need to master details of the work in hand and, more important, future prospects. He arranged to stay with David Harris who reminded him that he had only a week in which to prepare this vital speech.

He seemed in no hurry. He saw all his old digger pals and gave them a riotous retrospective party to compensate for the dull affair in Cape Town to celebrate his thirty-seventh birthday a week earlier. He thanked them for their congratulations and swigged champagne from a pewter tankard, 'just to bring back the taste of the beer, for beer was good when I'd just earned the price of a pint.' The boozy camaraderie was doubly welcome after the strain and formality of the Assembly, but in his more sober moments he spoke seriously of his confidence in the diamond industry. They cheered when he promised an early return to full employment in the diggings and repeated his pledge not to desert them for the Rand.

A crowd followed him when he marched jauntily to Ebden Street to confer with Gardner Williams who briefed him on mining returns in the first year. Several cronies waited outside to escort him on a tour of the saloons which usually ended in the small hours with everyone else under the table. He liked to put the gloves on for a little sparring practice, but turned down a challenge to go three rounds with a burly miner. David Harris had stepped in to warn him that the Vice-Chairman and Life Governor of De Beers might not look at his best on the platform with a 'shiner' or a thick lip.

Harris became more and more nervous as Barney kept putting

off preparing his speech. He reminded him in vain that the meeting would be attended by shareholders still unconvinced about the Amalgamation while Jameson and others might welcome a chance to ridicule him if he fell short of Rhodes's expectations. The financial Press had arrived in force, and the proceedings were certain to be reported far beyond South Africa since Rhodes had lately rented splendid offices in Lombard Street in the hope of securing an official quotation for the Company on the London Stock Exchange. Barney, however, seemed completely unaware that he was expected to give a full-dress performance before an international audience.

Instead of applying himself to the notes which Gardner Williams and the conscientious Harris had prepared, he spent his nights tippling and gambling after a few hours' work in the offices of Barnato Brothers. One morning he bustled in and demanded the state of the firm's bank balance. He then consulted his diary and commented sharply, 'You're £4,000 out. Let me have details of everything bought and sold this week.' He was shown the figures and frowned. 'You'd better find that £4,000,' he snapped. The accountant produced his pass books and sales records which seemed to be in order, but Barney was still not satisfied. He had always prided himself on knowing, almost to a sixpence, exactly where he stood, and this apparent discrepancy upset him. Harris tried to reason with him that the sum involved was minute in relation to the firm's turnover and hardly justified turning the office upside down when he had the far more important General Meeting ahead. He persisted, however, and had the satisfaction of being proved right although the circumstances were disturbing. It turned out that an employee had falsified the books to cover his misappropriation of a parcel of Kimberley Centrals.

Barney was still making merry at 4.30 a.m. on 19 July, the day fixed for the Meeting. He finally sprinted to Harris's office where he sat down by the light of a couple of candles to go over sheets of facts and figures. He read them through carefully and made notes on a few scraps of paper which he crumpled into his pocket, only looking up to shoot a question or two. As the clock struck seven, he hurried off to his cousin's house for a shave and cold bath, followed by half an hour's press-ups and shadow boxing. He then sat down to a hearty breakfast, pouncing now and then on notes spread all over the table. After dressing with exceptional care he strolled off to Ebden Street with his hair smoothly parted and a garden flower in his lapel.

He spoke fluently for almost two hours with hardly a glance at his notes, making his points like a veteran chairman. He brought bright tidings but was not tempted into bombast. He kept his hands still and for once restrained his Lyceum manner in reporting a first year's profit of nearly half a million pounds. To everyone's surprise he also acknowledged Rhodes's 'marvellous piece of finance' in capitalizing the company on a realistic level.

He sat down to cheers in which even Jameson joined, afterwards expressing astonishment that an illiterate cockney could give such an unimpeachable performance. The London *Financial News* gushed praise and commented that his 'fertile brain' was behind the Amalgamation for which he had so generously handed Rhodes the credit: 'The absence of the chief gave Mr Barnato the opportunity, which was all that was required, to establish his reputation in the eyes of the world as a master of finance.'

Before leaving the platform he had winked mischievously at his cousin and whispered, 'Well, Dave, how did I get on?'

'Much better than I expected—or you deserved,' laughed Harris who hurried home to catch up with his sleep, amazed that Barney's stamina enabled him to go off and drink champagne before settling down to the best of five frames at snooker.

While waiting for the coach back to Johannesburg which was flashing distress signals from the Stock Exchange and the diggings, he went quietly to the rescue of several out-of-work miners and a number of shopkeepers who were in trouble. He heard that a broker whom he had known from his 'kopje-walloping' days was lying seriously ill in a back room. Barney was distressed to find him suffering from incurable cancer. His friends had done what they could over medical expenses but the illness was certain to be long and painful.

He asked Harris to summon a specialist from the Cape and arrange for day and night nursing as well as the best of nourishment. When he next visited Kimberley, Harris told him that the man was dead and he had paid out over £700 in medical and nursing expenses. Barney handed him a cheque which he signed with tears in his eyes: 'I wouldn't have cared if it had cost three times that amount to have saved the poor blighter's life.'

At the same time he hated lending money, particularly to anyone who tried to impose on a slight acquaintance. In the end, while still keeping his 'stoney-broke pocket' filled with sovereigns for genuine cases, he overprinted a warning on all his visiting cards: 'I will stand any man a drink, but I won't lend him a fiver.'

10

BARNEY ARRIVED BACK IN JOHANNESBURG to a semi-hysterical reception. He was waylaid by storekeepers, builders and stockjobbers who needed reassurance even more than financial aid. The share market was still becalmed with little sign as yet that the pyritic-laden gold yields might be improved. At pre-luncheon sessions in the Rand Club, the long bar counter reflected a parade of even longer faces. Rhodes was still in England finalizing his Charter and hinting strongly that he might turn from the slump-hit goldfields and concentrate all his energies on De Beers and his new British South Africa Company. Urged by Rudd, he had sold £300,000 worth of his mining stocks in six weeks. This plainly added to the mounting vote of no confidence in Johannesburg's future.

Barney refused to wring his hands. There were few takers for his Market Hall stands but the Waterworks Company's pipes had at last begun to function and a small number of building plots were being sold in Doornfontein. He still bounced into the Stock Exchange every morning and stubbornly bought blocks of shares which helped a little to stabilize prices although few were brave enough to follow his example. But his own personality acted as the stronger antidote to despondency. 'When things go badly, don't cry but laugh,' he urged a meeting of company promoters, including Eckstein and his Corner House colleagues who seemed as defeatist as the near-bankrupt storekeepers and with far less cause.

In July 1889, the hard-pressed citizens were able to take a welcome break from their anxieties. From London's East End, Barney had imported a Jewish bruiser, one Woolf Bendoff, who had fought the best in England and considered himself unlucky to lose to Jem

Smith. Barney and some of his friends offered to back him against J. R. Couper, the champion of South Africa, who commanded enthusiastic support from a local syndicate headed by Abe Bailey. 'Professor' Jamie Couper was frail-looking and had a deceptively gentle manner. Barney's racial sympathies and nostalgic affection for Whitechapel naturally made him belittle his chances against a man of Bendoff's gigantic physique. There had been a slight hitch when Kruger threatened to ban the contest, arranged for 26 July, but Barney sent an envoy to Pretoria and guilefully persuaded 'Oom Paul' that it might look very like cowardice to run away from this blustering Englander who boasted that he could whip any man in the Transvaal. The odds steadily lengthened against Jamie Couper. Despite Bendoff's suspiciously pneumatic waist, he was bowling over sparring partners and threatened to beat the little challenger with one hand tied behind him.

On the day of the fight, Barney felt so exuberant when he bustled in for breakfast that he assured Fanny he was almost tempted to take on Couper himself! He had dressed with special care for the occasion; his checked suit and brown curly bowler were sporty-looking and he wore a cowboy's woollen shirt from his Kimberley wardrobe to go with his bow tie. The drainpipe trousers set off his muscular calves as he jumped into his carriage to pick up Leo Lowenthal who would be one of the umpires. He forgot to take his hip-flask of brandy but refused to turn back as it might bring bad luck. On the way to Eagle's Nest, six miles out of town, they passed the post-chaise in which Woolf Joel and Lou Cohen were sipping champagne. Barney gave them a good-humoured catcall and waved gaily at the hundreds of fans who were driving or walking to the corrugated iron enclosure where the fight was scheduled to start at 7.30 a.m. Johannesburg had almost emptied itself within an hour. Few stores would open and the Stock Exchange had suspended all business for the day.

Touts were selling £5 tickets for £20 or more by the time Barney arrived, and all roads leading to Eagle's Nest were choked with wagons abandoned by their owners who had joined the excited crowds on foot. A stampede of gate-crashers started so many free fights that the boxers could not climb into the ring until 9.30. Couper kissed his wife and solemnly promised to 'win or die', but his backers continued to lay off their bets when he stripped off, looking even more drawn than usual. A roar of derision went up as he withdrew his dentures and solemnly handed them to Abe Bailey. At the ringside Barney shouted advice and encouragement in Yiddish or cockney to the strutting Bendoff, while briskly laying the odds with wads of banknotes. Finally running out of cash, he placed a few extra bets from a reserve of diamonds tucked into his waistcoat pocket.

Couper 'tapped the claret' from Bendoff's nose in the very first minute. He then peppered him with well-placed punches and warily dodged his opponent's heavier blows. As the fight went on, Barney began chewing cigarettes which he forgot to light. He could only hope that Bendoff would land a pile-driver to end it all. The big Londoner's face was now punctured by so many cuts that it resembled Rhodes's all-red route to Cairo. He had to retire after twenty-six rounds of a contest which had become hopelessly one-sided.

When Jamie Couper left the ring with winnings of over £7,000, he opened a liquor saloon on Commissioner Street as well as a boxing academy. Barney sparred with him most mornings and used to impart Stock Exchange tips which made Couper several thousands until the market burst.

That autumn Rhodes at last secured the Queen's signature to a Charter for his British South Africa Company. In mid-September 1889, a fortnight later, Barney registered the Johannesburg Consolidated Investment Company Ltd but with far less confidence. These companies, launched with very different motives, exemplified the divergence of personality and attitudes that would continue to separate the two men. Rhodes was the hero of the hour in London where shareholders glowed with visions of the gold and diamonds which must flow out of Matabeleland and Mashonaland. They would not glimpse a dividend for many a year but had to put up with it. 'Get out if all you want is money,' Rhodes once shouted at a complaining shareholder.

De Beers had subscribed £210,000 of the first issue of a million one-pound Charter shares, but Rhodes regarded this as only a

down payment and continued to sign company cheques for anything that took his fancy, from guns to school grants. Lord
Rothschild, unconsciously echoing Barney Barnato's doubts
during the Amalgamation parleys, once remarked sharply, 'We
are not a philanthropic association. Our business is to get diamonds.'
Rhodes ignored him; he was then busily thrusting his railway and
telegraph northward from Kimberley while dealing with 'the
naked old savage' who showed signs of going back on the Concession. 'I hear Rhodes is planning to visit Lobengula,' Merriman
wrote scathingly to a friend. 'Pity he doesn't take Barnato with
him!' Neither followed his advice. Rhodes persuaded Jameson to
represent him in Bulawayo where he treated the King for gout.
Between pain-killing injections of morphia, 'Old Lob' later permitted the Chartered Company's surveyors to start digging and
consented to a column of seven hundred armed police and settlers
marching unmolested across the Mashona plateau.

Barney was rather less disturbed than 'Natty' Rothschild by
Rhodes's tendency to use De Beers as a kind of Sancho Panza
while he tilted at his costly windmills in the new territories. He
only began to show alarm when these subsidies passed the
£500,000 mark. As he was often travelling between Johannesburg,
Kimberley, Cape Town and England, he appointed David Harris
as his proxy at De Beers' board meetings which Rhodes called
peremptorily when he needed cash in a hurry. Barney was
growing a little anxious about his notorious casualness with money.
He kept no books and often left valuable securities lying about in
old discarded suits or buried in jammed drawers.

For the moment, however, he was impressed by Rhodes's
triumphant flotation of the British South Africa Company and
imagined that the London Stock Exchange would similarly
endorse his own faith in Johannesburg as 'a financial Gibraltar'. He
failed completely to appreciate that a Royal Charter which
guaranteed glory *and* profit might look far more dazzling to the
City's hard-headed but chauvinistic bankers than speculative
mining properties. Their lack of faith astonished him and certainly
caused him to miss opportunities.

He did not exaggerate in declaring in later years that he could
have bought up practically the whole of the Rand at knockdown

prices. More than once he was tempted to gamble the whole of his firm's diamond revenues on the future of Johannesburg and already thought of opening a Barnato Bank. This idea had slowly fermented in his subconscious when many diggers and trades-people began to approach him for loans after they had been turned away or threatened with foreclosure by the town's bankers. A bank with his own name over the portals could become a shop window for his big enterprises while simultaneously boosting local morale. It made a rough kind of sense although he was more influenced by showmanship than any deep appreciation of banking. What he seemed to have in mind was a grandiose hybrid of pawnshop and company promotion rather than the normal banking service built upon underground vaults of stability.

His nephews had some difficulty in restraining this effervescence. Woolf coolly appraised market trends but nettled his uncle by constantly advising retrenchment. Barney, who liked cheerful faces around him, was turning more often to Solly whom he had affectionately nicknamed 'King Sol'. They grew even closer when Solly married and started working much harder, obviously with an eye to a future partnership. He chose a beautiful young actress as his bride. She was Nellie Ridley, a Lancashire lass who had come out to Kimberley with a touring company. Thanks to Woolf's wife, Olive, who played an understanding chaperone, the courtship was smooth but Solly had nevertheless to go to England to seek approval from the Ridleys who raised almost as many objections as his own parents. Following the precedent set by Fanny and Olive Joel, the bride agreed to embrace the Jewish faith and bring up her family in that religion.

Although two children, Doris and Woolf, were quickly born to them, Solly was hardly more domesticated than his Uncle Barney whom he accompanied regularly to race-meetings and late-night poker games. It was, however, an unwritten law that he and Woolf should be interchangeable in Kimberley and Johannesburg or ready to deputize for Barney if he happened to be away at the Cape on parliamentary business. Solly made no secret of his preference for Kimberley. While Woolf delighted in the adroit in-fighting 'between the Chains', his young brother would never lose his early infatuation with diamonds. He was the only member of his family to watch diamond-cutters at work in Hatton Garden and Amsterdam whenever he visited Europe.

He took an unending delight in the wooden box, two foot by nine inches, kept in the De Beers safe in Kimberley. This was fed with diamonds until it reached the top when digging stopped automatically until more sales were made. Thus supply was rigidly restricted to demand and the price per carat maintained. It led to an arrangement for buying all the company's diamonds, with Wernher, Beit and Barnato Brothers taking half the output between them. Solly was chosen to represent his firm. He passed congenial days in Kimberley buying diamonds and often sailed to England to supervise the London side of important deals. But he was now more needed in Johannesburg to act as a gentle brake on Barney at a most critical stage in the firm's affairs.

Their investment of over £2m in the Rand was worth barely half that sum by the autumn of 1889. The Barnato Market Hall would not be open for several months and looked unlikely to justify itself. If the present slump continued, customers would have still less money in their pockets. The building had to go on, but Solly was opposed to injecting any more cash into non-productive gold mines. He favoured a diversification of the firm's interests to provide more working capital. He wanted to develop what they already had rather than encourage Barney's appetite for snapping up claims which could be floated on the stock market. It took some argument on Solly's part to register Johannesburg Consolidated Investment which he envisaged as a holding company to own and administer the various properties bought by Barney and himself during the early months of that year. 'Johnnies', as it was soon familiarly known to brokers, would have a four-fifths interest in Barnato Buildings.

The original capital was a modest £175,000, the company's records testifying that forty stands in the future gilt-edged suburb of Doornfontein were valued at a mere £4,408. Barney thought the new company such small beer compared with his gold mines that he considered a staff of two perfectly adequate. John Tudhope, a former member of the Cape Government, was appointed general manager, assisted by a clerk to do the office chores.

Solly kept a keen look-out for useful subsidiaries. He invested capital in a liquor firm and also set up a separate branch to deal with building materials and transport. An associate firm handled food wagons to take advantage of the government's new subsidy during the drought. A more important long-term investment was made in the newly-registered Argus Printing and Publishing Company.

But it had been a disquieting year of boom and slump. Preparing over Christmas for his trip to England, Barney had to reassure shareholders that he was not deserting the Rand but planned to convince the London Stock Exchange that they were missing 'a good thing'. Before taking the coach for Kimberley en route for the Cape, he put on a typical clowning act at a Veterans cricket match on the Wanderers Club ground. Stationed in the outfield, he dribbled with the ball and even shinned up a telegraph pole pretending to retrieve it. His batting was decidedly unorthodox although he made the winning hit with a six. He was soon run out but refused to leave his wicket. 'Bloody silly, that,' he protested to the umpire, 'just as I was beginning to knock the bowling about.'

Stopping briefly in Kimberley to make his ritual inspection of an almost-full box in the Board Room at De Beers, he calculated swiftly that his own firm stood to make a profit of about £100,000, while Gardner Williams confirmed that the underground system of mining would shoot up the working profits of the company to well over a million in their second year.

He was, therefore, full of good cheer when he arrived in London. He had a warm welcome from brokers now that De Beers had an official Stock Exchange quotation, and it did him no disservice to be a fellow-Life Governor with Rhodes whose pioneers and prospectors were being lauded almost like heroes of a new Armada by the Press. But it was a very different story in the high-ceilinged City banks where he had to pace yards of deep carpeting while waiting to be summoned. Life on the Johannesburg Exchange had a rough camaraderie which he missed in these offices with their hushed and sepulchral flavour of old money. His attempts to arouse enthusiasm for gold mines were met by a chilly reminder that many investors were still nursing wounds suffered from an over-capitalized Rand.

He had jauntily chosen 'Unassisted' as the telegraphic address of his new London office, but the joke had suddenly boomeranged. He found Harry panicking about reports that the gold had turned to dross. As for the Chartered Company, it might win glory for Rhodes but could ruin De Beers unless he were restrained. Harry also disliked investing hard cash in the Waterworks Company which had so far produced no dividends. Barnato Buildings he dismissed as a white elephant that was eating its head off. He was particularly alarmed by the scale of his brother's gold-mining adventures which had cost them over a million sterling already. In short, they would do well to consider leaving Johannesburg and concentrate on the more profitable diamond business.

Barney closed his ears to this litany of gloom. He had a large mahogany table installed in the main office at Draper's Gardens because he disliked desks and preferred to spread his papers where he could pick them up almost blindfold. He received Hatton Garden merchants and stockbrokers from Throgmorton Street and left them dazed with his machine-gun monologues. He was elated when the news reached him that Rhodes had become Prime Minister and formed a 'Cabinet of all the talents' in which Sivewright would serve and, more surprisingly, Merriman, who had qualms about the Mashonaland 'filibuster', but emerged as Treasurer in the new administration. In his exuberance, but no doubt with a weather eye on the London Stock Exchange, Barney ordered framed portraits of Rhodes and enlarged graphs of De Beers' progress to be hung in the anterooms of his offices.

He gave dinners for stockbrokers and diamond merchants and their wives, followed by visits to Covent Garden where he usually took two boxes. They all sat together until the interval when Barney would unblushingly invite most of them to adjourn to the second box from which they might enjoy a better view of Fanny. With her curls mounded high and spanned by a tiara, she was always superbly gowned and jewelled but suffered acute embarrassment at Barney's affectionate but blatant insistence on placing her on display. Shy by nature, she missed her own servants and felt confused by the comings and goings in their hotel suite. Barney talked business incessantly with Harry, Jack Joel and a stream of brokers on returning from the City, often settling down to a long card session after dinner unless they were going to a theatre.

He relieved the strain of his first weeks in London with several visits to the East End, gladly accepting an invitation to give a benefit performance of *The Octoroon* at the Novelty Theatre in aid of his old school's rebuilding fund. During rehearsals at The Black Lion, one of his early haunts, his vigorous realism almost throttled the actor playing the auctioneer. 'Turn it up, Barney, turn it up,' he croaked, to the delight of the audience.

They would go to the theatre or the music hall two or three nights a week, but the highlight of the trip, for him at least, was a backstage audience with Irving. Barney spoke warmly of having seen him long ago in *The Bells* when he had wept throughout the performance. 'I sat in the pit and you were on the stage then,' he sighed. 'Now we are both on the stage, mine being the stage of life.'

'I did four characters that night,' Irving recalled.

'Three,' Barney corrected him.

Irving regarded him with some hauteur. 'Excuse me, my friend,' he said starchily, 'but you will perhaps admit that I ought to know what I did.'

'I don't give a continental what you thought you did that night,' grunted Barney. 'I'll tell you exactly what you did, the times you came in, the doors you went out, and every scene you played.' He then took off his coat to mime each entrance and exit until Irving raised both hands in mock defeat and laughingly admitted his error.

Barney played supper host that night to a party of friends. The obsequious wine waiter produced a carafe of hock. 'Johannesburg '77,' he confided, explaining that he liked to keep it for discerning patrons from South Africa. Barney went red in the face. 'Take it away,' he shouted angrily, 'and bring us a couple of magnums of bubbly. D'ye take me for a *schlemiel* (Yiddish: fool)? Johannesburg wasn't even built then!'

His dislike of being cheated often led to scenes over trifles. He would argue strenuously over the mileage for a penny bus-fare and once threatened to punch the nose of a Whitechapel coster who included a bad apple in the pound he had bought. Still nibbling a core, he stopped a barrel organ in Wentworth Street and 'played' a tune while he tap-danced in time. He then went on his way, whistling, after dropping a sovereign into the monkey's little red bag.

He wallowed in sentimental trips to Whitechapel which were all the more welcome after Harry's grumbling. A social and gastronomic tour started as soon as he turned into Petticoat Lane where he skipped about poking his fingers into barrels of pickled cucumbers and devouring a salt herring, a fistful of glistening black olives or a dollop of soft cheese. There were delicacies like *smetana*, the most succulent sour cream this side of paradise: the crusty ripeness of rye bread, the juices of *gefüllte* fish, the *lockshen* and meat balls, and so many other delights secretly lusted after during the years of exile. Names and faces came back in a flurry as he stopped for a word and a joke over a glass of lemon tea which he sipped with the ritual lump of sugar on the tongue. He would invariably dash into Bonn's for a slab of the cheese cake he had so often coveted in his boyhood but could never afford.

He gorged all the local gossip at the fried fish parlour run by his kinswoman, Polly Nathan, who told him about families in want and orphan girls who needed dowries. Through her and the local rabbis he was able to help scores of people. In the streets and cafés he was surrounded by a laughing crowd who could not believe this was 'Barnato the millionaire' as he ripped open his collar and danced in the roadway while he juggled with rings of *beigels*, the crusty rolls he had missed so much in Johannesburg. To many of them he was still little Barnett Isaacs who had come home. One evening he spotted an old lady who remembered him as a child sitting on the kerb outside the barber's shop in Wentworth Street and pathetically grateful for something out of her shopping bag. He rushed over to clasp her round the waist. 'Rivka, you were the prettiest girl in the Lane then and you're even lovelier now,' he laughed. 'Come to Africa with me! I'll make your fortune!' He pressed a five-pound note into her hand and gave her a sound kiss.

Once back in his West End hotel, he would drink too much and become restless for Solly's companionship or the 'shop' breakfasts in his own home. Fanny came to recognize the pattern. He would count the days and hours before sailing joyfully for England. Within a few weeks, unless fully occupied by office work or a round of music halls, fights and race meetings, he began to mope about and wish himself back in Africa. He was seldom happier than when sailing 'home', either to Southampton or Cape Town, a kind of Falstaff and Flying Dutchman combined. His money made him feel at home everywhere—and nowhere. It was specially true of his visits to England where he was less important and too remote from the hub of his own little empire.

This particular trip was further overshadowed by reports of political tension in the Transvaal. As a result, the City withdrew even further into its shell.

11

ARLY IN MARCH 1890, Kruger visited Johannesburg on his way
to confer with Sir Henry Loch, the new British High Commissioner, at Blignaut's Pont on the Vaal. Already disgruntled,
he set out from Pretoria in a Cape cart. He was not only chagrined
by the depressed state of the mining industry, but geographically
his situation had become claustrophobic. He felt himself locked in
on three sides. The British in Bechuanaland had closed him in from
the west. Rhodes's pioneers in the north evidently planned to
occupy all 'Charterland' up to the Zambesi while the concession-
hunters exploited their gains in Matabeleland. Within his own
borders he was threatened by the Uitlanders of the Rand who
already outnumbered his burghers by three to one and would
assuredly bring down the Republic if he were unwise enough to
give them votes. He was, therefore, all the more desperate for
access to a sea port and humiliated at being unable to help the
Netherland Railway Company complete the line from Pretoria
to the coast.

This cherished project was still in jeopardy, although Rhodes's
impudent offer to buy the port of Delagoa Bay for £700,000 had
been reluctantly turned down by the Portuguese owing to German
pressure. Moreover, the Cape Government had recently agreed
with the Orange Free State to continue the Port Elizabeth line
through Bloemfontein right up to the borders of the Transvaal. If
this were extended to Johannesburg, it would compete with his
own line, which was not under British control, and would have
the advantage of being nearer to the gold-mines.

These irritations festered within Kruger as he jogged towards
Duiwelstad (Devil's City), his name for Johannesburg. The mining

slump had robbed him of transfer dues, ground rents, licence money and other profitable revenues which could only partly be replaced by imposing heavy customs duties on all Cape produce while the gold industry was bled white by the sale of monopolies for dynamite and other essentials. His overpaid Civil Service was choked by grasping Germans and Hollanders whom he trusted more than the Cape Afrikaners with their avowed sympathy for Rhodes. These alien bureaucrats, backed by many of Kruger's relatives, were given plum jobs and ample opportunities to fatten on the voteless citizens of Johannesburg who paid 90% of the taxes yet could not even persuade the Volksraad to put up more pillar-boxes which one member denounced as 'extravagant and effeminate'. A trifling matter like a proper scale of cab fares had to be submitted to Pretoria where it was passed along a chain of lobbyists and other interested parties.

As he rolled and bumped towards Johannesburg, Kruger was less concerned with the appalling roads than the Uitlanders' manifest signs of affluence. The tiny black eyes, sunken into elephantine bags of skin, glanced indifferently at shops bright with bunting but noted the trees and gardens which framed the stoeps of a few newly-built villas in the suburbs. Hunched and unsmiling as he puffed at his long-stemmed pipe, he ignored the rubble and vile sewage which the so-called Sanitary Board had not troubled to remove even for this ceremonial visit. When some burghers raised a faint cheer he disdained to remove his scarred chimney-pot of a hat and spat continuously out of the window in disregard of his flanking escort of State Artillery.

Some ten thousand spectators had assembled on the Wanderers Ground where he stepped on to the platform as a standard-bearer waved the four-striped *Vierkleur*. The round of applause gratified him enough for him to open his wrinkled, over-tight frockcoat and raise a gorilla-like arm in what seemed a friendly wave. But his voice was harsh as he started to address the crowd; 'burghers, Afrikaners and Uitlanders . . .' It touched off a storm of boos and hisses. '*Bly stil*,' (be quiet), he shouted angrily but to no effect. His unfortunate opening reference to the difficulties of getting the railway running to Johannesburg was lost in catcalls. Apart from the franchise and the compulsory use of Afrikaans for all official business, this was the sorest spot of all. While Kruger laboured at his wretched little line from the capital to Delagoa Bay, Johannesburg was still being fobbed off with excuses for not extending their railway from the south that would bring coal and machinery and help to keep down the price of foodstuffs which were still hauled by wagons at a mile and a half an hour.

He was shouted down by a chorus of demands for votes, railways, sanitation and an end to the hated monopolies. When some young men began singing 'Rule, Britannia' with 'God Save the Queen' for an encore, he turned his back on the crowd, picked up his hat and stumped furiously from the platform. A jeering mob followed him along Rissik Street and all the way to Government Buildings. Someone then pulled down the Republican flag and trampled it underfoot while a number attempted to storm the house of the Landdrost, Carl von Brandis, where the President was to spend the night.

Charles Leonard, the lawyer, and George Farrar, representing the leading mining interests, naturally received a very dusty answer when they arrived to present their familiar catalogue of civic grievances. They needed to raise their voices above the boos and whistles of a mob whom the police had failed to disperse. Over a final cup of coffee that night Kruger growled at von Brandis, 'You can tell your Uitlander friends, Carl, that I will not give the vote to a pack of baboons. And never again will I set foot in Johannesburg.'

The screws had already tightened by the time Barney returned early that summer. A Second Chamber was to be established in the Volksraad which would make enfranchisement still more remote, but most Uitlanders were more disturbed by a continuing low gold yield paralleled by a dizzy rise in the cost of living. Barnato Buildings was, however, completed and the firm moved into an island of shiny new offices surrounded by 'To Let' notices. There were as yet no takers for stands in the Market Hall, and brokers grumbled at the higher rents demanded for the spacious new Stock Exchange building. Barney Barnato still tippled champagne but his optimistic forecasts had gone very flat.

His Eagle Gold Mining Company was one of many casualties. With little ore to justify its original capital issue, the shares now stood at threepence. He had no alternative but to close it down.

Louis Cohen, always accident-prone, had the misfortune to choose one of the few really bad eggs in the whole Barnato basket. He had paid £6,000 for his Eagles, and they were now worth barely £100. He went about the town vilifying Barney for having 'robbed an old friend' but did not hesitate to visit his offices and beg for his money back. Barney had no sympathy for a poor loser, but for old times' sake or perhaps to curb Cohen's damaging tongue, he agreed to exchange the bedraggled Eagles for 200 of his healthier Primroses which, at current prices, would at least provide a bonus of £75. It was meagre enough, but few of the Rand magnates showed even such benevolence in those months of slump. Cohen would see Primroses blossom to over £8 each, but one cannot confirm that he had the patience or resources to preserve them. Unlike Barnato, Robinson and the Corner House financiers who could withstand the shock of losing fortunes on paper while they waited for sixpenny shares to go to a fiver or higher, most small-scale punters would tend to buy too hastily and often sell before harvest time.

Barney found other ways of helping Cohen whom he came across one day 'between the Chains' with neither the cash nor credit to take part in even the dribble of dealings going through. Barney greeted him with affection and took him off for a cheering drink while Cohen recited a tale of lamentations like a Hebrew funeral service.

'We can't talk here,' Barney interrupted him. 'Let's go to your house for a bite. I want to taste some of your wife's wonderful *lockshen* soup again.'

Cohen hesitated. He feared that the larder might be empty and also suspected, from past experience, that Barney only wanted a free meal. Mrs Cohen managed, however, to prepare some spicy Jewish dishes which went down admirably with Barney's bottle of brandy followed by lemon tea. He burst into the kitchen to thank his hostess and, slipping an arm round her waist, soon extracted a tearful résumé of their bleak financial situation. He returned to the dining-room, pulled off the tablecloth and used a pencil stub to scribble a few names and figures. 'Lou,' he said quietly, 'you ain't behaved well to me and I can't forget it, but I'm going to make you some money quick.'

Next morning he hustled Cohen into the Stock Exchange Hall and briskly netted him £150 in commissions within the hour. He then called on four bank managers to whom his old partner was grandly presented as 'my broker'. 'The previous day I had been a nobody without credit,' Cohen said later. 'After his introduction my credit was well above par. There was no reason why he should have done this, for I had annoyed and offended him.'

He saw another side of his benefactor on the following Sunday when Barney proposed a long walk which might profitably combine business with pleasure. Barney was still worried about the Waterworks Company. Suspecting that water was either being wasted or not paid for, he decided to tour Johannesburg and its environs to see for himself. They had started at first light and covered about fourteen miles on foot when poor Cohen insisted on stopping for a drink. They ordered whisky and Barney added some water which he pronounced to be of excellent quality. The barmaid agreed, innocently confiding that nobody had called for six months to collect the rates. Barney made another entry in his little book. 'Now, Lou,' he laughed, 'tell me the honest truth. Have *you* paid for water in the ten months you've been in your house?' Cohen shook his head. Next day he was served with a summons.

Before the end of 1890 salvation miraculously came to the Rand through a team of Glasgow research chemists. Working in the Robinson and Sheba Mines, they discovered that pyritic-laden gravel could be effectively treated with potassium cyanide. When the solution was poured on plates of zinc, it resulted in almost total recovery of the gold which had previously refused to amalgamate in the presence of pyrites. A new Eldorado emerged from the ashen-grey tailings.

Every mine on the outcrop was soon working at full blast again, particularly when it was noted that coloured skins seemed almost immune to cyanide. Consequently, hundreds of natives hastened back to sign on for a year in the galvanized iron compounds with a guarantee of good wages. Engineers, assayers and metallurgists could almost name their own salaries, while many others who had fled during the slump and drought were returning by the wagon-load, desperate for jobs and living quarters.

Barney was exceptionally placed on all fronts to benefit from this dramatic upward swing. As lessor of the Stock Exchange building, he and his associates had an inside berth on the Committee when any major flotation was in the wind. He had business sites in the town centre as well as building plots in the suburbs served by his Waterworks Company. Easily the largest owner of real estate on the Rand thanks to his early investments, he was now undisputed leader of a sellers' market which would become a frantic scramble as white-collared workers, engineers and tradesmen clamoured for houses away from the narrow crowded streets and mine dumps.

His cheaply-bought estates in Yeoville, Houghton, Doornfontein and Berea at once mushroomed in value while his building subsidiaries soon found it difficult to keep pace with the demands of a population that multiplied almost as quickly as the flowers and trees. Parks were swiftly laid out to luxuriate in Johannesburg's generous sunshine and rain while architects were still blue-printing a city of fine buildings with electric tramways running along good roads which would replace the potholed reminders of mining camp days. Nothing, however, could be done about the too numerous street-crossings, a legacy of the profitable corner sites bought by Barney and other speculators and enthusiastically approved by a government ravenous for ground rents.

Every inch of office space in Barnato Buildings was now snatched at the asking price. Each morning wagons streamed into the Square from every part of the Transvaal, the Free State and Natal with wood, wool, forage and all manner of produce to be auctioned off. The stands in the new Market Hall could have been rented or sold ten times over, but even this handsome revenue was insignificant compared with the potential value of Barney's group of big-yielding mines. They had picked up immediately after news of the cyanide discovery, but a far richer bonanza would follow within the next two years as engineers sank shafts and bore-holes to gold-bearing formations 3,000 feet and more below the surface. These 'deep levels' could be worked almost inexhaustibly as they dipped under the previous boundaries of the outcrop to reveal more and more conglomerate like the layers of a huge tilted cake.

It opened a glittering epoch for the Rand. Ground hitherto thought valueless or abandoned during the slump of '89 could be pegged and deeply intersected to hit the Main Reef well south of the original outcrop. But this dazzling potential was only gradually appreciated. The early few who sensed the significance of the dip in the reefs were sometimes able to buy claims for hardly more than the licence fees. They were outnumbered, however, by those content to stick to the outcrop.

The deep levels were only reachable with patience and vast finance, and Beit was not far out in estimating that each of his mines demanded an average outlay and working capital of a cool million pounds to produce the maximum results. The small claim-owner, unlike his predecessors in Kimberley's blue earth, had no hope of competing with magnates like Barnato and the Corner House group who could afford to buy, absorb and digest under-capitalized groups.

It was thought that the 'deeps' might yield £8m a year, but not even the most sanguine could have predicted that the capital value of Rand companies would soar to over £300m by 1895. The share turnover was relatively small until Barney took a hand and started almost a lone-wolf operation to animate the Johannesburg money market. Acting on the advice of geologists, he purchased several farms suitable for pegging but soon decided that company scrip was far more satisfying and less expensive than sinking shafts. Any large-scale development would henceforth be mainly financed out of capital subscribed by local investors anxious to share in 'Barney's luck'. Few were finicky about insisting on monthly gold figures like those ritually supplied by Beit. The Great Barnato was patently the man for all who wished to scoop dividends, jumping paper profits and the promise of much more to come. No other financier in Johannesburg could command such a following. People forgot stray mishaps like the Eagle Company and pointed instead to Primrose.

Publicity helped. Barney constantly reminded potential investors of his staunch faith in the Rand when the Corner House was practically derelict and 'between the Chains' looked like the Wailing Wall in Jerusalem. He now strutted along Pritchard Street whose windows would soon rival Bond Street and the Rue de Rivoli. If in the mood he would dash into the Standard Bank for a quick drink and a whisky with the very deferential manager.

The mud-thatched branch was being replaced by an imposing building with glass swing doors and 'every modern convenience in the way of electric bells and speaking tubes'. Barney liked to clown with the old six-shooters which were still kept as sentimental relics to focus attention on the shiny, steel-lined strongroom. The manager now spoke lyrically of an Assay Department available to customers for testing and smelting gold and ores, complete with furnaces, chemicals and weighing machines.

It almost tempted Barney to revive his pipe-dream of a Barnato Bank which might transport him to the godlike heights of Rothschild and soothe a pride still bruised from his last visit to the City of London. But he was realistic enough to appreciate that no bank could offer a bigger and safer reward than the series of companies now being registered under his banner. Moreover, it gave him a patriarchal glow to be acclaimed by so many beaming shareholders.

His every movement was enthusiastically reported in the local Press, whether he held forth about 'the deeps' with special reference to his own companies, or gave a dinner-party at the Central Hotel to celebrate the annual Kimberley *v* Johannesburg cricket fixture. A Cape Town newspaper described him with approval as 'the head of the richest firm in South Africa' and he never stopped bragging about his pioneering days in the diamond fields. Although he spoke appreciatively of Rhodes, he did not care to be reminded too often that he was only one of four Life Governors at De Beers. Whenever he was asked about the Amalgamation, he always preened himself on having forced Rhodes to pay an extra million for Kimberley Central. Only Solly and Woolf guessed that he would never quite rid himself of the suspicion that he had won the chips but somehow lost the pot itself in that historic poker game.

He gave no hint of anything but abundant self-satisfaction at his business breakfasts which always stretched into luncheons on

Sundays. At Norman House, still the only non-bungalow in town, his invitations were eagerly canvassed by brokers, engineers and visitors from Europe. He harangued each group simultaneously and at top speed, bustling about in his pyjamas and dressing-gown while he chain-smoked cigarettes until they singed his moustache. He rarely stopped to sit down at the table, preferring to devour a baked potato while a servant relayed mugs of black coffee laced with rum and a green parrot in its solid gold cage screeched, 'What price Primrose today, Barney?'

He maintained his early morning sparring sessions with Jamie Couper who marvelled at his stamina and once remarked to David Harris, 'Barney never keeps still. He's as lively as a parched pea in a frying pan.' He liked to parade the streets with Solly or one of his mining engineers, talking business while Barney Malone, the pugilist, Cohen and others formed a flattering retinue to escort him round the saloons. It usually ended with a triumphal entrance at the Stock Exchange where he was received by more back-slappers. Walking with his elbows held high and forward, he bristled with energy. Once he left his entourage without warning to dash across Simmonds Street for a word with Eckstein who hinted that Beit wanted an appointment at Barnato Buildings to discuss a very attractive proposition.

'Appointment? What appointment?' laughed Barney. 'I'll go right over and see him.' With his straw hat on the back of his head, the bow tie askew as usual and his shirt sprouting like a ruffle from a low-cut waistcoat, he exploded among the frock-coated staff of the Corner House where Beit was presiding like a dignified bishop at a solemn conference with his senior executives. He did not keep Barney waiting. The business talk lasted some hours which dis-located several meetings lined up by Solly.

'It saves time going over to the other bloke's office,' he explained later to his nephew. 'If things ain't going my way, I can always say I have an important engagement and bugger off. Here I'm in a corner and can't move until he's talked my *tukkas* (Yiddish: backside) off!'

His favourite form of relaxation was still a game of poker played for high stakes with men as tough as himself. It added spice to the proceedings if not always geniality, as he discovered during one colourful session which made local history. Barney's ample funds and card sense made a formidable combination, but his endurance was an even greater hazard for opponents. He would play the clock round if necessary to finish up on the winning side.

One night, however, he was confronted by a hard-bitten diamond broker named Sager who had often clashed with him in Kimberley. Solly and the other players withdrew from the game when Barney and Sager kept raising the stakes until chips worth several thousands of pounds turned on a single hand. Barney finally called the bet but he had run out of chips, as Sager reminded him very firmly. He turned impatiently to Solly who had by then lost all his money and could not help. Barney then offered to back his call by cheque. Sager refused. 'Cash or stand down,' he snapped, reaching for the pot. Barney roughly seized his wrist and almost broke it. After a violent argument it was decided that both players should seal their cards in envelopes which were handed to a third party for safe keeping until the banks opened. Barney hustled in next morning with a wad of notes to cover Sager's bet but the unsealed envelopes revealed him as second-best. Sagar refused to sit down for a revenge session or cut for double or nothing. He had suffered too many punishing experiences in the past to risk another.

Soon afterwards Barney set off for Kimberley to preside at a De Beers shareholders' meeting in the absence of Rhodes who was away 'on important business' in Mashonaland. He spoke warmly of the Chairman and tried to soothe those who mourned poorish dividends and the heavy subsidies to the Chartered Company. There was gloom over a diamond pipe recently found at Wesselton which would threaten the Company's monopoly. Rhodes recommended buying out the owner for what Barney thought too high a sum, but it proved a splendid investment. 'The worst of Rhodes,' he privately admitted afterwards to Woolf, 'is that when you have been with him for half an hour, you not only agree with him but imagine you've always done so.'

Others were less impressed. Lord Randolph Churchill had come out to South Africa at the end of that summer of 1891. Already a very sick man, he was advised by his doctors to cut down on cigarettes and alcohol and generally to take things easily. He planned to do a little shooting and perhaps look over some gold mines which might replenish his purse. The trip proved far from relaxing either for himself or those unfortunate enough to entertain him. On the way out, his ship caught fire. Commissioned by the *Daily Graphic* to send home letters at £100 a time, he started off with outspoken criticisms of the Castle Line's 'negligence' which infuriated Sir Donald Currie and his co-directors.

In Mashonaland, where he had gone for some shooting, he was most hospitably received by Dr Jameson who had recently given up his practice to become Resident Commissioner in Salisbury. Lord Randolph formed a poor impression of 'Charterland' and wrote several pessimistic articles about the Company's prospects. He disliked roughing it, even on safari, and saw no charm in sitting on a barrel for a dish of coarse ox meat and some inferior whisky while Jameson bored him with unconvincing and exaggerated accounts of Central Africa's potential. He soon went down to Cape Town to stay briefly with Rhodes who could not have found him too congenial. Lord Randolph had already dismissed him as 'a mere cypher' and his *Daily Graphic* letters were destroying the London investors' confidence in what he called 'this God-forsaken country'. He confessed privately to a friend that he had only chosen to stay with Rhodes because he happened to stock his favourite vintage of champagne.

He found more consolation in the Rand's deep levels which he toured in the company of his mining consultant who shrewdly advised him to buy farms away from the outcrop. Lord Randolph's eyes bulged at the prospect of restoring his finances. From Mafeking he wrote gloomily to his wife that he was 'done with politics and would now try to make a little money for the boys and for ourselves'. He lacked the capital and patience to peg the 'deeps' on a long-term basis but did the next best thing by buying 5,000 of Beit's Rand Mine shares at par with the help of a £5,000 loan from his friend, Lord Rothschild. They would increase twenty fold in value by the time he died in January 1895. Altogether, these shares and those he bought in the other enterprises fattened his otherwise modest estate by over £70,000. The shares had to be sold after his death in January 1895 in order to pay his debts.

Lord Randolph's enthusiasm for the Rand was in inverse ratio to his view of the territories that some admirers had already begun to call 'Rhodesia'. He sailed for England just before Christmas 1891, not at all displeased to have Mr B. I. Barnato as a fellow-passenger. Barney, then brimful of confidence in his own series of over-subscribed company issues, had almost as many Press reporters to see him off as the politician. He jocularly flourished his return ticket to prove that he was only taking a short business trip and would soon be back to resume operations.

His habitual shipboard zest mated most amiably with Lord Randolph's new gold fever. Barney found him a flattering listener for his racy but well-informed chatter about the mining industry. They passed several convivial hours together amid the brandy fumes and clouds of cigar smoke. The result was an unusually pompous interview with a reporter from *South Africa*. 'Since I had the pleasure of being introduced to his lordship,' Barney pontificated, 'I can state that I have never conversed with a more agreeable, pleasant and social gentleman.'

He quickly noted that Lord Randolph's dabblings in gold had started a pleasant little flurry in the City which was far more significant than his vicious attacks on the Chartered Company. Barney would loyally support Rhodes and Jameson at De Beers' meetings but had never felt more than a twinge of their missionary zeal for Central Africa. It seemed to him a troublesome luxury out of all proportion to its cost, a view most unpleasantly confirmed that March when the Chartered Company faced bankruptcy.

Rhodes's private secretary, Harry Currey, burst into the Barnato offices in Kimberley one morning and startled David Harris by informing him brusquely that the Standard Bank threatened to dishonour the Chartered Company's last cheques unless De Beers could forthwith subsidize or guarantee their account to the tune of £220,500. Harris had willingly consented to act as Barney's 'alternate' on the Board in his absence but without envisaging emergencies like this. He took alarm and offered to cable Barnato for his approval, but Currey (briefed, no doubt, by his master) argued vehemently against delay. He explained that Rhodes and Beit were in no position to finance the company any further from their own pockets. Together with Philipson-Stow they had approved the guarantee by De Beers, and it only remained for the last Life Governor to come into line.

Poor Harris, fearing Barney's wrath, stammered that his authority as proxy was limited to the firm's production and marketing of diamonds. Currey interrupted to remind him that they had only two hours in which to save the Chartered Company's credit. Nothing less than the future of the new lands was at stake, not to speak of the Prime Minister's good name and credit.

Harris decided to take a chance. He hurried away to Ebden Street where he summoned a quorum to pass the necessary resolution. A wire was sent off to Cape Town informing the bank's head office that De Beers would at once advance £70,000 and pay the balance in monthly instalments over the next three years.

When Rhodes got back from England he thanked Harris who replied modestly that he was 'only the mouse in the lion's cage'. Barney could hardly have acted differently himself without splitting irrevocably with De Beers. He did not reproach Harris, 'in the circumstances', but remained curiously tight-lipped long after the loan had been repaid in full and with interest.

Within a few months of this episode, De Beers itself was threatened by a dip in prices due to a trade lull in England and an American share recession. A Syndicate was quickly set up to replace the previous arrangement for marketing the Company's output. Wernher, Beit and Barnatos would together guarantee to buy almost half the total production under a five-year contract involving at least £20m worth of diamonds. Someone in London then quibbled over a point which would have made a difference of £5,000 or so in the purchase price. Rhodes contemptuously tossed the wire into a wastepaper basket and growled to a secretary, 'Cable them that I thought they were diamond merchants, not retail grocers.'

It was magnificently imperial but did not endear him to Barney who was growing less enchanted with the Oxford brand of '*chutzpah*'. He particularly disliked being summoned to emergency meetings, usually at short notice and even on trains, when Rhodes needed cash. As it happened, this latent irritation coincided with a closer relationship with President Kruger who, as Barney soon discovered, spoke very much his own language, albeit through an interpreter.

12

———

IMPATIENT OF RED TAPE, Barney took to driving over to Pretoria for the permits which often held up his engineers, architects and building contractors. A bureaucracy that could have given pointers on 'squeeze' to any Chinese Customs official had few terrors for him. He went blandly through improper channels and seldom came back empty-handed. After the electric vitality of Johannesburg he liked to relax briefly in the drowsy old-world atmosphere of this quaint town whose brick houses were neatly framed by gardens and orchards. A scent of roses lingered pleasantly as he strolled past the church in the Square on his way to the Transvaal Hotel. There he held genial court among bearded members of the Raadsvaal and a small corps of 'stoney-brokes', as he called them, who always swooped on him the moment he arrived in town.

He soon began to pay courtesy calls at Kruger's simple villa, whether or not to request favours. The acquaintance had started over some bottleneck concerning the Waterworks Company. It was smoothed out so quickly that Barney felt encouraged to buy an interest in the concession granted by Kruger to his son-in-law to bring water from the Vaal River. Another point of contact was Sir James Sivewright, now Commissioner of Crown Lands, whom Rhodes had instructed to try and drive some sense into Kruger's tough skull about completing the railway from the Cape. With deep shafts going down everywhere in the Rand, it was irksome to send machinery on by wagon from the Transvaal border.

Kruger was more obsessed than ever with his Delagoa Bay line. It was still making tortoise progress in 1892 but he would not hear

of giving priority to 'Rhodes's Railway' to Johannesburg. Barney
listened to Sivewright's reports of his meetings with the stubborn
old Dopper and proposed an ingenious plan. The Rand's growing
prosperity was yielding the Republican treasury about £300,000
a year. It would undoubtedly go much higher once the deep levels
were at full blast, but that would not be for a year at least. In the
interval there was not enough to spare for what Rhodes derisively
called 'Kruger's little hobby'. Barney used Sivewright as his
mouthpiece to propose that the railway from the Cape might run
to Pretoria with a branch line to Johannesburg. That would save
Kruger's face in front of his burghers. As a *quid pro quo*, the
Colony would help him complete his own railway from the
coast.

Kruger seemed well satisfied. The monthly output of gold was
rising steadily and most experts spoke optimistically about the
deep levels. Obviously his treasury would benefit from this
revenue as well as the ground rents and service charges from the
houses which 'Johnnies' and other speculators were putting up.
Meanwhile, he was still busily handing out concessions to old
friends like Sammy Marks who paid him £1,000 a year to distil
liquor in a Pretoria factory. It did so well—at the expense of the
consumer public—that Marks sold his concession within four years
for £120,000. The President gave him many other exclusive
titbits, from brickmaking to the manufacture of jam, and allowed
him to act as go-between for the Dynamite Concession. This
monopoly went to Beit's rascally cousin, Edward Lippert, who
now avenged himself handsomely for his abortive carpet-bagging
in Matabeleland. He charged £5 a case for dynamite which might
have been imported for 35s. to save the mining industry at least
£150,000 a year.

The Johannesburgers, however, temporarily forgot such miseries
in anticipation of their railway. Thanks to a Rothschild loan, it was
completed a good two years before the Dutchmen were able to
link Pretoria with the coast. When the six-coach train at last puffed
into Park Station in September 1892, over two thousand cheering
people gave it a wild welcome from which the Government
pointedly stood aside. Barney was boisterously fêted by citizens
who tended to exaggerate his share in the negotiations. 'I did it

only because I want fresh fish twice a week,' he protested as they tried to garland him.

Many now turned to him for guidance when they became ensnarled with the bureaucrats. He was an ideal lobbyist for the Johannesburg Chamber of Commerce and the mining interests who soon discovered that he could talk to the President on a genial man-to-man basis. By avoiding politics, he alone seemed able to crack the granite. They would sit for hours on the stoep of the white house, drinking cups of coffee, while Barney puffed at his cigarettes and Kruger constantly refilled his pipe bowl from the moleskin pouch and blew his huge nose with a bandanna handkerchief. They coughed in unison and periodically interrupted their friendly dialogue with a fairly accurate use of the huge spittoon between them. Leo Weinthal, the editor of the *Pretoria Press*, usually acted as interpreter and had the gift of defusing Barney's occasional indiscretions. Sometimes he laughed out loud at some quip in Yiddish which he translated to such effect that the semi-deaf Dopper would have it repeated more loudly or even call in his wife to hear it all over again.

Kruger used to grasp Barney's hands warmly in greeting. At first a little wary of this De Beers Life Governor who ran the diamond industry with Rhodes and seemed to dominate Rand finance, he had quickly noted that Barney kept aside from the National Union and did not weary him with chatter about the franchise. 'Men come to the Transvaal to make money, not to vote,' he had publicly declared, a practical sentiment which further endeared him to 'Oom Paul'. He also pleased him by driving over to Pretoria to request quite trivial favours and only rarely overstepping the mark.

But he was pulled up sharply when he warmed to the theme of a Municipal Council for Johannesburg on the English model, with a proper Mayor, Aldermen and Councillors. Hinting tactlessly that this would please the Uitlanders, Barney went on to disparage local officials who clogged the city's arteries. Kruger hawked noisily and growled that he would never permit a 'State' within his own Republic. 'Have I not given them their railway?' he roared, rapping the table. 'Instead of going on their knees in gratitude, they invite me to a Ball in honour of Queen Victoria!'

Barney, always a passionately loyal British subject, had to bite
his tongue over that gibe. It so happened that he had recently
welcomed an unexpected opportunity to render a small personal
service to the Queen. She was driving through the streets of Berlin
with her daughter, the Empress Frederick, when a Polish girl
almost threw herself under the carriage wheels to toss a petition in
the Queen's lap. It was a plea for clemency on behalf of her
husband who had been sentenced to seven years on the Breakwater
for buying stolen diamonds. He had interrupted their honeymoon
in Paris to return to Kimberley for this final disastrous coup,
leaving her destitute.

The Queen was moved and referred the matter to her Colonial
Secretary. He wrote to the Cape Governor who could not inter-
vene officially but asked Barney to help in any way possible behind
the scenes. He paid the girl's passage money and settled her in a
Cape Town hotel where she was diligently coached to tell her
pathetic story to an impressionable corps of journalists. He then
worked so effectively to have the case reopened on the grounds of
some rather dubious new 'evidence' that the sentence was reduced
on appeal to four years. The girl at once sued for divorce, married a
wealthy South African and emigrated with him to Canada. 'So
much for a broken heart,' Barney used to laugh when telling the
story. Some of his cynical enemies sneered in private that the
Governor had made the ideal choice of an intermediary for a case
involving I.D.B., but Barney would long take pride in what he
called 'my Royal Commission'.

He had always promised himself that if ever Fanny had children
they would be born and educated in England. They were married
very quietly at the Strand Register Office on 19 November 1892.
When Fanny had told him she was pregnant after so many years,
he fussed over her as if she were in late middle-age instead of
thirty-four, and engaged doctors and nurses months in advance.
Meantime, he took a large suite at the Hotel Metropole in
Northumberland Avenue where he entertained an overflow of
callers from the office. Shortly after arriving in London, he had to
face the Waterworks shareholders who had called a special meeting

at Winchester House. They grumbled throughout Sivewright's bumbling alibis, but Barney mollified them by painting a bright picture of Doornfontein and other properties bought on their behalf. He also announced that John Tudhope had been switched from 'Johnnies' to replace Sivewright who was now too busy with his ministerial duties.

Sivewright was no loss to the Company. Soon afterwards, he gave one of his friends a concession to supply refreshments on the Cape Railways without going through even the formality of inviting tenders. Merriman and some others refused to continue serving with him. Rhodes repudiated the contract but demanded a vote of confidence. He was re-elected and formed a new Cabinet without Merriman who had fretted for a chance to return to the Opposition benches.

Barney digested all this gossip from Solly who was a diligent correspondent. Solly also reported excellent production from most of their mining properties but warned that Beit seemed to be creaming the deep levels to which he had at last converted Rhodes. The latter soon enlarged his first Rand company into Consolidated Gold Fields and agreed to exchange his share of the profits for stock worth around £1,300,000.

It seemed obvious to Solly that the time had come to sink shafts before floating too many new companies. Barney was finally won over. One day, while sitting at his table in Draper's Gardens, he turned to Harry and said thoughtfully, 'Gardner Williams tells me he has a friend in the States, name of Hammond, who can smell a gold mine a thousand miles away. Let's send him a cable and find out why he's supposed to be worth $50,000 a year. We'll guarantee his expenses if he agrees to come.'

John Hays Hammond accepted the invitation with some hesitation. A native of San Francisco and Yale-educated, he had won fame as a brilliant engineer in Nevada. Fearing that Grover Cleveland's tariff policy would lead to another trade depression, he was keen to emigrate and had almost decided to try South Africa when Barney's cable reached him. He made a few enquiries which put him very much on guard. This Barnato was rumoured to have made a pile from I.D.B. and had a name for window-dressing his companies.

He appeared at Draper's Gardens, spruce and high-collared, one Monday morning in April 1893. He was agreeably surprised that Barney did not seem quite the brash cockney bookie he had been led to expect. Instead of the checked suit and florid buttonhole he wore his best City frockcoat and cravat with a dignified smile to match. The brother, Harry, was rather less prepossessing although tailored, laundered and pomaded in the best Pall Mall clubman style.

Barney's pincenez twinkled as he made the visitor welcome, but Hammond cut short the small-talk. 'I haven't much time, Mr Barnato,' he said sharply. 'I've another appointment in half an hour.'

'When d'ye plan to go back?' Barney asked, rather startled.

'I've booked passage for Friday,' snapped Hammond. 'Now, let's get down to cases.'

Barney nodded. He liked this blunt American and found him refreshing after the obsequiousness of most of his staff, who so often promised more than they could fulfil. Nevertheless, he had to control his temper when Hammond went on brutally, 'I've been told you've over-engineered the market for your stocks. That's not *my* kind of engineering! Before we discuss any terms, it must be clearly understood that my professional reputation is not to be used for the purpose of rigging the stock market for your mining securities.'

Barney beamed, spreading his hands in mock protest as he raised innocent blue eyes to an understanding Jehovah.

'By my life, I'm glad to hear you say that, Mr Hammond! If you'd do whatever I told you, what bloody use would you be to me? Why, you'd probably do in the mine for someone else, if he'd make it worth your while.'

Hammond had to laugh. The talk became less affable when Barney offered him a salary of $25,000 per annum for three years. Hammond demanded double that figure and Barney finally agreed, ignoring his brother's mumbled protests, but they became deadlocked when the American refused to sign for beyond six months. He had heard of service agreements which Barney had torn up when engineers failed to produce the spectacular results he expected. A broken three-year contract could rob him of his benefits and also diminish his prestige. He now insisted on his freedom to accept other engagements as a consultant if they did not run counter to the company's interests. Above all, he warned the brothers that he expected them to back his advice with very substantial development capital for all properties he cared to recommend.

Barney lit another cigarette and glanced over to Harry who looked glum but nodded. 'Right,' he said cheerfully. 'Let's crack a bottle of bubbly to celebrate. The contract will be ready for your signature tomorrow morning. Tonight you'll have dinner with me and I can promise you a little treat afterwards.'

Having learned that Hammond was a very keen boxer, he took him off to the National Sporting Club in Covent Garden of which he had become a patron soon after its opening in 1891. He was at the ringside for the historic battle between the Negro, Peter Jackson, and Frank Slavin. Until then he had nourished the quaint delusion that, pound for pound, no coloured boxer would ever master a white man. Thereafter he offered to lay £1,000 to £800 on Jackson against anyone.

He was honoured and delighted when the Committee asked him to act as judge at one of their Monday Nights. Whenever he was present the boxers liked to give of their best and not only because he always started the shower of 'nobbins' with a fistful of sovereigns. The Fancy knew that few members were handier with the gloves or as ready to hurry off to the dressing-room to console a fighter who had taken a hiding.

Hammond enjoyed his evening. He was also touched when his new employer impulsively offered him, his wife and two boys their passage from New York. 'You can have return tickets, just in case,' he said jovially. They arranged to meet that autumn in Cape Town. 'He's the best man in the business,' Barney assured his brother. 'He'll make Rhodes and Beit sit up, you mark my words.' For days afterwards he babbled about the millions of ounces of gold that would soon be extracted from the Rand by 'my new man, the highest-paid engineer in the world'. If the City still showed no eagerness to anoint his undug reefs with official quotations, there was no mistaking their respect, however guarded, for the array of companies, headed by De Beers, that now adorned the mahogany panel in the waiting room at Draper's Gardens. Diamond, gold, real estate, waterworks . . . the rubric dazzled callers as well as a widening social circle.

Barney was being asked to a round of dinners but refused to be imprisoned in any social aspic. In the restaurant of the Savoy Hotel he once found himself sitting beside Lady de Grey who was trying to enrol him for one of her charity galas at Covent Garden. After listening in a slight daze to some very broad chatter about his Kimberley days, she asked if it were true that he had once been an acrobat.

'Not 'arf,' he assured her proudly. 'Look, I'll show you.' He peeled off his tail coat, turned up his shirt sleeves and walked round the Palm Court lounge on his hands. Encouraged by the applause, he gave two encores.

He felt restless at formal receptions and favoured the stag parties where one could have some fun. At another Savoy dinner, this time in a private room with a congenial company of stock-brokers and sportsmen, he took over from a hired music-hall artist whose act had fallen flat. He gave one of his recitations and followed it up with a non-stop performance of juggling and bawdy anecdotes which lasted until he dropped off to sleep. The others turned down the lights and crept out rather than disturb him. He snored on until 3 a.m. when he undressed to the skin, wrapped himself in a tablecloth and slumbered like a babe until the cleaners arrived. While his clothes were being valeted, he had a cold bath and shave and called for some herrings for his break-fast. He then bought six dozen roses and went off in a hansom to make his peace with Fanny.

Her pregnancy was too far advanced to risk a visit together to the East End for an 'annual fixture' he hated to miss. This was the pre-Passover Eve party of 'Chometz Bottel' to celebrate the ritual changeover of food and utensils for the eight-day festival. On this day all the local Jewish public houses took out their front windows and dispensed free 'rum and shrub' to passers-by. Barney loved to wander among the crowds who jammed Petticoat Lane from early morning, buying the festival foods, drinks (no malt liquors being permitted at Passover) and new crockery. The stalls, lit by naphtha flares, were laden with fish, fruits, poultry and *matzos*, while costers with wheelbarrows did a roaring trade in olives and the yellow salted cucumbers from Holland.

Barney was always an honoured guest at the 'Chometz Bottel' given by the well-known kosher butchers, Manny and Harry Barnett, over their shop. A running buffet of drinks and rich delicatessen stayed open until well past midnight. The poorest mingled with millionaires like the Sassoons and Montefiores, but Barney preferred to seek out 'Joe' Lyons, the teashop king, who had been a keen actor in his younger days and still amused himself by writing plays and sketches for the Pavilion Theatre in White-chapel Road. There were others like Willie Clarkson, the wig-maker, with whom he liked to exchange racy jokes. And everyone made much of Israel Zangwill, the bearded and sardonic author who had left his teaching job at the Jews' Free School because the Rothschilds and their fellow-Governors resented his outspoken satires on Jewish life. Barney rarely opened a book but he had wept over 'Children of the Ghetto' and kept pumping Zangwill's hand.

Before sitting down to the formal Passover Night dinner with the Barnetts and their family, he had rushed into Polly Nathan's to arrange for several hundred best 'middle pieces' of fried fish to be delivered to the Jewish Orphan Home. The *seder* always made him feel humble and very sentimental. The huge table was decorated with bitter herbs; roast shank bones represented the Paschal lamb and *mitzvah matzos* the bread of affliction. There were mashed almonds, raisins, apples and cinnamon compounded into small dumplings to commemorate the sufferings of the Children of Israel who had made bricks without straw during the exodus from Egypt. Wearing skull caps, wretched refugees from Galicia ate their fill and took new hope as they chanted the traditional saga of the long pilgrimage through the wilderness and the crossing of the Red Sea. For a few hours, as Zangwill put it caustically, 'the grubs and butterflies met together for Auld Lang Syne in their beloved hatching-place.'

Barney cried when he thought of the sufferings of his brother-in-law who had recently died of cancer. It seemed but yesterday when he had carted those boxes of cigars in a wheelbarrow from the old King of Prussia to a backyard in Cobb's Court. But he shed his gloom as Fanny's confinement approached. He had become impatient to return to South Africa and kept pestering the doctors for daily bulletins. To occupy his mind he made elaborate arrangements for a party to follow the baby's circumcision. The painful operation proved unnecessary. Fanny was smoothly delivered of a daughter on 16 March 1893, and Barney quickly forgot his disappointment in the joy of becoming a father. With a suitable blend of sentiment and business he named the child Leah Primrose after his mother and his favourite gold mine.

During Fanny's convalescence he threw himself into a whirl of meetings with Hatton Garden merchants and stockbrokers. It was also imperative to reorganize the office for the increasing business which would follow Hammond's anticipated development of their Rand interests. Harry could now be written off as an active partner. He was far too nervous in times of crisis and had once fled to Brighton to avoid meeting some restive Waterworks Company shareholders. Jack Joel was married and had settled comfortably in London. He was conscientious but plainly needed Woolf's specialized experience of Kimberley and Johannesburg, above all his flair for Stock Exchange intricacies.

Woolf would continue to commute frequently between England and South Africa but he and his wife obviously preferred to make London their home. Only a few months earlier he had turned down the nomination for a vacant seat in the Cape Assembly as representative for Kimberley. He was far too reserved for politics and would never forget Barney's election campaign. There were other reasons. His uncle revelled in the limelight and would always be happiest in a box at the theatre; Woolf symbolically preferred the fourth row of the stalls next to the aisles. He now held a dozen directorships, in addition to De Beers, and could not contemplate spending weeks at the Cape away from his desk, although he wilted in the sizzling heat of a Johannesburg summer.

He was something of a hypochondriac and had long been terrified of death by cholera, but Barney was an even greater hazard to his peace of mind. His constitution, never robust, could not withstand the dual strain of deputizing for his uncle during his lengthy absences abroad and attempting to keep up with his cracking pace as soon as he set foot ashore. Now worth the better

part of two million sterling, Woolf decided to buy a pleasant
Georgian house in Upper Brook Street within walking distance of
brother Jack's mansion in Grosvenor Square. It would give him
and his stylish wife the opportunity to entertain graciously on a
scale befitting a City magnate.

Barney would of course continue to rely on the full support and
companionship of Solly whose lacquer gloss seemed impenetrable
to every pressure from Kimberley or the Rand. He never lost his
temper in or out of the office. The local reporters found him an
unfailing source of sprightly copy. He dressed nattily in white
ducks and favoured gold-tipped cigarettes in a diamond-encrusted
holder even lengthier than Lord Randolph's. South African dandies
hastened to copy his white evening waistcoats with the gold and
onyx buttons. For formal occasions he wore a silk hat, spats and a
white slip under his morning coat which nipped a waist kept trim
by a butterfly's appetite for food and drink.

In Johannesburg he and his wife gave lavish dinners and brought
out their gold plate for the Jewish Festivals and special banquets.
He shared Barney's sentimental affection for the Primrose Mine
and had a solid gold replica of its tower as a centrepiece for his table
decorations. While his uncle made no secret of his indifference to
culture, Solly had a majestic library of finely-bound, unread
editions at 13 Wilhelm Street. He sorely missed the London clubs,
the City's plushy ambience and the Empire Promenade, but made
the best of Johannesburg's attractions. He was an early patron of
the polo games and Auckland Park Trotting Club, and went to
every first night, boxing match and Turffontein race meeting,
invariably at Barney's side and seldom without a friendly bet
between them.

The stakes at his private card parties became the talk of the Rand.
He was both skilful and phenomenally lucky but remained cool
whether winning or losing. After an unusually bad run during one
all-night poker session, he kept his nerve and once again ended up
as the biggest winner. Fritz Mosenthal dropped £20,000 in that
game but did not turn a hair as he signed a cheque and held out
one of Solly's crystal goblets for more champagne. '*Mozel tov,
momzer*' (Yiddish: good luck, bastard) he laughed.

Solly believed in taking chances and scoffed at his Uncle Harry's timid doubts about engaging Hammond at such an incredible salary. Barney himself was waxing more enthusiastic by the hour. He rented an elegant house in Johannesburg for the Hammonds before hurrying off to attend a session of the Assembly, but spent more time with tame journalists whom he spoonfed with notes about his companies and Hammond's brilliant reputation.

The Americans docked at Cape Town with an almost regal collection of baggage. The one-man reception committee made Hammond wrinkle his nose in distaste. Barney had shaved in haste and still reeked of stale liquor. He had barely allowed himself time to slip an ulster over his pyjamas before jumping into a high-wheeled Cape cart. The Hammonds squirmed with irritation but softened when he genially pinched the children's cheeks and made them laugh with his ventriloquism. He whisked the party through Customs and insisted on personally carrying Mrs Hammond's bag, tossing her absurd compliments as he talked nineteen to the dozen at her husband. They piled into the cart while he swore at his pug dog, Blue Rock (named after the Kimberley deposits), and exchanged affectionate insults with his green parrot who seemed to be overawed by the visitors and had to be coaxed to scream, 'What price Primrose today, Barney?'

It was all very disconcerting for Hammond who only thawed when they were ushered into the elegant suite reserved for them at the Queen's Hotel in Sea Point. While they unpacked, Barney took the two boys off to his office to dazzle them with the showcase of diamonds soon to be shipped off to England. They were only a selection, he explained grandly, from the haul bought by his firm from De Beers during the past three months.

The Americans settled in very smoothly. Natalie Hammond, a woman of taste and beauty, soon charmed Fanny and Solly's wife, Nellie, who together introduced her to everyone in Johannesburg. Within a very short time she was giving dinner-parties notable for a *cordon bleu* cuisine and wines impeccably selected by her husband. Barney used to go on to their excellent Sunday luncheons after breakfasting with his own business friends, but there were times when his coarse jokes plainly embarrassed Hammond. His wife was more tolerant and obviously liked him for his cockney perkiness and good nature. He would drop everything to sit with her boys when they were ill and transformed the nursery into a place of fun with his juggling tricks and high spirits. He would rarely appear without gifts for the invalids and huge be-ribboned baskets of fruit or flowers for their mother. The daughter of a Confederate general, she handled him firmly, however, when he threatened to take over her Sunday luncheons. She instituted a system of 'fines' on anyone talking shop, and Barney had to come to heel. It was something Fanny would never be able to achieve.

For the first few weeks Hammond was too busy studying the terrain to worry overmuch about his employer's idiosyncrasies. He had brought his former assistant, V. M. Clement, over from California and put him in charge of the New Primrose Mine. Together they blue-printed plans to sink shafts far deeper than anyone had previously attempted on the Rand. A vast programme of capital expenditure was initiated, not only for new plant but to acquire several more properties on the dip side south of the outcrop. Hammond was supremely confident that these claims, which could be picked up far more cheaply than those on the outcrop, would be workable to a depth of 5,000 feet and more for several miles around. Above all, he thought Barney might do worse than sell his holdings in the outcrop companies and reinvest along the site of the reef before Beit, who had similar theories, could buy up the best ground with the millions he was busily raising from French and German syndicates.

Hammond worked with pioneering enthusiasm. The Comstock Lode in Nevada seemed negligible to him when compared with the Rand. Johannesburg was obviously sitting on the largest treasure house of all time. He engaged more and more experts to deal with ventilation and water at the deepest levels and began thinking seriously about electricity. His orderly mind was jarred, however, by the higgledy-piggledy structure of mining finance. Of the many registered companies at least a hundred had yielded no gold at all, notwithstanding their high share quotation. The others produced about one and a half million ounces a year which he thought might be boosted tenfold with efficient management and better machinery. But working costs were absurdly high and he set about cutting wasteful methods in all Barney's claims. Coming with a fresh eye, he was astonished by the official restrictions and open corruption which slowed down operations and inflated overheads. But the vicious monopoly system operated by Lippert and many others outraged him far less than the Uitlanders' grievances. Voteless, they were even 'prohibited from using English for official business and paid massive taxes for public services far inferior to the meanest towns in California.

Barnato seemed to him incredibly complacent about the undemocratic *status quo* and even more infuriating in his handling of business routine. He gave not a fig for protocol and frequently broke appointments which Hammond had arranged with geologists and engineers. The fastidious Yale man disliked being received at home by an employer who conducted his meetings in a dressing-gown or with braces dangling from his trousers, and usually with that maddening parrot on his shoulder.

Barney would put off decisions to buy new properties while he was coining money on existing promotions. He also appeared to have a permanent coterie of sharepushers and sporty characters for whom he would interrupt the most serious technical discussion. Hammond had found his booziness and vulgarity uncongenial from the start. He disapproved even more of Barney's plain intention not to expand into the South Dip while his existing companies, good and bad, continued to outshine all others on the Stock Exchange.

This attitude was logical even if it did not make long-term sense. Beit's Rand Mines, easily the best potential of all the deep-level concerns, still had little appeal for Johannesburg. The local brokers showed no enthusiasm for his closely-reasoned forecasts about the 'deeps' and preferred to stimulate company shares that would attract gamblers seeking a more dramatic turnover. The Great Barnato filled the bill to perfection.

Barney had other reasons for trying to slow Hammond down. He valued his sharp nose for properties and a Yankee drive for efficiency, but would never quite overcome his suspicion of all experts after missing that first golden crop on the Rand. He was, after all, paying Hammond a princely salary and would not object to increasing it after six months, but other matters had priority. He would suddenly drive off to Kimberley on diamond business or interrupt a technical conference because Solly had picked up some tempting subsidiary which might justify another capital increase for 'Johnnies'.

Hammond's growing frustration was also understandable. He resented being unable to show more than a few blueprints and bulky reports for his months of hard work. When he wished to buy plant or arrange for Barney to inspect some promising claim, it was irritating to be fobbed off with the vague suggestion that he should make a survey in Mashonaland, a whim that had suddenly crossed his employer's mind and would leave it as quickly. Above all, he hated being ridiculed in the clubs as 'Barnato's American white elephant' because so few properties had been bought since his arrival.

In February 1894 he decided not to renew an agreement which, in his view, had injured his professional standing. Barney happened to be feeling euphoric. He had just been re-elected at the top of the poll for Kimberley and was about to leave for England with Woolf and Fanny who was expecting another child. Before sailing he told a friend in Cape Town that he would lay heavy odds on the birth of a son but could not risk smallpox, typhoid and other local terrors. 'In London I can get everything that money can buy,' he said. 'Here I'm seven thousand miles away from it all.'

He did not take Hammond's resignation threat too seriously. 'Look, I'm too busy now,' he told him with a winning smile. 'But I'll talk it over with Woolfie on the boat. I'll cable you definitely—on my life, John!—the second we get to Madeira. We'll wire you from there—definitely, d'ye hear?—about new terms, more cash and a lovely fresh agreement. You'll be a happy man, John, a very happy man.'

Hammond was soothed but thought it prudent all the same to check on the boat's estimated time of arrival at Madeira. When no cable arrived, he went off in a rage to Solly's office and handed in his formal letter of resignation. Solly implored him to wait a day or two while he wired his uncle, but Hammond refused. Barney was told the news by reporters at Plymouth but laughed it off. He told them cheerfully that, far from resigning, 'my consulting engineer' was planning to make an extensive survey of the Rhodesian gold-fields on the firm's behalf.

Hammond received several offers but finally decided to act on a wire from Rhodes inviting him to visit Groote Schuur. Yale and Oxford took to each other on sight. They sat chatting outside on a wooden bench while sipping an excellent Rudesheimer. Hammond had expected to drive a hard bargain but Rhodes disposed of all the formalities with a patrician casualness which did not conform with his ruthless reputation. It was difficult indeed to identify this cultured, bookish Prime Minister with the man who had ordered Jameson to mow down the Matabele and driven Lobengula to his lonely death on the banks of the Shangani. Now his kraal was in ashes and the Union Jack flew over Bulawayo. 'You must come up to Matabeleland and Mashonaland with me,' Rhodes coaxed his visitor. 'But first you will oblige me by looking over all our properties on the Rand.'

There was no difficulty about terms. Hammond asked $75,000 a year, fifty per cent more than Barnato had paid him. Rhodes agreed without hesitation and also promised him a share in Consolidated Goldfields' profits as well as the right to buy any new share allocations at par. Mindful of his recent experiences, Hammond still demanded powers to buy up mining interests at his own discretion, a franchise he had sorely missed with Barnato Brothers. Rhodes nodded, pulled an old envelope out of his pocket and scrawled in gold letters, 'Mr Hays Hammond is authorized to make any purchases for going ahead and has full authority, provided he informs me of it and gets no protest. C.J.R.'

Barney was more incensed by what he considered Rhodes's duplicity, particularly when Clement also defected to Gold Fields, than the actual loss to his own mining interests. Hammond had initiated some excellent plans which were quickly carried into effect. His departure in fact stimulated Barney and Solly to promote several new companies after sinking a number of deep shafts in locations he had recommended.

But Hammond had transferred more than his services as a consultant. He probably influenced Rhodes to embrace Americans in the celebrated Scholarship scheme which was originally restricted to thirty-six 'young colonials'. There can be little doubt that his growing involvement in Transvaal politics also acted as a catalyst for both Rhodes and Jameson. Until October 1894, when Hammond arrived to report to them on the mineral potential between the Limpopo and the Zambesi, neither was too seriously concerned with the Uitlanders' clamour for the vote and more self-government. They were still too eager to consolidate their gains in the new domains and hoped to dazzle the Chartered Company shareholders with visions of another Main Reef.

Hammond sharply disabused them. The Chartered Company would have to rely on Rhodes's Consolidated Gold Fields and Beit's Rand Mines for their funds, but he warned them that even these sources might soon be in jeopardy. While they sat smoking and drinking coffee round a camp fire he spoke passionately of an explosive situation in the City of Gold. 'Unless a radical change is made,' he prophesied, 'there will be a rising of the people of Johannesburg.' He saw Kruger as the one dangerous obstacle to all progress on the Rand.

Some historians, aided by hindsight, have suggested that the disastrous Raid was conceived during these camp fire talks. One can only speculate on whether events would have taken a different course had Barney sent Hammond that promised cable from Madeira.

13

———

WHEN BARNEY FIRST ARRIVED IN ENGLAND in March 1894, he planned to stay only long enough to see Fanny through her second confinement. He remained fourteen months during which he became the leader of a frenzied investment boom. It seemed a good omen when, that June, his first son was born. He was named Isaac Henry Woolf. At the last minute Barney prankishly added 'Ladas' after Lord Rosebery's recent Derby winner, but the boy would always be called Jack.

While waiting for Fanny to recover her strength for the return journey, he set about raising more capital for the Johannesburg Consolidated Investment Company which was rapidly expanding its real estate holdings. He had planned to double the original capital of £175,000 and could easily have done so in South Africa, but his feelers in London and Paris encouraged him to seek a glossier City hallmark. Within a few months the company's capital was successively increased to £850,000 which enabled 'Johnnies' to acquire various mining assets from the family firm. The volume of business made it essential to move out of Barnato Buildings into new headquarters at the junction of Harrison and Fox Streets. Colonnade Building, a sprawling block entered through cloistral-like arches, soon became only second in importance and turnover to the Corner House itself.

Barney had made his City début precisely when the European bankers had, for different reasons, suddenly become Rand-conscious. The Bourse, excited by the latest gold figures, gave more support to the Wernher-Beit syndicates, while Rhodes, still sporting the laurels of his Matabele campaign, had transformed the whole climate of opinion in Throgmorton Street. The

London Stock Exchange had previously hesitated to issue official quotations for gold shares and kept their dealings in 'Kaffirs' to a minimum. When Rhodes arrived in England that autumn, he came not only as Prime Minister of Cape Colony and the symbol of Empire but as Chairman of the thriving Consolidated Gold Fields Ltd.

His prestige was at its highest. Even his Chartered Company shareholders, disappointed by Hammond's glum reports on the minerals of Mashonaland, were consoled for their lack of dividends while he was being fêted by Cabinet Ministers and eulogized in *The Times*. Patriotism, though still unaccompanied by five per cent, seemed fully justified when their hero was received at Windsor Castle by the Queen who thanked him graciously for adding many thousands of square miles to her dominions. He was made a Privy Councillor and would soon be permitted to give his name officially to the newly-won provinces of Mashonaland and Matabeleland.

At the Burlington Hotel in Cork Street he held court in a vast suite which cost him £25 a day. Barney called on him as a courtesy but could not refrain from airing his grievance over Hammond's defection for which he would always hold Rhodes personally responsible. He shouted angrily, 'Suppose you had a first-rate chef and after dining with you I lured him away. You'd think I was a rotter, wouldn't you? And you'd be bloody right!'

Of some three hundred mining companies registered in South Africa at the peak of the boom only a handful were yielding ore in any quantity. But nothing could assuage a share fever which mounted with reports, mostly fanciful or premature, of huge outputs from 'the deeps'. After one company was launched in the City of London, a director had cabled Johannesburg to enquire when crushing would actually commence. Back came the reply: 'As soon as you've returned the samples.' The faintest whisper of shaft-sinking was amplified by brokers and financial writers for the benefit of share-hungry investors no longer concerned with quarterly dividends or the dull safety of Consols.

Barney was ideally cast for the rôle of ringmaster in the 'Kaffir

Circus'. He typified the dynamism that activated both the London Stock Exchange and the more volatile Bourse. He had caught the market's scent from the moment the City bankers endorsed his 'Johnnies'. When further capital was decreed by speculative demand for what was, after all, a company mainly concerned with landed properties, his instinct assured him of an even keener appetite for mining shares. He had therefore instructed Solly to sink more shafts and buy up any likely deep levels whether or not for immediate pegging.

The results were spectacular. In the course of a few months he brought the number of enterprises under his banner up to almost thirty, headed by 'Johnnies', New Primrose and New Croesus. Others were either low-grade ore producers or simply finance concerns launched on the tide of speculation, but they looked impressive in such good company. The firm's holdings represented something like £10m of nominal capital with a peak market valuation of close on £62m. Such a growth rate naturally delighted promoters and shareholders alike. As soon as a mining property was acquired, it was simplicity itself to float a company in the Transvaal and then introduce shares at a high premium in London and Paris. Since the Barnatos, Joels and their associates held most of the original stock, little was left for the investing public whose appetite grew with nibbling. Thus the promoters could increase issues which shareholders were more than eager to buy even at inflated prices. Everyone was happy; the brokers fattened their order books; shareholders saw their 'Buffels' shoot up almost overnight from £3 to £9; and the Barnato-Joel clan could make a huge cash profit by selling at will part of their holdings while still retaining substantial blocks purchased at par.

It seemed foolproof and, notwithstanding sneers from the disappointed, the firm could not be accused of thimble-rigging. Barney did not float bogus companies or issue false valuations. They subscribed the entire issue of Barnato Consolidated with £1,250,000. Its shares went so high within weeks that Barney could justly claim, 'I might easily have issued capital for five million.'

Intoxicated investors now turned from practically every other security in favour of bouncing Kaffirs. The Barnato Group quickly became the odds-on favourite, with such a variety of stock that many lost all sense of discrimination and simply directed their brokers to buy 'Barneys'.

He had long enjoyed popularity in Kimberley and Johannesburg, but he was nobody in London until his share 'tips' filled the pockets of thousands of punters. He loved being recognized in the streets and used to stop his carriage to acknowledge cheers and distribute largesse. The bus drivers now flicked their whips in greeting, sweetened by the £100 cheques he regularly contributed towards their Christmas 'beano'. Hansom cabbies almost fought to drive him to the National Sporting Club or the Empire where he became a familiar figure in the noisy Promenade. Before long he bought an interest in the celebrated music hall, not as an investment but primarily to book acts for South Africa, usually underwriting all fares and salaries.

He invested some cash in *The Duchess of Coolgardie* at Drury Lane and, true to form, soon made suggestions for 'improving' it. Later he persuaded the manager to let him walk on as an extra in the Johannesburg scene of *Cheer, Boys, Cheer*. This brought on an attack of stage fever. When the Rothschilds organized a charity show, he headed the list of donations with a cheque for 5,000 guineas but failed to land a part for himself. Instead, he put on a one-night benefit performance of *The Bells* at the Vaudeville and, of course, took Irving's rôle. It was a disaster. 'South African audiences must take their pleasures sadly,' wrote one unfeeling critic. But Barney was consoled when Ada Blanche sang a new song, 'Golden Africa', at the Empire in which she called for a round of cheers for 'Barnato, boys, and the land of Livingstone'. The chorus sounded suspiciously like a puff for one of his own companies:

> 'The shafts are sunk, the stamps work, boys,
> The golden quartz pans out
> In many a merry ounce, boys,
> For they know what they're about.'

He was even more delighted when George R. Sims, playwright, balladist and the most influential gossip-writer of his day, asked permission to call his pedigree bulldog pup after him. One evening at the National Sporting Club, Barney thanked him for the compliment and said jokingly, 'I hope he won't injure my name.'

'Don't be afraid, he'll never do anything to upset you,' laughed Sims. 'So mind you don't disgrace *him*!' Like everything else he touched at this time, the name proved lucky and 'Barney Barnato' won first prizes whenever he was shown.

He was rather less fortunate on the turf but considered his £10,000 a year well spent, although he missed the camaraderie of the Johannesburg tracks and could not dictate to his manager, Lord Marcus Beresford, whose patrons included the Prince of Wales. His trainer was Joe Cannon who did the best he could with a dozen middling animals run in Barney's appropriate colours of primrose with old gold cap. Worcester cost 2,000 guineas and later won some good races including the City and Suburban. He was a bad-tempered colt and only his owner had any faith in him to win even a three-horse race at Brighton. Just before the off, Woolf Joel advised him to back the favourite as well. 'Not me!' snorted Barney. 'I didn't get rich by backing two out of three.' He promptly took £700 to £400 against Worcester who won easily.

He rushed off to collect his winnings and was splashing champagne into a glass when a coster touched his sleeve. 'M'lord,' he mumbled, 'I saw your 'orse win like a good 'un but he let out and kicked over me whelk stall on his way back.' Barney, bred in Petticoat Lane, could usually smell a tall story but decided to give this man the benefit of the doubt. 'Go and see Mr Cannon and tell him all about it,' he said genially, scribbling something on his race card. 'Here, show him this and he'll give you a pony (£25). And next time we meet I'll expect a plate of whelks on you. I love 'em.'

He also won a useful prize or two with Miss Primrose but was too far away in the stand to see the mare run her first race at Newmarket. By the time he had snatched a pair of binoculars from a complete stranger, she was already past the post. It was typical of him not to invest in field glasses when he could borrow them. Although he would cheerfully take half a dozen guests to the theatre and entertain them to supper afterwards at the Savoy, he still relished pinching pennies. It gave him enormous pleasure to discover a dingy chophouse in Tokenhouse Yard off Leadenhall

Street where one could lunch for eighteenpence, including a tankard of porter.

A generous host at all times, his own tastes remained simple. Reporters were usually regaled with champagne, oysters and fistfuls of cigars, but one scribe had a shock when he arrived at the Berkeley Hotel in Piccadilly for an interview. Barney invited him to share his breakfast of two herrings and some scraps of watercress, served by four waiters who constantly refilled the free pots of coffee while Leah Primrose sat on her father's lap and kept tweaking his ear.

Barney had moved into the Berkeley when his tenancy ran out on his Curzon Street house. He became so angry over a repair and make-good clause in the lease that he retaliated childishly by having all the ceilings painted black. In the end he had to foot the bill for the re-painting, but enjoyed his brief satisfaction. This episode prompted him to acquire the freehold site of 25 Park Lane overlooking Stanhope Gate from the Duke of Westminster. Solly had repeatedly urged him to buy or build a house in a fashionable part of London, arguing that the multi-millionaire head of a flourishing group of companies could not continue to entertain adequately in restaurants and expect his family to camp in hotel suites or rented houses. Barney hesitated. He would never quite lose the pedlar's instinct for carrying his possessions on his back or his dislike of putting down roots. He retained a lifelong superstition against building a house of his own which he considered unlucky. Besides, he regarded South Africa as his main base of operations.

Solly, who himself had an eye on a mansion in Great Stanhope Street also adjacent to the 'Rothschild Row' end of Piccadilly, argued that their business expansion would require his uncle's presence in London for at least six months every year. Barney only made up his mind when Beit bought himself a mansion in Park Lane which he filled with Murillos and Romneys, closely followed by J. B. Robinson who took a long lease of Dudley House and spent lavish sums on Old Masters.

Society had quickly embraced the wealthy 'Randlords' who now dominated the City. Welcomed in the most exclusive Clubs, they were also pursued by hostesses who took their cue from the Prince of Wales's predilection for cosmopolitan financiers and sportsmen. They were open-handed and had a pasha-like exoticism about them that lent spice to the conventional Season. Rhodes had ridden in Rotten Row with a shabby brown bowler and a rat-catcher's jacket over his white flannels, but this was dismissed as charmingly idiosyncratic by all save a few diehards. Barney was more formal on the whole, and he did not tip as ostentatiously as Rhodes who once gave a favourite waiter £75 to keep importunate visitors out of the Burlington, but the velvet rope was always unhooked for him by restaurant managers with a nose for publicity. His racehorses and Stock Exchange coups were being so widely reported by newspaper gossips that he was swamped with invitations and finally saw the logic of returning hospitality in a home of his own.

He remained sensitive, however, to the faintest signs of con-descension. The Park Lane site had cost him £70,000 and he became very incensed when the Duke of Westminster expressed concern that he might build something unworthy of the neigh-bourhood. The agent even demanded a clause in the agreement stipulating that the house should cost at least £20,000. 'Tell the duke,' spluttered Barney, 'that I'm going to spend that on the stables alone.' Once he decided to go ahead, he lavished funds on the architect, T. H. Smith, who soon exceeded his preliminary estimate of £40,000 to put up the house and a further £30,000 for decorations.

Built of Portland stone, the five-storeyed mansion would com-mand a splendid view of Crystal Palace and the northern heights of Highgate. The interior was designed in the Renaissance style with slightly florid touches of Louis XIV. There would be an imposing staircase of marble four flights high and lit from the top by a glass dome, a ballroom of some 2,000 square feet, a conservatory and winter garden. Barney wanted two billiard rooms and also insisted on having the entire mansion heated by radiators to keep out the London chill. Fanny's only stipulation was that the children's quarters, including a special kitchen, bathroom, nursery and schoolroom, should be on their own floor.

It would take almost two years to build and furnish. Barney continually breathed down the architect's neck and amused himself by checkmating the hordes of parasites who imagined he would be an easy target for their bric-à-brac and pictures. He knew nothing about art and, apart from commissioning portraits of his family and himself, only bought one picture in his entire life. It was Sydney Cooper's banal 'Group of Sheep' which he purchased on impulse because 'one of them looks like me'. Otherwise, his artistic taste was confined to Louis Wain's drawings of cats which he cut out of the *Daily Graphic* and pinned over his dressing-table.

Such heresies failed to deter the dealers. One eager tout steered him into a gallery and confided that the Constable had just arrived. Barney showed interest for the first time. 'What's the copper 'ere for, I wonder?' he enquired. At the theatre with a party of friends he noticed a most attractive young woman who kept fluttering her eyelashes at him. She buttonholed him during the interval and hinted broadly at her valuable collection of paintings some of which she was prepared to sacrifice. 'You really must find time, Mr Barnato, to come and see my Watteau,' she murmured behind her fan. Barney took a closer look at her décolletage.

'D'ye mean it?' he asked, dropping his voice.

'Of course.'

'Fine,' he said warmly, favouring her with a wink. 'When's your old man out? Or p'raps we'd better meet somewhere outside?'

Woolf was, by contrast, very much the sophisticate. He was regarded as the best-dressed man in the City of London and prided himself on his buttonholes and brocaded waistcoats. He smoked ten-inch Havanas or scented Egyptian cigarettes and had a witty languid manner that made him popular with clubmen who sometimes found Barney overpowering. One of his friends was Alfred de Rothschild whose grotto of art treasures was the envy of the world's connoisseurs. Woolf thought that such taste and expertise might be usefully conscripted but his uncle bristled. He despised this Rothschild as a fop who conducted his private symphony orchestra with an ivory baton and amused himself by driving a carriage drawn by four zebras.

'I don't need *his* help,' he growled. 'Why, his house would go into my hall.'

He was showing signs of megalomania as the millions rolled into his companies. Passing Dudley House where several carriages were waiting for Robinson's guests, he observed casually to a companion, 'I'd half a mind once to buy that property. It's got such a splendid place for the baby's perambulator.' Possibly to gain newspaper publicity, he also wrote to the Duke of Wellington offering to rent Apsley House 'until my own place is ready'. As expected, the Duke's agents sent him a stiff refusal, but he had already taken the lease of Spencer House in St James's Place. 'It's not a bad position,' he told a journalist. 'Exactly half-way between the Prince of Wales in Marlborough House and the P.M. in Arlington Street.'

This imposing Doric mansion, built in the eighteenth century by Kent's pupil, Vardy, overlooked Green Park. In the dining room with its ionic colonnades and walls hung with green silk damask, the Barnatos gave some excellent parties. They kept an elegant table but Barney preferred plain fare to all the pink-frilled cutlets, plovers' eggs and enamelled cups of Turkish coffee. He took some pride, however, in the celebrated Painted Room with its exquisitely ornate ceiling and liked to warm his back by the fire, his elbow barely reaching the marble chimneypiece, while he joked with his friends or rattled off instructions to a relay of clerks from Draper's Gardens. The handsome library, remodelled by Sir John Soane, failed to tempt him. He put up a card table under the gaze of Sydney Cooper's sheep and tore through columns of figures before breakfast. 'You must come and see me again,' he told an interviewer, 'when we've got some of our own silver in—lots of stuff on the way from Cape Town. We ain't unpacked half our things yet.'

The atmosphere at Spencer House was distinctly greenroomish. Apart from rabbis and others from the East End who called frequently to ask for help, he kept open house for actors, journalists, racing trainers, boxers and theatre managers. One of his regular visitors was the dramatist, Haddon Chambers, who had rashly agreed to collaborate on a play based on his early days. Progress was slow because Barney could rarely be cornered except on his cross-Channel trips to see French bankers when he would walk up and down the deck pouring out his ideas. At home he insisted on acting out every scene while Chambers made notes between constant interruptions from callers or the children.

The play would never be completed but it gave Barney some outlet for his nostalgia. He was also supremely confident that the public would flock to see the production if he took a part himself. 'I'll do a bit of sword-swallowing,' he suggested, 'to fit into the scene about Payne's Circus.' He had Charles Wyndham in mind as the star and hoped to see it staged at the Criterion. 'Otherwise, I'll buy a theatre and form my own company,' he said grandly.

Chambers resigned himself to very odd hours but, like almost everyone else in his inner circle, he loved Barney for his kindliness and complete lack of side. 'He is always the same, wherever he might be or whoever he's with,' he once said. 'He seems to take a bit of Shoreditch with him everywhere.' In his velvet dressing-gown and white socks, chain-smoking and talking simultaneously to half a dozen callers while Leah and her nanny romped on the carpet with a terrier, he was never too overawed by Lord Spencer's ormolu and marble to break off and entertain them by standing on his head or walking round the elegant salon on his hands, usually sticking a monocle in his eye by way of finale.

He insisted on shaving himself and only allowed his valet to look after his clothes and iron the nap of his topper. He expected at least five years' wear from all his hats and gave up buying expensive gloves after losing one. He bitterly resented paying wages to the deferential butler and a squad of footmen who seemed to do nothing but stand about. For a time he tried putting on the boxing gloves with one or two of the younger ones but stopped in disgust because they were far too nervous to hit him. 'It's no fun,' he complained, 'punching a bloke who bows and thanks you as if he's afraid of losing his ruddy job.'

His mail bulged with invitations from donation-hunting duchesses and every variety of begging letter. One morning he pounced on an appeal from a man who claimed to have given him his first shave in Kimberley and now wished to invest his life's savings of £400 in anything The Great Barnato might care to recommend. Barney looked puzzled until the name clicked. 'Why, it's old Jacko,' he told his secretary. 'Remember him all right! Worst bloody shaves I ever had! But a good lad all the same. See that he gets his lot before they go too high. Tell Mr Woolf to double his money for him.' Another correspondent proved less fortunate. He was a London agent who asked several thousand pounds for an estate near Rome which carried an Italian dukedom with it. Barney thanked him and replied, 'I might even go above your price if you can arrange to throw in King Humbert's crown as well. However, I'm not too interested, having just offered a million quid for the Mansion House.'

A number of friends, particularly attractive women, soon discovered his amiable habit of impulsively handing out diamonds like cigarettes. One evening, after an exceptionally heavy day in the City, he went off to dine at a club in Pall Mall. Too weary to go home and change, he had rushed into an outfitters near his offices and bought himself a new collar and cravat. When he arrived, one of the company could not take his eyes off the stone in his tie pin.

'By Jove, that's a cracker,' he enthused. 'Good old Kimberley.'

'Nothing at all,' Barney assured him modestly. 'It's yours as a souvenir if you'll put up all the champagne for the six of us at dinner.' He solemnly handed over the pin before taking his leave. 'Good luck to you,' he chuckled. 'I paid ninepence for it when I bought this collar and tie.'

He made practical use of his diamonds on his frequent visits to Paris. During that rosy spring of 1895 when 'Kaffirs' continued to spiral into the bluest of skies, he launched the London-Paris Financial and Mining Corporation with a nominal capital of £500,000 which was quickly doubled as Gallic investors caught the Rand bug. In his suite at the Continental or the Bristol the wires hummed to London, Johannesburg, Wall Street and St Petersburg while champagne corks popped round the clock. One French interviewer rhapsodized, 'Sir Barnett Barnato has appeared and already a new force enriches the thin blood of Europe's finance markets.'

Reacting instinctively to the lobbying and manoeuvring which made the Bourse so much more congenial to him than the London Stock Exchange, he cultivated the most exclusive *cocottes* in Paris. They gave him the affectionate nickname of 'Toto' (Little One), but the relationship was mainly businesslike on both sides. His lower left vest-pocket was lined with diamonds for these young women who might drop useful hints about his enterprises. When he took a party to the Restaurant Paillard he was always warmly greeted by diplomats and politicians who hoped to pick up a few golden crumbs. He would rarely leave Paris without making an appearance at the Opéra, usually as the guest of Sir Edgar Vincent, head of the Ottoman Bank.

Barney enjoyed, but was not seduced by, social grandeur which he was often astute enough to put to practical use. He was far more at ease with his Whitechapel friends than the greedy dowagers and men-about-town whose hospitality softened him up for some share tip. He felt honoured, however, when a St James's club welcomed him under the special rule authorizing admission of 'a few gentlemen calculated to lend distinction' to their gatherings, but avoided becoming pompous. When Stuart Cumberland, one of his corps of friendly London scribes, proposed him for membership of another exclusive Club, he hesitated over the space reserved for 'Occupation' on the application form. Winking at Cumberland, he scribbled 'Toff'. The Secretary winced. 'Will you kindly explain what that means?' he demanded.

'Oh,' replied Barney innocently, 'that's Hebrew for financial gentleman.'

He retained his old warmth for the East End where he now had an enormous roll of pensioners no longer able to work. Every Friday morning a clerk would leave Draper's Gardens for Spitalfields with a gladstone bag filled with envelopes of money. Each was delivered personally with a kindly message from their benefactor. He was besieged by the sick and elderly whenever he appeared east of Aldgate Pump but kept alert for *schnorrers* (Yiddish: scroungers). Recognizing one who always whined for alms and had never done an honest day's work, he shouted angrily, 'A bob? I'll give you a bob for your wreath. No, they're not allowed in our religion. Better yet, I'll leave you a shilling in my Will.'

He increased his donations to synagogues and communal charities after his father's death. Old Isaac had succumbed to a painful illness which made Barney pray that his own end would be swift and sudden. For some weeks he would not go out to dinner or the theatre and made elaborate plans for burial beside his father's grave in the Jewish Cemetery at Willesden Green where

Joel Joel had also been laid to rest. He became morbidly convinced that the house in Park Lane would bring him ill-fortune. 'I shall never live to see it built,' he declared time and again. Perhaps to appease the gods, he bought some hideous gargoyle-like figures for the roof when someone assured him they were good-luck totems. As an additional insurance he and a very nervous Fanny were swung aloft in a crane to cement photographs of themselves under the cornerstone of a gable.

He continued to work and play at a furious tempo. At the end of a strenuous day in his office or among the Hatton Garden diamond merchants he would snatch a chop at Rule's or hurry into Gatti's for a dozen Whitstables washed down by a pint of champagne before spending an evening at the National Sporting Club or the Empire 'Prom'. Often he slept for only three or four hours before driving off to Victoria to catch the boat train for Paris. Invigorated by a cold bath and twenty minutes with his Indian clubs or chest expanders, he would be rubbed down with alcohol by a footman who carefully middle-parted his yellow hair and waxed the ends of his moustache. But no matter how busy, he would steal into the nursery at Spencer House to play with the children. Leah loved to listen to the ticking of his watch while the baby gurgled whenever Barney stood on his head and made animal noises.

If he had an early appointment at Draper's Gardens he would try, usually without success, to arrive ahead of his nephew, Jack Joel, who prided himself on being at his desk even before the office boy. He had an excellent memory second only to Barney who, interviewed by a financial correspondent about details of his various enterprises, once said breezily, 'I'll give them to you in three minutes flat.' He then rattled off a score of balance sheets almost as fast as the journalist could take them down in shorthand. 'I've got them all in my head or at my fingers' ends,' he boasted with every justification. 'I need no notes.'

But it was more than a trick of memory. Like many another man born poor and needing to reassure himself, he continually totted up his assets and kept them fresh in his mind. Louis Cohen, while on a visit to London, asked him if it was true that he was supposed to be worth £20m. 'Yes,' agreed Barney, after scribbling on his pad, 'but I still need another five million to feel quite comfortable.'

'What good will it do you?' protested Cohen. 'Why go on slaving?'

Barney whisked out a snapshot of Leah and his baby son. 'Because, when I'm dead, I want them to be able to say that their father was a clever chap after all.'

He always found time to joke with the most junior members of his staff and sympathized with their troubles. In a roundabout way he once heard that a clerk with a large family had fallen into a moneylender's hands. He secretly paid off the debt and handed back the I.O.U. 'The best of us have owed money,' he assured the grateful victim. 'Even millionaires.'

He was driving along Pall Mall one day with Haddon Chambers when his dog-cart collided with a van. Thrown out of his seat, he dusted himself off and unconcernedly lit one of the Barnato Havanas which Robert Lewis of St James's Street now imported specially for him. A few days later he was breakfasting with Chambers at Spencer House while revising a scene in 'The Play' when a servant brought in a letter from the owners of the van who happened to be a Sisterhood in Lambeth. They enquired about Mr Barnato's health and gently reminded him that the repairs had cost fifteen shillings. Barney sent them a generous cheque with a warm letter composed by Chambers.

Rhodes was also given to quixotic acts of philanthropy but he lacked Barney's intensely personal identification with suffering. As Natalie Hammond had perceptively noted in her diary after her husband left Barney, 'Mr Rhodes's sympathies are for the human race, and not for the individual. In this respect he is unlike Mr Beit and Mr Barnato. He can be as bloodless as fate when people are not of use to him. He simply has no place for a disused member.' Barney would have ample cause to endorse that judgment which applied not only to Rhodes but to many in the City of London.

They made much of The Great Barnato when his shares were the best gambling chips on the market, but this did not account altogether for his popularity among a widening circle during the Kaffir boom. He tended to regard his shareholders rather like

members of a mammoth clan with himself as their wise and bene-
volent patriarch. It was a simple-minded view easily reconciled
with a sentimental man who had survived so much hardship
without becoming callous. He liked being cheered by the gallery
when he entered his box at the theatre and was deeply touched
when the Barnetts and others suggested that he might stand as
M.P. for Shoreditch. 'No, Kimberley is my seat,' he told them,
'and South Africa has long been my home.'

Cupboard love attracted some guests to the dinner-parties at
Spencer House while many others guzzled on his Stock Exchange
tips, but a number found genuine pleasure in his company despite
his ignorance of books, music, pictures and the usual social graces.
Voluble and cocky he might be, as well as an unabashed huckster,
but he remained the genial, bouncy Cockney, irrepressible as
yeast, whether dining at the Carlton Club or seizing a pickled
cucumber from a Petticoat Lane barrow.

A remarkable cross-section of City, theatrical and sporting
interests attended the dinner given in his honour at the Criterion
before he left for South Africa in May 1895. The 250 guests were
welcomed by the Lord Mayor of London while, screened off from
the men, Fanny and other ladies listened to the speeches con-
gratulating her husband.

Barney could not refrain from behaving like a bull in a talking
shop. After recalling his early days in Kimberley and the Transvaal,
he went on to paint the rosiest picture of South Africa's wealth
and potential. In a characteristic aside he reminded the company
that his own gold mining interests were now worth over £20m.
'And I'm proud to say that I've never issued a prospectus so that
I'm pleased to find that so much confidence exists in my name
alone.' A dangerous boast, as he would soon discover.

When he arrived at Waterloo with Fanny, his children and two
parrots to catch the boat train, they were followed by a long
procession of hansoms and carriages. Their special saloon car was
choked with flowers from well-wishers and they were given an
almost regal send-off at Southampton where Sir Francis Evans,
Chairman of the Union Steamship Company, went aboard
specially to wish them *bon voyage*.

Twenty-two years before Barney had sailed steerage in the

Anglian with his shabby kitbag and Joel's dubious cigars. He still had the same gusto and high spirits as he raced up and down the promenade deck, clowning for the benefit of crew and passengers alike. Among those on board was Philip Tennyson Cole, the society portrait painter, who tried to sketch little Leah but found her almost as restless as her father. 'Look up at Mr Cole or I'll throw you in the water,' Barney threatened her. 'If you do, you won't get another daughter,' she replied pertly. In the end Cole agreed to paint her as well as her parents. 'Charge what you like,' Barney said grandly, which Cole found refreshing after his recent experience of J. B. Robinson who had commissioned four portraits from him and growled, 'Five hundred guineas for the lot. Take it or leave it. And that includes the frames, of course.'

Cole could not resist Barney's high spirits. 'His disposition was so mercurial and alive with electrical force,' he wrote later, 'that even his ugliness became attractive.' He was able eventually to complete his portrait but Barney proved a most elusive and fidgety sitter. The artist had to endure a long series of broken appointments from the moment Barney bustled down the gangway at Cape Town, holding Leah's hand and with the green parrot perched on his shoulder. A brass band trumpeted him to his hotel, but the welcome grew even more uproarious when the train steamed into Kimberley to a chorus of fog signals and the cheers of several hundred workers from De Beers. They thrust bouquets at Fanny and hauled the carriage through the streets to the Company's head office where Gardner Williams stood outside to offer an official greeting.

Barney replied with genuine emotion. Although born within the sound of Bow Bells, he would always be regarded by many in the City of London as a flashy colonial financier. Here he was on first-name terms with almost everyone; store-keepers, diggers and brokers who still remembered when he had trudged back from the claims with only a few stones and his bottle of Cape Smoke in the 'poverty bag'.

14

―――――

JOHANNESBURG MOBBED HIM. Almost everyone on the Stock Exchange seemed to be coining money from his companies. All his London speeches and interviews had been reported back in full, together with titbits of gossip about his racehorses and the Park Lane mansion. He quickly laughed off rumours that he might retire to England and pointed to the growing bulk of his firm's holdings on the Rand. 'Johnnies' was flourishing and would show a profit of close on a million that year.

Johannesburg pumped extra zest into his arteries enabling him to work at a much faster tempo than in London. Within hours of his return he had taken charge of all the firm's enterprises, darting and swishing his baton like a demented conductor, but with Solly as his very able first violin. In Colonnade Building the lights burned far into the night with clerks handling cables from all the world's money markets.

Barney showed no outward sign of exhaustion. When the cycling craze hit Johannesburg he was among the first to ride strenuously round the Wanderers Ground every morning, accompanied by Fanny who was now in her third pregnancy. He hoped for another son but little 'Miss Barnato', as he playfully called her, remained his prime favourite. One night, after a late session at the Rand Club, he was driving back to Norman House when he suddenly recalled promising her a new doll which he had forgotten to collect that afternoon. Overcoming his superstition about turning back, he drove to the shop on Pritchard Street and apologetically woke up the owner. 'You wouldn't care to be in my shoes,' he explained with a laugh, 'if I arrived home without that doll.'

Barney needed all his good humour to deal with the Waterworks Company crisis. The summer rains had failed and the city was enduring its worst drought in years. Hotels refused to serve tea or coffee and men drank their whisky neat, smuggling out the soda bottles for domestic ablutions. The Company could not cope and limited its supply to an hour each morning while a small gang of water pirates raided outlying dams and wash holes to retail buckets at several shillings a time. Even Solly lost his cheerfulness and feared that, unless the rains came soon, the Company's unlucky directors stood in danger of being lynched.

Other local grievances had festered during those hot and dusty months. President Kruger welcomed the Rand's gold but had no time for the miners. He was even more stubborn in opposing the National Union who complained bitterly that nobody could vote until he had lived fourteen years in the Republic although boys of sixteen were being called up to serve under an alien flag.

The Chamber of Commerce turned desperately to Barney who was credited with enormous influence in Pretoria. He was genial and sympathetic but quite unhelpful. His year's absence had made him even more oblivious of Uitlandish psychology. He loved South Africa but, regarding himself as a British subject before all else, felt far less emotionally involved with nationality issues than those who resented being treated as 'squatters' by a government that squeezed them tirelessly. With his own faith in the power of money, he failed to see why a thriving community should concern itself with 'politics'. It seemed madness to him to upset the *status quo*. 'The old man (Kruger) has kept his team together and has them now well in hand. We don't want to swap coachmen at this or any other river.' He was, however, strongly put out when Kruger gave a banquet in Pretoria to celebrate the Kaiser's birthday and declared, 'I know I may count on the Germans in the future.'

Barney deplored this pro-Germanism but still chose to dismiss it as a political gambit against Rhodes and the Cape Afrikaners. 'The Transvaal Government,' he blandly assured his friends, 'is not a government at all, but an unlimited company of some twenty thousand shareholders which has been formed to exploit a large territory, and after being unable for thirty years to pay any dividend or even to pay its clerks, has suddenly struck it rich. There was neither capital nor skill in the company itself for development, and so it leased the ground to those who had both.' As for the fuss over franchise, 'If I had a company going on all right and shareholders satisfied, d'ye suppose I'd do anything to bring in a lot of fresh shareholders? They had a hard time in the early years and one thinks they are entitled to all they can get now. That's all right and quite in my line.'

His personal popularity combined with the flourishing state of the stock market added weight to his views, however unpalatable. 'If the people want English education for their children, let them pay for it,' he said with a shrug. 'I'll do my part but you can't expect a Dutch Government to treat its own language as foreign.' He also professed indifference to the laws debarring Jews and Catholics from holding military and official posts and excluding their children from State-subsidized schools. Having been educated at the Jews' Free School himself, he saw no problem in providing special establishments which he and other wealthy co-religionists could easily endow.

Sheer force of events caused him to change his mind. He was received with the usual cordiality on the presidential stoep in Pretoria but made no headway when he protested that the dynamite concession alone had added £600,000 a year to mining costs. When he mentioned that the monopoly for manufacturing potassium cyanide, an essential solvent of gold, was also causing quite unjustified hardship, Kruger reminded him gruffly that this industry would be an insurance for the Republic in case the Rand gold ran out. Barney resisted the temptation to point out that, if that happened (and most geologists thought it unlikely for a century at least!), the State's cyanide factory would then have no value at all. 'What use is it to talk to a man like that?' he muttered to Solly when he got back.

Far more serious during those prickly summer months was the government's plain intention to force the Cape and Orange Free State railways out of business. Although the Delagoa Bay line from the coast to Johannesburg was shorter, it was inefficiently run and had poor landing facilities as well as inadequate rolling stock. Most of the personnel were Hollanders who knew little English and even less about railways. Not surprisingly, the Cape railways could still carry freight more cheaply even on their longer haul.

Kruger retaliated by allowing the Netherland Company to treble the rates on the fifty-mile run between the Vaal and Johannesburg, including a tariff of 3d. a ton of coal per mile. This was obviously designed to force importers to use the Delagoa Bay railway which would then have a clear monopoly. The Cape Government promptly lowered the rates on their line as far as the Transvaal border. When the Netherland Company imposed still more punitive charges, the Cape Railway unloaded their freight at the Vaal River 'Drifts' (fording places) and took it on to Johannesburg by ox-wagon, as many as two hundred plunging through in a single day.

Barney was approached to check this dangerous and costly game of beggar-my-neighbour. His indifference to the franchise agitation was shared by many who, as he had cynically remarked, were more concerned with cash than votes, but nobody doubted his deep concern for the welfare of Johannesburg which his faith and capital had helped to transform from an overgrown mining camp into a prosperous city of 150,000 people with fine buildings and shops and a network of roads extending over fourteen square miles. He now had the largest holding of real estate in the town and its suburbs which depended upon a stable economy, but the more imminent threat was to the Rand's mining interests. The preferential rates in favour of the Delagoa Bay line benefited only the Netherland Railway shareholders while crippling the mining companies. If overheads continued to rise, they would have to cut down on their development of the deep levels and perhaps abandon the low-grade ore-producing properties in which speculators had invested so heavily.

Barney failed to see why Kruger chose to promote the interests of his inefficient and grasping Dutch officials at the expense of the gold industry on which his treasury depended. He did not take into account the President's firm dislike of the Uitlanders or his eagerness to ruin 'Rhodes's Railway' and place a barbed wire fence around his Republic. It seemed obvious to him that self-interest must soon convince 'Oom Paul' that the Rand could not be run indefinitely at the pace of the ox.

He felt almost cocksure when he drove off in his gilded coach, armed with time-tables, traffic returns and bulky dossiers, itemizing delays and obstructions on the Johannesburg section. He had been thoroughly briefed by the Chamber of Commerce and saw himself bringing off a masterly coup. The inefficient Netherland Railway Company was the real cause of the trouble, he told the Mercantile Association. 'Why, if they would carry coal, as they ought to at one halfpenny a mile, extend their system by another line and look after their business as I look after mine, I could spend two millions a year in developing low-grade properties that now barely pay.' By seeing the whole problem in terms of a differential between a halfpenny and threepence a mile he was guilty of his usual tendency to over-simplify. As Stuart Cumberland once remarked, 'In his idea, books should be all pictures and little paragraphs, and newspapers all headlines.' It was not the best apparatus for handling an impermeable opponent who could strike with gorilla strength or go to ground like a porcupine.

Kruger scarcely glanced at the time-tables and gauges which his visitor produced with an eager torrent of explanation. Once or twice he nodded through the cloud of tobacco smoke but could not be drawn on the subject of delays or prohibitive rates. 'That is not my affair,' he grunted. 'It is entirely a matter for the Netherland Railway Company. I am always pleased to see you, Mr Barnato, but such questions are for the railway manager.'

Every argument cracked against a bedrock refusal to accept official responsibility for the Company's policy, although it was common knowledge that the government had a major share holding and dictated every move in the freight and tariff game. Kruger's own ambivalence was nakedly exposed when Barney and his Chamber of Commerce friends, seeing no hope of shifting him, persuaded a Raad member to propose a Bill for expropriation by the State. Kruger at once summoned a secret session and urged members not to be misled by 'interested adventurers'. He convinced them that the purchase of the railway could only damage the State's independence. 'We can do many things through the Company,' he added darkly.

Barney himself now had to accept that the track from the Vaal to Johannesburg was symbolic and meant far more to the President than the gold industry itself. It had become a sjambok to chastise the Uitlanders, Rhodes and the hated Cape Dutch who still talked of federation. 'I felt sure there was some very special motive in blocking me every time,' Barney declared after the plan for expropriation was finally rejected by the Raad. 'If the Pretoria people will mix up trade and politics in this way, they will burn their fingers very soon.'

Nevertheless, he would not consider any enforced change of government. He could see the advantage of supporting a progressive like Lukas Meyer to replace Kruger, but still thought it far too risky to attempt to upset a régime which, with all its pig-headedness, had the burghers' support and kept the excitable National Union of Uitlanders in line. He laughed at Colonel Frank Rhodes who had been sent by his brother to learn 'management' at Consolidated Gold Fields but, as everyone knew, spent all his time conspiring with Lionel Phillips and other hotheads who were talking about organizing rifle clubs to frighten Pretoria.

'If Johannesburg keeps quiet, all will come right in time,' Barney assured Solly who seemed far less optimistic. 'Some day the Executive Council will get tired of taking two years to settle cab charges or the exact procedure which the police are to adopt about street gambling booths and houses of ill-fame.' He continued to assert that the ordinary Uitlander did not give a tuppeny damn about the franchise while he had a full stomach and a bulky pay envelope for his week's work. Despite the Dynamite Concession and all the other monopolies, the Rand's mines were prospering, while his own newly-formed companies led by Barnato Consolidated Mines, had the investing public falling over itself to buy stock. There was not a cloud in the sky although he would not have minded one or two to break the drought and relieve the pressure on his unpopular Waterworks Company!

Barney now began chasing the butterfly which had so long

fluttered just beyond his reach. Early that summer Robinson had
floated his South African Banking Company with such success
that Barney could no longer be held back. That August he announced plans for the Barnato Bank, Mining and Estates Company
which, it was stated, had acquired interests in Barnato Consoli-.
dated, the New Primrose and 'various other properties' and could
be expected to pay at least the 20% dividend all his shareholders
had automatically come to expect. Launched on 2 September 1895,
this so-called Bank took off like a gigantic balloon amid scenes of
near-hysteria. The share capital was to be £3½m in £1 shares,
with a million held in reserve. Barney and his associates and
nominees subscribed £2,500,000 for shares bought at par.
They doubled overnight and then trebled in value as investors
flocked to buy more stock. Although orthodox financiers would
have preferred some kind of prospectus, even the most conserv-
ative houses in the City of London thought *The Economist* too
squeamish in describing such new enterprises as 'blind pools'.
Nothing could stop the breakneck advance of an enterprise
whose capitalization would sweep to over £12m within a few
weeks.

It was a remarkably odd 'bank', with no money on general
deposit repayable by cheque. Even the façade of separate headquarters was deemed unnecessary. Under fine analysis it was
simply a glorified trust company to which Barney sold huge
blocks of shares in his various South African concerns. A number
like the Primrose Mine had flourished, but others were still highly
speculative. Lumped together, however, they made quite an
imposing package. Delighted investors asked few questions and
Barney hardly exaggerated in claiming afterwards, 'If I had
proposed to make a tunnel from the Bank of England to Johannesburg, they would have snatched up the shares without waiting to
hear a single detail of the scheme.' No single figure on the financial
stage had until then—or has perhaps since—commanded a more
uncritical personal following.

The blend of 'Barnato' and 'Bank' made a heady elixir. The
ingredients were skilfully mixed. Barney and his associates formed
a 'pool' to acquire one-quarter of their interests in the Bank at £2
a share for which the subscription was fixed at £3. The jobbers

then took over and sold to self-intoxicated investors for prices that shot up like a fairy-tale beanstalk.

That September the offices in Draper's Gardens seemed like an overflow from the nearby Stock Exchange. Barney had arrived from Johannesburg already assured of the Bank's successful flotation, but even he was amazed by the City's overwhelming endorsement. In a single morning the British public invested nearly £2m in his companies without sign of any let-up. Extra secretaries and clerks had to be engaged to deal with letters offering to support any of his enterprises. As soon as it was rumoured that he might start a line of steamers between England and the Cape, many did not wait for details but impatiently posted their cheques for shares. There was no foundation for the story but it served to enhance his prestige.

His self-esteem, nourished by a ceaseless accumulation of paper profits ('I make a fiver every minute of my working day,' he confided to an interviewer), began to convince him and others that his name and the Rand's gold could together keep the boom going indefinitely. To fit his new banking identity, he now drove to Draper's Gardens in a silk hat and morning coat with an orchid in his buttonhole like Joseph Chamberlain, the Colonial Secretary. For amusement he also sported an eyeglass in place of his pincenez. On chilly mornings he wore his sable-lined topcoat which flapped around his ankles as he bustled about, pausing only to warm himself before the log fire in his room. Before long he would fling off the coat, open his wing collar and discard his waistcoat to do a few brisk handstands.

Leaning forward in his chair with his first cigar drawing nicely, and comfortable at last in shirt-sleeves, he would search for his pincenez which had meantime slipped behind his neck on the attached chain. He talked at top speed with Hatton Garden dealers, stockbrokers and financial journalists, only interrupting himself to fire a question about share prices and his investments in the goldfields of British Columbia and Australia which Woolf had recommended for a pleasant flutter. Messages poured in every few minutes from Throgmorton Street while he paced about with a cigarette end on his lip and dispensed champagne to relays of visitors.

The Park Lane mansion was raising its giraffe neck but he showed no haste to see it completed, still unable to rid himself of his premonitions. The birth of his second son, Woolf Joel ('Babe') Barnato, on 27 September, was followed eight days later by an elaborate buffet supper to celebrate the circumcision. The Lord Mayor of London was among the guests whose carriages choked St James's Place and several of the surrounding streets. To commemorate the occasion, Barney also arranged for a man from Cartier's to bring over a magnificent diamond parure for Fanny's approval. One of his acquaintances, a low music hall comedian who currently had the run of Spencer House, was invited to give his opinion of the necklace.

'Don't you think something better, perhaps?' Barney asked him anxiously.

'Certainly,' agreed his friend, straight-faced, tossing it across the table. 'But wouldn't this do for the baby to play with?'

A day or two later, Barney had far more serious decisions to make. Without any warning, while business was quiet on the world's exchanges because of the Jewish Day of Atonement, the bottom fell out of the entire Kaffir market.

15

———

A THROMBOSIS HAD LONG THREATENED the bloated and over-heated gold exchange. The fatal seizure, however, came so suddenly and in such odd circumstances that only the most naïve could fail to suspect foul play. Vast blocks of Rand shares were thrown on the market on the Fast day of Yom Kippur when the Johannesburg Stock Exchange was closed and turnover generally very restricted in most other leading money centres. The Paris Bourse was the focal point for this attack on gold shares which slumped even more dramatically with comparatively few buyers about. Within a few hours all mining securities were being sharply marked down. Some showed losses of up to 50% before the end of October, with Barney's companies prominent among the victims. 'Johnnies' had recently increased its capital to acquire holdings in more diamond, gold and property concerns. Its shares toppled at once from £7 to £3. The Barnato Bank, formed barely a month earlier, was specially vulnerable with its mixed bag of mining enterprises, several still unproved. Its whole *raison d'être* had been speculative fever. Shareholders who had bought stock at over £4 saw it crumble to 30s. and even less.

Barney tried without success to discover the source of the panic selling. Like many others after the Jameson Raid, he suspected that Rhodes and Beit had initiated a gigantic bear operation designed to make them millions by selling short at the top of the market in the expectation of buying back at bargain prices after a Transvaal revolution. Timing and place gave some substance to this theory. The Yom Kippur selling wave synchronized almost to the hour with Kruger's reckless decision to close the Drifts on the Vaal River. On 1 October, his Customs officials turned back seven wagons bound for Johannesburg. He proclaimed his intention of continuing this embargo until the Uitlanders paid the high railway tariffs imposed by the Netherland Company or used his own Delagoa Bay Line. It was an illegal action which, as Rhodes anticipated, could not be ignored by the Colonial Office. Joseph Chamberlain protested to Pretoria and sent out troops, the Cape agreeing to bear half the cost of the expedition and to supply a number of fighting men.

Rhodes would always deny that he was guilty of 'sordid motives' for the Jameson Raid. He undoubtedly sold large holdings of Chartered stock that summer and might have counted on Kruger's downfall to send the shares up again, but nothing could remotely justify the venom of Henry Labouchère, the anti-Imperialist M.P. and newspaper proprietor, who later indicted him as 'this Empire jerry-builder who has always been a mere vulgar promoter masquerading as a patriot, and the figure-head of a gang of astute Hebrew financiers with whom he divided profits.'

Rhodes was a very sick man that September and fearful of not living long enough to bring the Transvaal into a federated South Africa. He needed cash for arms and supplies and may well have unloaded gold shares as well as his Chartered Company stock. A depressed market would certainly have caused alarm and despondency in the Republic and stimulated the more sluggish Uitlanders to take action. 'So long as people are making money individually in Johannesburg,' Colonel Frank Rhodes had written bitterly to his brother, 'they will endure a great many political wrongs.'

It is more than likely that Wernher, Beit and Co. played the leading rôle in the Yom Kippur sell-out. They had the largest holdings of gold shares and controlled most of the dealings on the Bourse through an intricate network of nominees. No substantial move in Kaffirs could have been possible without their prior knowledge and approval. Moreover, Beit was at this time planning to become a naturalized British subject and, with all the frenzy of a convert, saw nothing but Union Jacks everywhere. Ignoring Wernher's warnings against political involvement, he was now determined to support Rhodes's take-over plans which he agreed to underwrite. He therefore had a good enough motive to raise money in a hurry with the prospect of making far more from the adventure than the 'Patriotism plus five per cent' promised to the Chartered shareholders.

The circumstantial evidence pointed to Rhodes as the planner, with Beit as a stock market executive unrivalled in large-scale operations which had to be performed swiftly and with maximum secrecy. The combination had proved most effective in gaining control of Kimberley Central, but any hopes they might have entertained of manipulating the Rand market with the same facility were completely upset by Kruger and Barney Barnato. Working from quite different positions, both surprised Rhodes by reacting out of character, thereby completely dislocating his time-table for an uprising in the Transvaal.

Confronted with Chamberlain's ultimatum, Pretoria gave in over the Drifts on 7 November 1895. Rhodes saw his 'Chartereds' wilt even more after Kruger's unwelcome capitulation when all had seemed ready to drive him out of Pretoria. He was only partially consoled by securing for the Chartered Company a strip of Bechuanaland through which he proposed to extend his railway from Mafeking to Bulawayo. Jameson hurried down from Salisbury as Resident Commissioner, ostensibly to keep his eye on possibly hostile native chiefs. He soon incorporated the Bechuana-land Border Police into his own forces which were neatly poised in the village of Pitsani to move quickly into the Transvaal, with Johannesburg itself barely two hundred miles away. The wounds remained unhealed on both sides, but Kruger offered no further provocation once the Drifts were reopened.

Worse, from Rhodes's point of view, Barnato had managed almost single-handed to check the gold share slump. Moving with tremendous energy throughout that crisis month of October, he bought Kaffirs on the declining market and thereby prevented a catastrophic breakdown in prices. Many shareholders lost their profits but were at least able to cut their losses. Without his bullishness the whole market would certainly have collapsed. Having survived more than one slump both in diamonds and gold, he was absolutely confident that this recession was temporary and had no relation to the Rand's enormous potential. The 'bears' could only be routed by a steady nerve backed by cash.

He had both. It cost him well over £3m of his own fortune to buy gold shares which he could easily have off-loaded for a fair margin of profit. At one Settlement, when Kaffirs had come heavily under fire and few dealers were ready to carry over their stocks, he sent two brokers into the House with authority to lend generously to suitable buyers. He was not acting entirely altruistically, of course, in this huge salvage operation, but the Throgmorton Street glee clubs were soon singing a ballad which, despite the sting in its tail, expressed the feelings of many shareholders:

> 'I'm beautiful, bountiful Barney
> And Beit may go to pot!
> Beautiful, bountiful Barney
> And Robinson may trot!
> The public all run after me
> For I know how to blarney.
> I tell you straight, he's up-to-date,
> Is beautiful, bountiful Barney!'

The Lord Mayor of London, Sir Joseph Renals, who had had a far from memorable year of office, thought the City should show more appreciation of the little cockney financier who had saved the gold market from disaster. He often dined at Spencer House where no doubt he had received useful advice about his holdings in many public companies, and particularly certain speculative Australian mining interests. Sir Joseph decided to give the last of his year's banquets at the Mansion House in honour of his friend. It would be held on the very day the Vaal Drifts crisis ended which gave a pleasantly victorious touch to the whole occasion, although many in the City of London and a number of distraught shareholders thought Renals was rather overdoing things by offering Barney Barnato the same laurels as Clive and Wellington.

From Spencer House he drove in style with Fanny, who wore a tiara and other magnificent jewels. She was the only woman guest present except the Lady Mayoress seated beside Barney. Apart from the aldermen, burgesses and a sprinkling of other dignitaries, most of the old-established houses appeared to have previous engagements. Carl Meyer represented the House of Rothschild, but none of the partners had deigned to accept. 'The City bankers were like snakes in Ireland and did not show themselves,' commented one newspaper gossip. *The Times* wrote acidly next day, 'Mr Barnato's action in repurchasing large amounts of certain securities was not a feat of such shining valour and transcendent virtue as to call for public recognition from the citizens of London. The Mansion House is not the proper place for glorifying a successful operator in a department of the Stock Exchange.'

Barney beamed on the company in the elegant Egyptian Room while a Hungarian orchestra played background music and flunkeys served venison, boar's head and other delicacies on the City's celebrated plate. He had only two regrets. His parents were not there to share this incomparable hour of triumph, although Harry represented the clan together with Woolf and Jack Joel. He would also have to wait for his Illuminated Address, because the inscription on the gold box was not ready in time.

He listened raptly to the Lord Mayor's eulogy which included the somewhat unfortunate remark, 'Mr Barnato is not to be judged by the eighteen months he has lived in London.' He bumbled on gamely, 'Mr Barnato is one of the few Englishmen—Englishmen by birth and not by adoption—who have contributed in a superlative degree to the great prospects of one of our greatest colonies. Coming to the Transvaal, we find in Mr Barnato the parent of some of the most successful enterprises that have helped honourably and honestly to enrich this old country of ours.'

Barney wiped away a schmaltzy tear when he rose to speak after a fanfare of trumpets which recalled dear old Charley on the night they had driven off together to break up opposition rowdies in Kimberley. He thanked the Lord Mayor but then could not resist making remarks more appropriate to a shareholders' meeting. He wound up an optimistic survey of the Rand's future prospects with a promise: 'To those who have placed their money in well-managed companies, I say they need not fear.' This was received with a spatter of forced applause which he took as a cue to hand the Lord Mayor a cheque for £12,500 towards the relief of poverty in Spitalfields regardless of creed. His firm soon afterwards donated £15,000 for other charities including the Hospital Sunday Fund.

He ignored disparaging newspaper reports of the banquet and

was delighted when the Lord Mayor nominated him a Lieutenant of the City of London. He promptly ordered full regimentals for the next Guildhall dinner and fussed endlessly over his scarlet gold-braided uniform. When the tailor arrived at Spencer House for a third fitting he was startled to hear the parrot screeching 'What do you think of Barney now?' while little Leah and several of the new Lieutenant's music-hall chums took turns to wear the plumed helmet.

Barney was back at the top of his form. Even the Waterworks Company, so near to breakdown and insolvency through months of drought, was functioning smoothly after a crisis that had had its moments of near farce. Solly, now Chairman, had shown all his uncle's enterprise that October by approaching two Americans who chanced to be preparing a mammoth fireworks display on the Wanderers Ground. They confirmed that Mr Pain's rockets had once precipitated the rains in Tucson, Arizona. Solly offered them a £100 reward to fire off some extra-size rockets and produce rain.

Sure enough, a couple of promising clouds arrived on schedule while hundreds of spectators looked skywards. A brief deluge soaked them, but not another drop fell in the two following afternoons when more rockets were fired. In the Raad angry members protested at a sacrilegious interference with nature, and one member growled that this Joel ought to be arrested for 'poking his finger in the eyes of God'. Kruger ordered a national day of prayer for Sunday, 2 November. Within a week the heavens duly opened and the drought was over at last.

The rains, together with an end to the Drifts crisis, had taken much of the steam out of the militant National Union's campaign, while Barnato's partially successful restoration of the share market prompted Frank Rhodes to admit despondently to his brother that 'the Jewish element is a damper on any political agitation'. It was clearly necessary to whip up some enthusiasm if Dr Jim were ever to dash across the border from Pitsani on behalf of the eighty thousand Uitlanders few of whom now seemed in too much hurry to be 'liberated'.

A few days after the Mansion House banquet, Lionel Phillips chose the opening of the new Chamber of Mines building in

Johannesburg to make a violent onslaught on the Kruger régime: 'It is a mistake to imagine that this much-maligned community, which consists anyway of a majority of men born of freemen, will consent indefinitely to remain subordinate to the minority in this country and that they will ever allow their wives, property and liberty to be subject to its arbitrary will.' His speech, widely reported overseas, did much to counteract Barney's efforts to shore up the stock market. Shares began to slip once more.

The physical and mental pressures had been unremitting for several weeks during which Barney slept little and almost worked the clock round on drink, snatched meals and his own adrenalin. Crossing to France once or twice a week to confer with Sir Edgar Vincent and other associates, he would hurry back to throw himself into the daily anxieties of Draper's Gardens. He had Tom Honey, his genial office chief, and Jack Joel by his side, but missed Woolf who had temporarily lost his health and confidence after a most unfortunate accident. While returning home from the City in his private hansom, he had kept urging the driver to hurry in his anxiety to change for a dinner-party. The horse had taken fright and bolted. The cab had overturned, killing the driver. Woolf escaped with severe concussion but lapsed into melancholia, blaming himself for the man's death. Although himself hard-pressed, Barney had urged him to take a holiday, promising to take care of the widow and children.

Woolf had departed for the Riviera where he stayed briefly with his Uncle Harry before moving into the villa of a gayer companion, Frank Gardner. He was soon in excellent spirits and pooh-poohed all rumours about the Transvaal, echoing Barney almost to the word. Both were too remote from Johannesburg to appreciate the very real significance of Lionel Phillips's speech which many mine-owners regarded as a manifesto. It roped in Solly Joel who had quietly nursed the idea of 'Kimberlizing' the Rand by some form of amalgamation of the competing gold interests. Through his growing cordiality with Beit and Mosenthal on the affairs of the thriving Diamond Syndicate, he had steadily become less insular than Barney. He had even made his peace with John Hays Hammond, now one of Rhodes's most fervent disciples, and was also on friendly terms with Phillips, George Farrar and Abe Bailey who were all leading members of the Uitlander movement. The firm's mining interests and the setback to 'Johnnies', his special baby, finally convinced him that Kruger's policies could only lead to disaster.

Psychologically he also felt in the mood to snap Barney's apron strings. He now held more directorships than even his uncle and was himself a millionaire. He ranked after Woolf in the hierarchy but, since his brother was now based in England, he was at the centre of power in Johannesburg. At heart he favoured the family's *laissez-faire* approach to politics but was still tempted to take his own line. He would not actually finance any coup, like Beit and Rhodes, and was not taken into the inner councils of the junta led by Jameson and Frank Rhodes, but saw no alternative to showing exactly where his sympathies lay. The share slump was already too advanced to make any slow change to a liberalized régime in Pretoria feasible, and he shared most people's distaste for a diggers' republic under someone like J. B. Robinson.

Always a gambler at heart, and with the kind of flamboyance that had made him fire Pain's rockets into the heavens, he was attracted by a political ploy for high stakes with the odds heavily weighted, it seemed, in favour of Rhodes, the Corner House consortium and the rest of the big battalions. Aware that Barney, notwithstanding his disenchantment with Kruger, would certainly have prohibited an open involvement by the firm in any rising against the Government, Solly quietly conveyed his intention to support the newly-formed Reform Committee, the ginger group of the National Union, who maintained the closest liaison with Rhodes and Jameson.

Woolf had meantime recovered enough energy to indulge in an athletic caper with his friend, Gardner. They drove up to La Turbie in the hills and decided to have a walking race back to Nice for £100 a side. The winner was to place his stake on the red at Monte Carlo and split any proceeds with his partner. Woolf won the race by seven minutes. After a change and bathe, they drove off to the Casino where the proverbial 'luck of the Joels' hit an almost incredible streak. Woolf placed his £100 counter on the red and won twelve consecutive coups together with several maximums on the 'nine' for good measure. In half an hour he had netted £16,000 before the table ran out of chips.

Back in London, he overcame his normal dislike of ostentation and, at Barney's insistence, agreed to give a showy celebration dinner at the Savoy. He and Gardner sat at each end of the table on raised chairs like croupiers, while their thirty-five guests were served by waiters dressed in red silk shirts, gloves, ties and buttons. The colour motif was maintained throughout the menu which included prawns, *queue; de langouste*, out-of-season strawberries and *mousse au jambon*. Each guest was presented with a pair of gold scissors to snip his own dessert from miniature vines, cherry and peach trees. The whole room was draped in red, including the electric lights, while the menu cards were printed in the same colour with a roulette wheel on one side and the lucky '9' on the other. This number and the ace of diamonds were fashioned in flowers as table decorations to blend with a mass of geraniums.

Barney was given an ovation when he stood up to propose the health of their host. An orchestra played 'The Man Who Broke the Bank at Monte Carlo' while fellow-guests sang a chorus recalling happier days:

> 'As I walk along Throgmorton Street with an independent air
> You should hear the folk declare
> "There goes the Millionaire",
> You should hear them sigh and almost die
> With envy as they loudly cry,
> "The man to start a bank is B. Barnato".'

There was some hilarity when he read out a telegram from the Casino inviting Woolf to come back and try his luck again. He solemnly advised his nephew to steer clear of the roulette table and stick, in future, to something more gilt-edged.

'The Barnato Bank, say?' someone called out rather unkindly. Barney laughed it off, still convinced that his newest enterprise would soon be back among the Lombard Street favourites.

That Christmas Eve he was in a hurry to be off to Brighton where he had taken a house for Fanny and the children. Guests had been invited to dinner but he would not leave before driving to

Marlborough Street police court to stand bail for a Hatton Garden
friend who was being charged under the Bankruptcy Act. The
magistrate glanced sharply at the jaunty little man in the checked
suit with the outsize rose in his lapel.

'Where do you live?' he snapped.

'Spencer House.'

'But that's Lord Spencer's house! Are you his major domo?'

'I'm my own bloody domo,' Barney shouted back, quickly
apologizing as the Clerk flashed him a warning.

'Are you worth £500 a year after the payment of your just and
lawful debts?' the magistrate went on doggedly.

Barney laughed and coughed into his bowler hat before emerg-
ing to nod agreement.

'What rent do you pay?'

'£2,000 a year.'

His Worship was beginning to see light but persisted with his
routine interrogation.

'What *are* you exactly, Mr Barnato?'

'A diamond merchant and director of a couple of companies,'
said Barney with a broad wink at the public. 'And I've also got a
bit of freehold in Park Lane.'

He was about to leave after posting bail when the Clerk
reminded him that he would have to sign the necessary release
papers. He rushed off to the prison as soon as he had wired Fanny
to explain why he could not join her before next morning. 'That
poor chap's going to have his Christmas dinner at home no matter
what he's done,' he told Jack Joel.

Christmas was being celebrated in Johannesburg in a sticky
oppressive heat but with the traditional holly and mistletoe. The
city had buzzed for days with rumours of an Uitlander uprising
timed for Saturday, the 28th. However, with rich fare on most
tables and the promise of excellent sport at the Turffontein Races,
followed by a fête on the Wanderers Ground, the tensions of the
past few weeks were temporarily relaxed. It was obvious that some
of the Reformers, comforted by a welcome halt in the share slump
and much-improved gold production figures, seemed to be

having second thoughts about using the rifles smuggled into Johannesburg in De Beers' oil-drums and coke trucks or attempting to seize Kruger's arsenal in the fort at Pretoria.

Towards the end of November, the leaders of the Reform Committee—Charles Leonard, Lionel Phillips, Frank Rhodes, John Hays Hammond and George Farrar—had provided Jameson with the draft of an impassioned, undated 'Letter of Invitation' in which they pleaded with him to 'liberate' the Uitlanders if called upon: 'Thousands of unarmed men, women and children of our race will be at the mercy of well-armed Boers, while property of enormous value will be in the greatest peril. The circumstances are so extreme that we cannot believe that you and the men under you (in that very convenient strip on the Bechuanaland border!) will not come to the rescue of people who will be so situated.'

Rhodes and Beit had contributed upwards of £300,000 between them for the purchase of arms, rations and remounts, but the date of the 'revolution' kept being postponed while the principals wrangled over which flag to hoist after the successful take-over. Hammond and most of the others wanted to keep the *Vierkleur* flying over the liberated Republic, while Jameson would not march except under the Union Jack. The flag issue was still undecided and many of the smuggled rifles (fewer than had been promised) were not yet unpacked by Christmas, only three days before zero hour. Meantime the whole affair was rapidly sinking into a '*fyasco*', as Rhodes later called it. He was plainly dissatisfied with some of Jameson's staff and even wrote him an irritated note: 'For God's sake, don't send any more damned fools like the bearer of this letter,' but Dr Jim could easily have riposted that Frank Rhodes, the gallant lady-killer, was not much better. Calling on him in Johannesburg for an urgent conference, Jameson had been turned away with a brief message, 'Dear Jimjams, sorry I can't see you this afternoon, have an appointment to teach Mrs X. the bike.'

While muddled wires in slightly theatrical but transparent code kept buzzing between Groote Schuur, Johannesburg and Pitsani, where Jameson sat chafing for action, Kruger was adroitly exploiting the situation. He abandoned his usual Christmas tour of the rural areas and went instead to Pretoria where he assured his more liberal burghers that he would avert revolution by introducing reforms. Those who urged stronger action against the conspirators were reminded that 'You must give the tortoise time to put out its head before you cut it off'.

Charles Leonard and F. H. Hamilton had set off for Cape Town on Christmas Day. The former had already asked for the dangerous 'women and children' letter to be returned to him, but Jameson evaded doing so by saying it had been sent to Rhodes for his views. In fact, he was keeping it in his pocket for future use. They arrived at Groote Schuur to inform Rhodes bluntly that few Johannesburgers would tolerate the Union Jack over the Transvaal. The distribution of rifles was chaotic, and the chances of seizing the Pretoria arsenal had become remote while thousands of Boers were still camped on Church Square and seemed determined not to return to their farms before the New Year.

Leonard strongly advised postponement of any armed action, at least until after their public demonstration arranged for 6 January 1896. By then it was hoped Kruger might have climbed down and met the Committee's demand for reform. Failing that or any show of force on his part, they would obviously have a better case for outside intervention.

Rhodes now understood that the whole plan had 'fizzled out like a damp squib' but still appeared reluctant to do more than advise his brother to restrain Jameson from taking immediate action. He could keep his force in Pitsani but was strongly urged to apply himself instead to running Matabeleland. Jameson, unfortunately, chose to interpret this hesitancy as diplomatic camouflage due to his friend's official position. Impatient to push on, he wired Rhodes on 28 December, 'Unless I hear definitely to the contrary, shall leave tomorrow evening.' Rhodes replied, 'On no account whatever must you move. I most strongly object to such a course.' It was tapped out over a dead wire, cut by Jameson's orders to ensure 'secrecy' for his filibuster.

The distinctly less warlike conspirators in Johannesburg had steadily swung to the view that a peaceful revolution could now secure their ends. At the long bar of the Rand Club they drank whiskies with some relief, confident that their restraining cables and, above all, Rhodes's stern disapproval had stopped Dr Jim from doing anything foolish.

Among the optimists was Solly Joel who had impetuously enrolled in a register of sympathizers kept by the Reform Committee in the offices of Consolidated Gold Fields. Like the tortoise in Kruger's parable, he too had stuck out his head.

16

———————

JAMESON'S DOOMED RAID maintains its special fascination for imperial masochists. The details are too familiar to demand more than a brief restatement. On the afternoon of Sunday, 29 December 1895, the little doctor paraded his men at Pitsani and read out the 'Letter of Invitation' from the Reform Committee, implying that it had just come to hand. Significantly, he left out the vital phrase, 'should a disturbance arise here'. They cheered him and sang 'God Save the Queen' at the prospect of rescuing 'thousands of unarmed men, women and children of our race' from the Boers.

At sunset Jameson rode off on his black horse with fewer than four hundred troopers—instead of the fifteen hundred he had hoped for—some pack horses, a field gun and a couple of seven-pounders. They carried only one day's rations but expected to pick up more en route, together with a promised column of Bechuana-land police from Mafeking. With visions of Clive and glory swirling about his head, Jameson was confident of entering Johannesburg itself in fifty hours. At dawn on the 30th he crossed the Transvaal border and expected to be acclaimed by the grateful Uitlanders on New Year's Day.

He had ordered the telegraph wires to be cut to ensure 'secrecy' for one of the most publicized raids of all time, but a drunken aide had mistaken the order, thus leaving Kruger an even clearer line to every stage of the raiders' progress. Apart from the Boer patrols who harassed him in the rocky, inhospitable terrain, Jameson was urged to turn back by messengers from the High Commissioner and the British Agent in Pretoria. He replied curtly that he had to keep faith with his countrymen 'in their extremity'.

They had received news of his filibuster with various degrees of exultation. 'He has upset my apple-cart,' lamented Rhodes who nevertheless tried to arouse British sympathy by cabling *The Times* a copy of the 'Letter of Invitation' which Rutherfoord Harris had conveniently dated 28 December. Lionel Phillips, bobbing between despair and optimism, began unpacking the cache of rifles while Colonel Frank Rhodes despatched two cyclists to assure Jameson that an armed detachment would soon be on its way. Hammond, determined that the Union Jack should not be flown even if the adventure succeeded, ran the *Vierkleur* up over the building of Consolidated Gold Fields. It was, however, hoisted upside down as a symbol of defiance by the Reform Committee. They all hoped the 'goddamned fool', as Hammond called him, might yet break through but took the precaution of cabling the High Commissioner to protect the lives of their fellow-citizens. While they agonized over the next move, the city was shocked by the derailment of an overcrowded train on its way to Natal with refugees. Many women and children were killed which made the notoriously inefficient Netherlands Railway Company even less popular.

Jameson's tired, sleepless and hungry cavalcade was on its third day with only thirty miles to go, and still without suspicion that they had been abandoned. Frank Rhodes had kept his word by sending out a corps of 120 men under Colonel Bettington to link up with them, but even this token gesture was thwarted by the timid Reform Committee who were now negotiating peace terms with Kruger. 'Bettington's Horse' were ordered to gallop back after covering only a couple of miles.

Kruger was in absolute control of the situation. Jameson's pathetic force headed straight for an ambush, while his friends in Johannesburg were at sixes and sevens and had swallowed the bait of an armistice. Lionel Phillips led a deputation of four to Pretoria where Chief Justice Kotzé assured them that his President intended to abolish food duties, lower railway charges and might even be amenable to a more liberal franchise. Technically, he explained genially, they were rebels but he would put forward their request to permit Jameson to enter the city peaceably before being allowed to go back to Bechuanaland. Meantime, they must persuade their

Uitlanders to disperse, in accordance with the British High Commissioner's stern injunction not to support this armed violation of a friendly State. Bluffing even such a shrewd horse-trader as Abe Bailey, the Chief Justice asked for an assurance that their Committee represented the community whose cause they were pleading. Phillips naïvely agreed to telegraph Johannesburg for the full list of names which, of course, included Solly Joel's as well as that of Harold Strange, general manager of 'Johnnies'.

Solly had been actively organizing relief services for a local population enduring the inevitable effects of food hoarding. Some had fled the city, but many others had arrived from outlying districts, terrified of being caught in the crossfire between Jameson and Kruger. Prices had soared with shortages and profiteering, and a fund was quickly started to distribute food and provide shelter for destitute refugee families.

Barnato Brothers headed the subscription list with a cheque for £5,000, Barney having cabled approval of this donation 'for the alleviation of distress in the community'. Nothing else supported the rumour, then current in Johannesburg, that Solly had turned to his uncle for advice at the eleventh hour. Having committed himself to a cause of which Barney disapproved, he would hardly have confided in a man as indiscreet and impulsive as The Great Barnato. It is even less likely that Barney would have knowingly subscribed to a relief fund which included prominent 'revolutionaries' like Farrar, Lionel Phillips and Abe Bailey and had bought rations for Colonel Bettington's troopers.

Solly continued to play poker in the Rand Club while most of his fellow-conspirators grew more nervous by the hour as conflicting reports of Jameson's advance came to hand. The Reform Committee had vainly tried to quieten the Johannesburgers who became exuberant at the false news that their deliverer had defeated the Boers and was only fifteen miles from their gates. Solly unconcernedly chalked his cue, won a brisk game of billiards and urged his friends to wait for more reliable information.

It came soon enough. On 2 January, the bedraggled invaders were trapped by two thousand Boers at Krugersdorp, Oom Paul's home town, and had to raise the white flag after a hopeless resistance which cost them seventy dead or wounded. Jameson and those who could still stand were marched off to Pretoria Gaol after being paraded twice round the Market Square for the benefit of a jeering crowd.

Johannesburg was stunned and angry, but could do nothing. Jameson was sent back to be tried in England, sailing from Durban in a ship mockingly named *Victoria*.★ The Kaiser at once cabled warm congratulations to Kruger who now felt encouraged to ignore the glib assurances given to the Reform Committee by his Chief Justice. At Groote Schuur Rhodes suffered agonies of self-reproach and despair as he wandered blindly among his hydrangeas. Night after night he paced his locked bedroom, gulping whisky while he tried to square an impossible circle of conscience. 'Jameson was twenty years my friend and now he has ruined me,' he groaned when he finally emerged but still refused to shelter behind the excuse that 'Dr Jim' had marched without his knowledge or approval. He had no alternative but to resign as Prime Minister since he had financed the Raid and been privy to the conspiracy at least up to Christmas.

Acting for Barney in his absence, David Harris went to Groote Schuur to remind him tactfully that the De Beers General Meeting was due in a few days. Rhodes, unshaven and tousled, stared at the accounts with bloodshot eyes. 'No, I can't make any public appearance just now,' he muttered, tugging at his collar. 'Would you be kind enough to preside for me?' On the 15th he sailed to face the British Government as well as the shareholders of Goldfields and a Chartered Company whose whole future was now threatened. But even these perplexities were eclipsed by fears for his brother and the others on whom Kruger plainly intended to take vengeance.

Warrants were issued for the arrest of the Reform Committee whose names had been so obligingly furnished by Lionel Phillips. Solly Joel was among those rounded up at the Rand Club on 9 January. He light-heartedly booked a return ticket valid for two days, and packed only a change of underwear, a spare silk shirt and some lavender water. At the last minute he included a bottle of

---

★ Jameson stood trial in England in 1896, and was released from prison on the ground of ill-health after serving only four of his fifteen months' sentence. He then returned to Rhodesia.

smelling salts because Hammond looked seedy and Fritz Mosenthal seemed close to collapse.

The sixty-four prisoners remained cheerful even when they were pelted with stones, mealie cobs and overripe peaches at each station on their way to the capital. Not all came from Boer hands. Many an Uitlander thought that Jameson had been betrayed by a vacillating, weak-kneed Committee who deserved no sympathy. They were herded into the foul antiquated prison but kept up their spirits on hearing that the High Commissioner had extracted the promise of a fair trial. Nobody doubted that they would be given a swift hearing followed by heavy fines to satisfy Kruger's burghers and his own notorious rapacity. Solly, the least concerned, thought he would have some fun. On entering the tiny airless cell he would share with his old poker rival, Mosenthal, he called peremptorily for the Prison Governor, du Plessis, a brutal relation of Kruger's, and demanded the complaints book. It seemed a very good joke at the time.

Barney received news of the 'fyasco' with mixed feelings. The Raid seemed to confirm all his earlier suspicions that Rhodes, Beit and their banker friends in Paris had engineered the selling spree at the end of September. He could not shed tears over their discomfiture and reminded Woolf of that night in Jameson's cottage when they had tried to argue Rhodes out of incorporating the Trust Deed in their Kimberley amalgamation. By mixing politics with business, he had not only ruined himself but disrupted the whole mining industry since the jailed Reformers represented some forty million sterling of capital between them. Although a little cooling-off in *tronk* (Afrikaans: prison) would do Solly Joel no harm for his share in the nonsense, it might be highly inconvenient at a time when the firm needed him badly, quite apart from his deputy, Harold Strange.

The Johannesburg Stock Exchange had closed for two days after the Raid to prevent a run, but nothing could check the inevitable slide in mining securities. It was now painfully clear to Barney that his rescue efforts during the previous autumn had been a waste of time and money. All Rand stocks were back to previous slump levels, but the fiercest spotlight beat on the Barnato Bank which had so far failed to provide any accounts or a single penny in dividends. At Draper's Gardens the morning mailbag bristled with angry demands for money back, abuse and even threats from those who had bought at £4 or over and now found themselves holding stock rapidly being marked down to par. Some openly accused Barney of having robbed them of their savings which had gone into building a palace in Park Lane. A stockbroker's clerk shot himself dead in a railway carriage after taking a flyer with his firm's funds. He left a note: 'Regret I have made a mess of it all. Barnato's Bank is the cause of everything.'

Even while the Kaffir Circus was in full swing, Barney had had his occasional qualms. He once turned to Woolf and remarked, half in jest, 'They think they know more than I do. If they drop a bit, they will come squealing to me to see them through.' The 'squealing' had come sooner than he or anyone else could have anticipated. To silence the Press which was now openly critical, and hoping to calm his shareholders, he agreed to address a special meeting at the Cannon Street Hotel on 14 January 1896. After a good breakfast at Spencer House, he dressed with exceptional care, popped a flower into his lapel and drove off in a hansom with Fanny who had for days dreaded this confrontation. Although her husband made light of his coming ordeal, it was unusual and disturbing for him to demand her moral support. With considerable nervousness she made her way through a huge tensed-up crowd to her seat in the gallery. Shareholders stood on the radiators and clung to window-sills, while hundreds more had to wait outside.

Barney bowed genially as he bustled to the platform amid a storm of cheers and jeers, waving cheerfully to the occasional friendly face. After polishing his glasses to look through his notes, he carefully undid the tightly-buttoned crimson waistcoat and began to address them with a pewter pot in his hand. It was an inspired touch of bravura. Those who had expected the traditionally soothing speech from a chairman under fire were astonished by his sheer audacity. A few growled, but even they could not help feeling reassured. Who else would drink a pint of ale at such a time? This was the old fireproof Barney who had made millions by his flair and would surely lead them out of the wilderness.

Reacting like a born actor to a mellowing audience, he rang the changes confidently between bombast and a kind of saddened half-logic, blending facts with hopes and skilfully returning to the attack on the well-tried 'hit 'em first' principle which his father had taught him so long ago in Cobb's Court.

'It is not likely after twenty-two years in South Africa that I am going to destroy the labour of that long time in twenty-two weeks,' he declared scornfully. 'Had I come to London to start a company merely to sell the shares, that would destroy the fabric I have spent half my life erecting in Africa.' He then took another swig at his tankard which contained iced champagne and not beer as everyone had imagined. It was proving a tonic. He looked flushed but his voice became firmer and rang through the hall to silence hecklers. 'My company is not a one-horse show,' he roared.

Then he spoke more quietly, adopting a dramatic note of earnestness that Irving himself might not have faulted. 'I devote myself to you,' he said, raising the tankard as if he were toasting each of them individually. 'I devote myself to you, and I promise you that I will not bring, even with the controlling interest I have in the company, my predominating vote against you.' Nobody knew exactly what that meant, but there was no mistaking his next solemn pledge. 'I tell you that the name of the Barnato Bank will not die out whilst the name of Barnato Brothers lives.'

Most cheered loudly and even the dissenters felt a lump in their throats—if not their accounts—as he surveyed recent events in the Transvaal to help explain away his Bank's temporary relapse. They were not quite sure whether they were cheering him, Jameson or the Empire when he delivered a highly effective curtain line about Cecil Rhodes who, 'whatever one might assume to be his faults, has done more than any living man for South Africa.' They roared approval as he drained his tankard and handed it to a waiter with a wink that was part Whitechapel and wholly Barney. A few jumped up to ask questions but he marched out with a springy step, his sturdy back as stiff as a plank.

He made his unexpected *glissade* into the ranks of Rhodes's supporters when British public opinion was incensed against Kruger, particularly after the Kaiser's provocative telegram which had prompted Queen Victoria to assure her daughter, the dowager German Empress, that Dr Jameson was 'an excellent and able man' and the Boers 'horrid people, cruel and over-bearing'. Three days before the Bank meeting, *The Times* had published a piece of jingoist doggerel by Alfred Austin, the new Poet Laureate. Entitled 'Jameson's Ride', it made strong men weep while emotional ladies like the Countess of Warwick almost burst out of their corsets with sympathy for the gallant doctor.

> 'We were wrong, but we aren't half sorry,
> And, as one of the baffled band,
> I would rather have had that foray
> Than the crushings of all the Rand.'

Barney could not altogether subscribe to such an unpractical sentiment, but his tribute to Rhodes seemed more than a manoeuvre to placate unruly shareholders. His pocket had suffered from the bearish attack in September and he had been hurt by what he regarded as a conspiracy to keep him in ignorance of a Raid which clearly involved the good name and resources of De Beers, but at no time would he utter a word of recrimination publicly or in private against the fallen Prime Minister. He refused to join hands with J. B. Robinson, who hoped to ingratiate himself with Kruger by ridiculing the Raiders, but was even more shocked by the vehemence of Merriman, Rhodes's former friend and Cabinet colleague, who now demanded his scalp for 'deceit and treachery' and reminded the Cape Assembly that he was 'unworthy of the trust of the country'.

Barney had other reasons for dissociating himself from those who wished to make Rhodes and Jameson scapegoats for Whitehall's discomfiture over the Raid. The Kaiser's telegram was followed by gleeful anti-British sentiments in several European Chancelleries. The French presented Kruger with a ceremonial sword which glorified a heroic Boer strangling the imperial lion. 'I know I couldn't fight,' Barney told a friend sadly. 'Little men with bad sight aren't much good, I fear. But if England were ever in trouble, I could at least buy her an ironclad or two.'

Elastic as always, he became more hopeful when Chamberlain invited Kruger to come to London and discuss their differences.

For some days he went about hinting that he would ask 'Oom Paul' to stay with him at Spencer House. But the stubborn old man still showed no sign of meeting any of the Uitlanders' grievances and would only parley with the British Government if they agreed to scrap the Charter and pay enormous compensation for the Raid. Plans for the proposed visit were indignantly dropped by Whitehall.

Barney's fleeting optimism was followed by weeks of depression intensified by the uniformly gloomy tidings from South Africa. All Johannesburg had been rocked by a violent explosion on Ash Wednesday. A train drew up at a goods siding in Braamfontein Station with 2,300 cases of dynamite ready for unloading and removal by wagon to the gold mines. It was left for three days under the hot sun before a shunting engine backed into a truckful of detonators. Within minutes the slum suburb, teeming with natives and near-whites, was devastated.

Hundreds were killed or horribly mutilated. Kruger visited the scene and announced a government donation of £25,000 to a relief fund. He was cold-shouldered by a sullen crowd who apportioned responsibility for the disaster between the infamous dynamite monopoly and the Netherland Company's criminal negligence.

Meantime, Jameson's failure had lit a fuse in Rhodesia where the Matabele chiefs and their witch doctors took advantage of the withdrawal of the Chartered Company police to massacre white settlers and their families. Famine now sharpened their appetite to avenge Lobengula. A widespread outbreak of rinderpest had killed off hundreds of their cattle, many more having to be slaughtered on official orders to check the disease.

Rhodes, although no longer Prime Minister or Chairman of the Chartered Company, sailed back from England to save the territories won through so much blood and treasure. The Cape had already sent up a force commanded by General Carrington with Colonel Baden-Powell as his Chief of Staff. They welcomed Rhodes whose riding crop seemed to stiffen the settlers' morale. Assuming the unofficial rank of colonel, he fought in the field with a kind of 'crazed gallantry'. Conspicuous in his slouch hat with a Norfolk jacket over the white flannel trousers, he seemed to be seeking death but showed no mercy towards the Matabele, killing with a relish that astonished even the professional soldiers.

Barney seemed more disturbed by these reports of atrocities in the new territories than by the plight of Solly and his fellow-prisoners who still awaited trial in Pretoria. Woolf, whose wife was expecting a baby (their son, Geoffrey, was born in Johannesburg that July), had reluctantly left London to take charge of Colonnade Building in the absence of his brother and Harold Strange.

Solly appeared to be in excellent fettle and still apparently amusing himself. He had infuriated the shabby-looking Public Prosecutor by attending the preliminary examination in an im-maculate white linen suit with a flower in his buttonhole, answer-ing questions with a studied impertinence which drove the Boer to near apoplexy. When Nellie Joel arrived at the gaol wearing a wide-brimmed hat crammed with cigars, a bottle of cream in her skirt and even a brace of ducks in the bustle, he organized a midnight picnic for his fellow-sufferers.

Next day Natalie Hammond appeared with a large Bologna sausage round her waist. She had pleaded for permission to take her husband, who was suffering from acute dysentery, to Cape Town for special treatment, but Kruger remained unmoved. He had granted bail for Solly and the other sixty prisoners with reluctance, so long as they remained in Pretoria, but flatly refused to release the 'ringleaders', Hammond, Frank Rhodes, Phillips and Farrar. Hammond, hopeful that his countrymen would soon make some high-level intervention on his behalf, had expected great things from Mark Twain who interrupted a lecture tour specially to call on him. 'How did you ever find your way into this godforsaken hole?' he asked the writer.

'Getting into gaol is easy,' laughed Twain. 'It's getting out that presents difficulties.' He was equally flippant when describing his 'enjoyable' visit to a reporter. 'I only wish I could join them, for I can imagine no place where one would be less badgered by the importunities of one's creditors.' In short he thought the experience afforded an ideal rest cure for 'the tired business man'. Apart from coining that happy phrase, his call brought no solace to Hammond who might well have died but for Barney's intervention.

Hearing of the American's illness, he had cabled Woolf to do all possible to arrange bail, offering personally to put up any sum required by the authorities. Recognizances were finally agreed at £20,000. No doubt Rhodes would gladly have done the same but without the smallest hope of acceptance by his old enemy who already regretted letting Jameson out of the country and had noted the surge of anti-Boer feeling in England following Rhodes's visit. But 'dear kind-hearted Barney', as Natalie Hammond affectionately called him, had so openly condemned the Raid as foolish and irresponsible, notwithstanding his nephew's imprisonment, that Kruger found it difficult to refuse him.

Barney wept with relief in London when Woolf cabled news of Hammond's release. He had long forgiven his defection, for which he would always consider Rhodes responsible, but discovered far less charity towards himself during the long wintry months of 1896. The British Press, once so flattering, sniped at him with every fall in Rand stocks. Unlike Rhodes, who had promoted a dream of empire and still had most of the Chartered Company investors behind him despite the Raid, Barney had promised a crock of gold to those who would follow him to the end of the rainbow. He was particularly vulnerable over the Barnato Bank whose share-holders had expected him to make good overnight the promise so recklessly given at the Cannon Street meeting. 'It's not my fault the price was forced up unduly on the opening day,' he burst out at one interviewer. 'However, as the public bought because of my name, I shall not allow the market to break.'

He felt no sympathy for those who had plunged beyond their means. One day, however, he received a pathetic letter from a country parson who declared that he was not a speculator but a trusting investor who had bought 500 Barnato Bank shares at 2¾ solely on the strength of its founder's cheerful representations. Now he would have to sell out and lose most of his life's savings.

Many similar letters had poured in. Barney was contemptuous of those who whined for their money back, but this appeal touched his heart. He replied that, 'in view of the exceptional circumstances', he would be willing to buy back the shares at the purchase price. The reverend gentleman, overjoyed, at once wired his brokers in Threadneedle Street: 'Buy 500 Barney's Bank at 1½ and take them up to Barnato Brothers who will give you 2¾ for them.'

Barney began to dread his days in Draper's Gardens. The time had clearly come for an over-delayed look at his whole group of companies, but he was temperamentally opposed to retrenchment. Nevertheless, with the exception of star properties like New Primrose, several of his gold mines lay in low-grade areas and had been outrageously over-capitalized. They should have been closed down, for a time at least, until conditions offered the prospect of a working profit. Instead, rather than admit failure, he had opted to work them at a loss, using heavy subsidies from 'Johnnies'.

He hungered wistfully for some bold and dramatic coup which would boost his own morale and restore confidence in the Rand. But any new flotation would have been suicidal, and it was obviously unpractical to attempt further salvage like that of the previous autumn. That spectacular operation had cost him a fortune with little but a Mansion House banquet and his City Lieutenant's plumed hat to show for it. Moreover, he could see the sense of the campaign by Abe Bailey, Solly and other fellow-prisoners to cancel all orders for mining machinery with the object of slowing down the industry. By threatening Kruger's treasury, they hoped to bring forward the date of their trial and quickly return to normal business.

It was good hard thinking but did not console Barney. Inaction was so foreign to his nature that he gave way to self-pity and began to exaggerate his troubles. However, he was still too much of a showman to wear a gloomy face at the National Sporting Club or the Savoy. He also kept the Press blithely informed of his plans to move out of Draper's Gardens which the firm had now out-grown. An entire row of houses was being demolished to make way for a handsome new building in Austin Friars, pleasingly adjacent to the Rothschild headquarters.

When the office depressed him, he liked to visit Joe Cannon's stables at Newmarket to see how his horses, particularly Miss Primrose, were getting on. There was nothing in his manner or style of living that winter to suggest that he was a very worried man. He drank rather more, perhaps, and had taken to roaming the streets because he was sleeping so badly. One cold foggy night, when the pavements were sheets of slippery ice, he was wandering along Oxford Street muffled in his overcoat when he heard a woman singing. She stood in the gutter with a whimpering baby in her arms. He gave her half a sovereign to buy some hot food and clothing. A few minutes later he saw her enter a gin palace. Blazing with anger, he rushed inside. 'You deserve to go to prison,' he yelled. 'Now come with me.' He hustled them into a nearby dairy where he ordered hot milk and broke off pieces of a bun for the shivering child. Before departing he gave the woman another half-sovereign and drove her back to her wretched lodgings in a hansom.

That February he made his Will which was surprising for a man in his early forties and enjoying exceptional health. His real trouble was psychological. He missed the habitual stimulus of speculation and was unsuited both by temperament and background to sitting quietly by while his shares drooped and the green parrot mocked him with the once-comforting cry of 'What price Primrose today, Barney?' Yet the market value of his empire still ran to several million sterling, not to mention the strong potential of real estate in and around Johannesburg and some useful properties acquired in Delagoa Bay just before the Raid.

In such circumstances only a disordered personality could account for his gloom. The excitement of making easy money had become so compulsive that he had begun to react like a drug addict from whom regular supplies have been withdrawn. He might well have broken down that winter but for Kate Joel who took his mind off money troubles by urging him to save Solly. By the end of March he made up his mind to return to the Transvaal. 'How can I face the poor boy's mother if I don't get him out of *tronk*?' he told the Barnetts at their 'Chometz Bottel' before sailing back to South Africa.

17

━━━━━

IN THE JOHANNESBURG STREETS and the Stock Exchange building
he was welcomed by Uitlanders who seemed to him over-
nervous about the approaching trial. He reassured them at the
public dinner held in his honour at the Grand National Hotel. Like
everyone else in the city he was impatient to have the trial over
and done with and had to work abnormally long hours in
Colonnade Building making decisions on problems which
had been shelved in the absence of Solly Joel and Harold
Strange.

He had no doubt at all that Kruger would show clemency in his
anxiety to restore the mines to working order. In this hopeful
frame of mind he went off to Pretoria to cheer up Solly and the
others. John Hays Hammond looked much thinner but had
benefited from his treatment in Cape Town for which he expressed
warm appreciation. 'Didn't you feel worried I might skip bail?'
he asked with a laugh.

'No,' said Barney, 'and between ourselves I think you might
have had more sense than to come back! That £20,000 bail is
nothing to me, nothing at all. You and I could make that in
London in a few days. Now you're in for God knows how
long.'

As the trial approached, he grew more sanguine by the hour. It
seemed a good sign that Kruger drove so cheerfully about the
streets in his fine new State coach lined with blue silk and bearing
the Republican coat of arms on its panels. Inside, with a fur rug
for his feet and wearing the broad blue Republican sash across his
chest, he waved almost genially to the crowds who tossed flowers
at his mounted escort. Barney interpreted it as a stage-managed

carnival setting for Kruger's coming magnanimity. He remained unsuspecting even when Gregorowski, the State Attorney from Bloemfontein, was sworn in to act as presiding judge. It looked as if Kruger had personally chosen a judge from the Orange Free State, rather than a member of the Transvaal Bench, to make good his promise of an impartial trial.

Gregorowski was a rather sinister figure with his egg-bald head and hooked nose. He had soon shown his intentions by privately enquiring whether anyone on the Pretoria Bench could lend him a black cap. (After the trial he would confess bluntly, 'I came up to put down rebellion.') Defence counsel played into his hands. It had been understood that the prisoners would be tried under the Gold Law which provided relatively light penalties for the offences charged. It was suddenly decided to invoke the ancient Roman-Dutch Law with its severe sentences, including death, for high treason. The accused were, however, assured of leniency if they pleaded guilty. Otherwise, in the face of overwhelming evidence, the prosecution threatened to insist on the maximum punishment.

The State Attorney, supported by defence counsel, put forward his detailed proposals on the eve of the trial. If the four ringleaders admitted the charge of having sent their Letter of Invitation to Jameson, he would drop the other counts in the indictment. The rest of the prisoners need only admit *lèse-majesté* for having distributed arms. It was strongly hinted that President Kruger desired only to condemn the Jameson Raid in the eyes of the world, and all sentences would of course be subject to his merciful prerogative. Lionel Phillips and the three other main defendants had most to lose but were moved by their counsel's strong argument that, in pleading guilty, they would thereby help their 'rank and file' friends to escape with nominal fines. Besides, the withdrawal of several charges in the indictment implicating Jameson in the rebellion might assist him in his own trial which would shortly be held in England. Moved by such quixotic and muddled motives, they finally agreed to throw themselves on the mercy of Judge Gregorowski.

Barney, aghast at these last-minute manoeuvres, had quickly scented a trap. 'It was an act of suicidal mania,' he stormed at

Solly. 'They're throwing up the game and tossing every chance away.' He sent a message to Kruger, declaring bluntly that no civilized Court of Law in the world would have accepted a plea of guilty on such a grave charge.

On the morning of 27 April 1896 he did not return the greetings of spectators as he pushed his way angrily through the ranks of armed troopers stationed outside the Market Hall. He sat stony-faced in the front row of the public benches as the four main defendants took their places in a special movable dock carried over the heads of the crowd by a squad of warders, dressed in funereal black. Solly and his friends, secure in the promise of generous treatment, chatted and joked among themselves as if they were in the stalls of a theatre awaiting curtain-up. They lounged to their feet when the little Judge mounted his dais, but Barney's hands kept trembling as he nipped at his hip-flask.

The proceedings were in Afrikaans but everyone in Court understood the dreaded phrase, *hangen by den nek*, which the State Attorney hammered home throughout his address. Hammond had to receive medical attention several times but, like all the others, remained confident that this macabre charade would soon be over and the 'deal' honoured. The hearing was adjourned until next morning, when the Judge would deliver sentence.

Barney spent most of that night drinking hard to quieten his fears. He shrugged off persistent rumours that the Pretoria gaol had been thoroughly cleaned with carbolic and the cells readied for the return of *all* the prisoners, but grew seriously alarmed as he drove next day to the Market Hall through a strongly reinforced body of mounted police. State Artillerymen at the doors were checking everyone for concealed weapons as they entered the courtroom. He sat down with a heavy heart and could not take his eyes off the head gaoler who had not been present on the previous day.

The Judge smiled at officials and even cracked little jokes behind his hand, prompting a Boer sergeant in charge of the prisoners to mutter in disgust, 'My God, he's like a dog who has bitten and chewed and guzzled.' He still wore a faint smile, grotesque with forced gallantry, as he advised women to leave the Court before passing sentence. He then slapped the scrap of black cloth on his

skull and condemned the four leaders to death, staring coldly at
them while his words were being translated. As soon as they were
taken off, he ordered the other prisoners to rise. Leaning back in
his chair, he favoured them with a derisive smile before scribbling
on his pad. The Court listened with horror to the scratching pen.
At last he delivered sentence of two years' imprisonment and a
fine of £2,000 to be followed by banishment from the Republic
for a period of three years. In the confusion and foot-stamping that
followed, few at first noticed that Barney had rushed headlong to
the dais and was shrieking curses at Gregorowski who looked
startled and bustled off without even pausing to gather up his
papers.

In the street outside, Barney continued to yell abuse at Kruger
and his judicial lackey while a crowd of Uitlanders, defying the
troopers, cheered wildly when he pledged himself to have all the
victims out of gaol 'in no time'. After several drinks and still
boiling with fury, he was holding forth at the bar of the Pretoria
Club when Gregorowski came in. Barney charged over and
addressed him as a 'Kaffir lawyer' hired to do the Government's
dirty work. Gregorowski, backing away, shouted, 'Mr Barnato,
you are no gentleman.' 'And you are no judge,' Barney screamed
back.

Johannesburg ran up flags at half mast. Some spoke darkly of
blowing up Kruger's villa, but most consoled themselves in the
saloons and drank the health of the unfortunate prisoners. When
Barney appeared 'between the Chains', excited brokers carried
him on their shoulders into the Stock Exchange Hall. Within
twenty-four hours, ignoring a lawyer's warning that his attack on
Gregorowski could lead to a charge of contempt of court or at
least defamation, he jumped into his gilded coach and drove back
to the capital.

His first call was on Mrs Hammond, distraught after being
rebuffed by Kruger's wife who had refused to intercede for the
condemned men. Stiff in a black dress and bugled bonnet, 'Tante
Sanne' went on clicking her needles like a Madame Defarge while
Natalie Hammond and Mrs Lionel Phillips made their tearful
pleas. 'If the Raid had succeeded,' she reminded them in a pumice
stone voice, 'my husband would have had to get out the white

horse he has not ridden for years and years and join in the fighting. Would you have thought of *me* then, ladies? Would you?'

Barney took Mrs Hammond's hand and sat with her for several minutes before trusting himself to speak. 'Don't fret, my dear,' he said gently as he got up to leave. 'I brought your husband to Africa and I'll stand by him until he's safely out of the country. That's a promise.' He was dressed in deep mourning with a crêpe band round his hat when he called next day at the presidential villa where he had spent so many cordial afternoons. Kruger did not clasp his hand this time or invite him sociably to sit on the stoep. Instead, he glowered behind his desk in the oppressively warm inner room with its wax flowers, coloured worsted mats and with the velvet plush curtains tightly drawn. He did not remove his stovepipe hat or unbutton the tight frockcoat with the broad Republican sash.

Barney opened amiably enough by apologizing for his attack on Gregorowski and was quick to deny playing any part himself in the Raid. 'They did not take me into their confidence,' he declared solemnly. 'They knew my views.' Kruger's frozen silence soon caused him to change his stance. He began to flay the Judge for imposing such vicious sentences on the strength of an archaic trumped-up law. He then went on to accuse the State Attorney of tricking the prisoners into a plea of guilty. Ignoring Leo Weinthal's signals, he became more vehement and repeatedly shouted down Kruger who grunted that the trial and sentences had been perfectly legal.

Barney then jumped to his feet and without warning suddenly threatened to ruin the Republic unless the death sentences were quashed and all the prisoners set free within a fortnight. He did not wait for Weinthal to translate Kruger's explosive reply. 'I'm not bluffing, Mr President,' he roared. 'I have twenty thousand Whites and a hundred thousand Blacks on my payroll. If I close down, I will put more white men alone out of work than you have burghers in your State. My concerns spend £50,000 a week which would be lost to you. Already, thanks to the political crisis, the mines have lost £20m in production. D'ye want to ruin your country for good and all? Do you?'

'The law must be respected,' grunted Kruger. 'I'll report your views to my Executive Committee. That's all.' He pointed his maimed thumb at the door and Barney hurried out without a word of farewell. Next day, to prove he was not bluffing, he issued an announcement on behalf of Barnato Brothers in all the Johannesburg and Pretoria newspapers: 'Preliminary Notice. Sale of valuable landed properties. Notice is hereby given that all our landed properties in this State will be sold by public auction on Monday 18 May 1896.' Similar notices followed on behalf of 'Johnnies' and the Barnato Bank.

A day or two later it was reported from Pretoria that the death sentences had been commuted. Kruger had found it difficult to resist the massive volume of pleas for clemency, headed by cables from the British Government, the American Secretary of State and several senators. But Barnato's threat undoubtedly forced his hand. After consultation with his advisers, he took the matter seriously enough to invite the little Cockney back for a further discussion. Barney would not budge from his demand for the release of all the prisoners, declining to wait until the Executive Council had finished their cat-and-mouse game. With some show of reluctance he finally agreed to extend his ultimatum by a fort-night. As a goodwill gesture he then flourished a cheque for £5,000 to relieve distress caused by the Raid.

The next few weeks were unbearably tense for the prisoners. One of them, Fred Grey, frantic with anxiety for his wife and six children, cut his throat. The others, particularly the reprieved four who were still being kept in suspense about their future, grew more despondent while the Executive refused to be stampeded either by Barney Barnato or the barrage of international protest. To help pass the dragging hours, Solly Joel toured the cells with a scribbling block, inviting his friends to amuse themselves by drawing a pig, blindfolded. Each sketch was solemnly autographed, together with the artist's place and date of birth. They were later collected and privately printed by Solly under the heading: 'Reform Committee. Sentenced, April 28th 1896. Pretoria Jail, Ascension Day, 1896. Showing our ideas of the Pig we bought in a poke from the Government of this so-called Republic.'

They had every cause for cynicism. Gloom enveloped the gaol when it was announced that the four leaders would serve fifteen

Reform Committee.

Sentenced. April 28th 1896.

Pretoria. Jail.
Ascension. Day. 1896.

Showing our ideas of the Pig we bought in a poke from the Government of this so called Republic

To amuse his fellow prisoners in Pretoria gaol after the Jameson Raid, Solly Joel invited them to sketch their 'ideas of the Pig bought in a poke from the Government'. The 'artists' included Frank Rhodes; John Hays Hammond; Solly Joel; and Harold Strange, General Manager of 'Johnnies'. They added their dates of birth.

years' imprisonment, almost a death sentence for a sick man like Hammond. Public opinion, briefly won over by the reprieves, now turned on Kruger who was so obviously reluctant to leave his prey. Barney, however, sensed victory, but was too practised a poker hand to relax his own grip. He adjourned all company meetings and went through the motions of disposing of his properties while making preparations, carefully leaked to Pretoria, to leave the Transvaal for good. All work had now been suspended in his properties, and employees given a fortnight's notice.

On 30 May, Kruger proclaimed that the 'junior' members of the Reform Committee would be released on payment of a £2,000 fine. When Barney heard the news he trotted exuberantly into the Johannesburg Stock Exchange where he was whisked on to the platform. 'I'm sorry the order of release doesn't include the four leaders,' he shouted above the applause, 'but I have every reason to believe they will be out before long.' Within ten days, while mayors from all the leading cities had assembled in Pretoria to present yet another petition, Kruger announced that the prisoners would be released on paying a fine of £25,000 each. They were given the choice of banishment or an undertaking not to engage in any anti-Republican activities for fifteen years. Frank Rhodes chose exile and was driven to the border that very evening under armed escort. His fine and those imposed on the three others were paid by Cecil Rhodes who, in conjunction with Beit, according to the accounts published by the latter's firm, met a bill of over £300,000 for the Raid and its aftermath. Rhodes repaid most of this from his own pocket. He later stated that he and Beit settled an account for close on £800,000 between them.

The relieved Uitlanders now seemed so disposed to forgive and forget the past that they even shouted three cheers for the President at a sign from Barney. He then led an almost delirious crowd of supporters to the railway station to greet Lionel Phillips and George Farrar, Hammond having arrived back earlier and taken to his bed. The horses were unharnessed from their carriage which was dragged to the Stock Exchange through streets lined by rejoicing citizens. That night a banquet was given in Barney's honour and Solly proposed the health of the men his uncle had helped to snatch from prison and perhaps the scaffold.*

Barney did not undervalue his own triumph. 'No one else could have done what I did,' he told a reporter. It was echoed even in far-off England where he had so recently been savaged by the Press. A London magazine published a cartoon depicting him as a music-hall conjurer hypnotizing Kruger. Watching from the stalls, Joseph Chamberlain murmurs admiringly, 'How on earth does he do it?'

The Jameson Raid had inevitably damaged the gold mining industry. Indirectly, however, it served to repair the image of the Barnato clan after the Bank débâcle. Barney had emerged as a popular hero, while Solly soon picked up another laurel by being elected Chairman of the Johannesburg Stock Exchange. Only a long-overdue revival of the Kaffir share market was required to gild the firm's prestige with profit.

* John Hays Hammond left South Africa to work in London as a consulting engineer before returning to the United States in December 1899. He served the Whitney and Guggenheim corporations and took a prominent part in public life. For a time he was considered as a presidential candidate. He represented President Taft at the Coronation of King George V and later became a valued member of the White House Circle during the Harding and Coolidge administrations. He died in 1936.

MOONSHINE.—June 13 1896.

BARNATO, THE CONJURER.
Mr. Chamberlain: "HOW ON EARTH DOES HE DO IT?"

18

―――――

A BRIEF SPURT IN SHARE PRICES gave Johannesburg an excuse to prolong its celebration of the Reformers' release. Then came the belated reports of uprisings by the *impis* in Rhodesia. Following his successful confrontation with Kruger, Barney felt tempted to give an equally dramatic solo turn. With Bulawayo itself under threat, despite Rhodes and the British brasshats, he now drafted a plan to raise a corps of volunteers from the eastern province of Cape Colony. This expeditionary force of 150 white officers and men, supplemented by 200 selected native auxiliaries, would be equipped entirely at his own expense.

Barney revelled in the part of commander-in-chief and perhaps regretted leaving his City Lieutenant's uniform behind in Spencer House. He spent excited hours with his maps, working out alternative routes to the north. According to his calculations, his rescue force might be in Bulawayo within a month, by which time he would have enrolled and equipped another company to support them. Woolf and Solly uneasily advised him to inform the authorities about his project before going ahead. An answering wire reminded him curtly that the military had the situation under full control. At dinner that night he told his nephews bitterly, 'It's awful to think of those poor women being slaughtered, but I can do nothing now. And my men could have been there quicker than any other reinforcements.'

He consoled himself by seeking a rapprochement with Kruger who had so far shown no haste to lower import and railway tariffs or remove the Uitlanders' political disabilities. Rhodes's military presence across the border, coupled with realistic Boer fears that Jameson might go scot-free or escape with a light sentence in a jingoistic British Court, had made Pretoria even more prickly. And Barney's own attack on Judge Gregorowski, followed by the threat to close down his mines, would never be forgotten. He was, therefore, given a frosty reception when he recited the now-familiar grievances about the railways and the dynamite concession which, he insisted, were holding up the gold industry's hopes of recovery.

Barney's waning optimism took another blow when Pretoria was reported to have allocated most of its budget for arms from Germany. This would further discourage and alarm European investors who already endorsed Chamberlain's severe view of Kruger as 'an ignorant, dirty, cunning and obstinate man who has known how to feather his own nest and enrich all his family and dependants'. Moreover, in his 'Statement of Policy' for that difficult year, Chamberlain had also denounced the Randlords as 'a lot of cowardly, selfish, blatant speculators who would sell their souls to have the power of rigging the market'. Although he would continue to use Johannesburg's discontent to whip up public opinion in England and South Africa against the Pretoria régime, it was becoming plain that he aimed to precipitate armed intervention under the British flag rather than see Krugerism replaced by an Uitlander Republic.

This volatile situation gave mining stocks little chance of recovery. Even under normal conditions and with goodwill on all sides, the inflated market would have needed time to subside. Huge capital investment was desperately required to restart production. But while investors were still taking heavy losses and remained wary of the Transvaal's political cross-currents, any hope of quickly attracting more funds could be written off.

Although crushing had recommenced on the reefs, Rand shares continued to melt like a child's snowman in the hot sun. With so many companies in the Barnato Group, even small falls represented losses of several thousand pounds each week, while some of the low-yielding mines, over-capitalized in the boom, were only kept going by loans from 'Johnnies' which still paid dividends.

Solly alone remained cheerful at the dispirited conferences in Colonnade Building. Although still ranking behind Barney and Woolf, the past few weeks had invested him with more authority.

His trial and imprisonment had made him a respected figure throughout South Africa, while his leadership of the Diamond Syndicate and an outstanding contribution to the success of 'Johnnies' had tested and proved his business flair. As Chairman of the Johannesburg Stock Exchange he was now poised to win over those who had never quite forgiven Barney's maverick tactics in the days of street dealings.

Woolf was London-based and therefore remote from the Rand's quick-changing moods. In any event he was too reserved to act as trouble-shooter. Solly's rôle became particularly vital at a time when his uncle, exhausted by successive crises since the previous autumn, seemed to have lost the old thrust. Barney was drinking heavily and had given up his training sessions with Jamie Couper who turned one day to David Harris and glumly prophesied, 'That marvellous vitality will run out. Some time such a bundle of quivering nerves will snap. Either life or brain must go.'

He was now suffering from a kind of financial hypochondria, ballooning every share dip into near disaster. 'I can't forget the work,' he confessed to Harry Raymond. 'It's too much now. I feel it, and yet I can't leave it off.' Fortunately, he was sleeping better again and cycled round the Wanderers every evening, but he now had an insatiable need of back-slappers in the bars and steadily grew more boastful as the liquor took effect far more quickly than in the old days.

He proudly gave his name to a new park that was being laid out in the suburb of Berea but it did not wholly compensate for the threatened collapse of the Barnato Bank. Before leaving for a holiday in England, Solly had bluntly urged Woolf and his uncle to close it down and also weed out the poorer companies in the firm's capital structure. Barney hated the very idea of retrenchment but agreed to defer his final decision on the Bank's future until Solly had taken careful soundings in the City of London.

Within a few days of his arrival, Solly arranged to buy the house he had long wanted in Great Stanhope Street around the corner from Barney's mansion which was still being built but already towered over its Park Lane neighbours. He also bought several horses with the intention of starting a stable. Time permitting, he explained genially to an interviewer, he hoped to buy a yacht and cruise in Mediterranean waters, one of the pleasures he missed in South Africa.

It was partly showmanship designed to stop panic talk, but he was serious enough in assuring his Hatton Garden friends that De Beers was about to declare a 42% dividend with half-year profits likely to top £1,200,000. It was far more difficult to convince the Throgmorton Street brokers who forecast a gloomy prospect for Kaffirs until Anglo-Boer relations improved. Few thought that possible with Kruger still in office. Solly tried to remind them of the Rand's tremendous potential and gave convincing details of his real estate development plans for 'Johnnies', but all talk ended depressingly with awkward questions about the Barnato Bank.

He reported his cheerless findings to Barney and Woolf in Johannesburg. They went into conference behind locked doors in Colonnade Building to plug any leakage which might panic the market. It was finally decided to wind up the Bank whose assets, such as they were, would be taken over by 'Johnnies', shareholders receiving five of its shares in exchange for eight of their own. Solly also unfolded a plan to build a vast luxury hotel like the London Carlton, together with a theatre capable of seating a thousand people. For days afterwards Barney could talk of nothing but 'my new theatre' which helped to take his mind off the Stock Exchange.

In this more cheerful mood he ran into Leo Weinthal who had just commissioned two marble lions for his house in Pretoria. Recalling that Kruger had hunted lions in his youth, Barney at once suggested that they would make an ideal gift for the President and simultaneously prove his own goodwill. Weinthal agreed to let him have them and suggested they should be presented to Oom Paul on his seventy-first birthday in October by which time Barney expected to be back from London.

He left for England at the end of July, confident of being able to soothe his Bank shareholders and generally to ginger up the City. With Fanny at his side he waved farewell to a group of well-wishers at the railway station and then joined David Harris who was also going to the Cape. Relieved by his cousin's improved spirits, Harris reminded him of his promise to help bright Kimberley youngsters to further their education. Barney thought that a new children's Wing for the Kimberley Hospital had a higher priority and at once signed a cheque for £10,000 towards the cost of accommodating 100 patients. There would be two special 'Leah Primrose' beds. He added £3,000 to endow scholarships for boys of local parentage, a generous postscript to the £10,000 he had previously given to help establish a Barnato School in Doorn-fontein for the benefit of poor children.

Since August was normally a slack period for the London Stock Exchange he did not fret overmuch at the continued drop in Kaffirs. Instead, he interested himself in the Park Lane mansion which helped to remind the public that Barney Barnato was still a multi-millionaire whatever they might have read about Rand shares. He waltzed with little Leah in the huge empty ballroom and played trick shots on one of the billiard tables. The builders assured him that the house would be completed and certainly ready for occupation within a few months. 'Make sure it is before the Diamond Jubilee next year,' he warned them fiercely. He drove back and forth between Spencer House and Draper's Gardens in his carriage and enjoyed himself at the races and theatres, oblivious of the crabbed little smiles exchanged in private by some of his former companions. At a Savoy party for a number of men-about-town and their partners from the Daly's chorus, someone proposed his health and ended with the gibe, 'We have such a galaxy of beauty present that they remind me of Barnato stock. Once you've got them, you've got to keep them.' Barney chose to take this as a compliment.

The storm broke early in September 1896, when it was an-nounced from Johannesburg, after a public meeting hastily called, that the Bank had been absorbed by 'Johnnies' without giving the British and Continental shareholders time to vote or investigate its affairs. They had received neither balance sheet nor dividends, while many who had bought at peak prices would suffer con-siderable losses by the not over-generous allocation of 'Johnnies' shares. One London newspaper summed up the affair as 'hurried burial without coroner's inquest'.

Barney was being reminded almost daily of his unfortunate promise, 'I tell you that the name of the Barnato Bank will not die whilst the name of Barnato Brothers lives.' He was nevertheless astonished and hurt by the abuse heaped on him by Press and public who chose to ignore his previous efforts to save the market and now hinted at sharp practice. One morning, throwing aside a pile of vicious threatening letters, he turned to Tom Honey and bitterly paraphrased Kipling:

'Twas Barney this and Barney that, and Barney everywhere,
But it's Mister bloody Barnato when I've anything to spare.'

Self-pity yielded to indignation when some of the brokers also turned on him. 'It costs me a fortune every time I come into the City,' he growled at Woolf who was equally shaken but urged self-control. 'Everyone who holds fifty "Johnnies" expects me to go into the House and buy a few thousands in order to get him out. It's a fool's game for which you don't even get thanks.' Poison pen letters arrived by the score and several anonymous writers threatened his life. One morning the butler at Spencer House handed him a parcel with a note attached: 'As you've had my boots, you might as well have the only garment left to me.' It was an old pair of trousers. Passing 25 Park Lane, Henry Labouchère was asked by a friend what the hideous stone figures on the roof were supposed to represent. 'They must be Barnato creditors petrified while awaiting settlement,' he sneered back.

Although Barney continued to brood over the Bank's collapse, that was only part of a deeper malaise. He had steadily developed a morbid terror of losing money, so long his symbol of success, but it was even more painful to sacrifice the adulation of shareholders. He completely failed to appreciate that the firm's losses, although considerable, represented only a proportion of the huge paper gains heaped up during the boom. In his semi-paranoic condition, every point dropped in Throgmorton Street had become a vote of no-confidence in himself and another step towards inevitable bankruptcy and disgrace.

He oscillated between aggressiveness and despair. After a dinner-party at Spencer House, Lady de Grey tried to console him over the harsh newspaper criticisms. 'If I were you, Mr Barnato, I would eschew them,' she murmured gently. 'You're quite right,' he grunted. 'Chew 'em up. I'll chew 'em up.' That became impossible in Paris where the collapse of his Bank and its depressing effect on all Rand stocks started a violent chain reaction. French anti-Semites, inflamed with memories of Dreyfus, now demanded little short of the guillotine or Devil's Island for the former 'Roi d'Or'. 'What is he doing here?' screamed the Marquis de Morès. 'He is cutting the throat of France. The collapse of the market has sent our millions to London. Barnato is at the Hotel Bristol until Wednesday. Let us drive him from Paris before it is too late.'

He kept away from his clubs, declining to become a trapped goldfish to be fed with a few crumbs of insincere comfort. Although continuing to support his pensioners, he even avoided the East End where some might ridicule him for losing his millions. Puffy-faced and occasionally unshaven, he would hurry each morning to Draper's Gardens and pounce on correspondence, often making a scene over some trifle. He was drinking hard and found it impossible to relax. When Jack Joel mildly suggested that he might benefit from a holiday at Harry's villa, Barney objected that he was far too busy. In fact, he spent most of his day mourning the Stock Exchange quotations or tippling in the City bars while his efficient staff looked after the firm's affairs.

De Beers was flourishing and the whole outlook of Rand mining had improved. Barney's lions, wrote Solly, now stood on either side of Kruger's house and had been unveiled at a special ceremony on 10 October, when the old man had emerged after his morning prayers to receive birthday greetings. He had signed a note of thanks written by his son, Tgard, which Barney showed to all his friends until he mislaid it.*

He had grown even more absent-minded and impulsive. One afternoon, while discussing some business matter with Tom Honey, he had a sudden craving for the excellent whisky jelly served at Birch's in Brighton. He hurried off at once and arrived without a shilling in his pocket. After consuming a couple of jellies and several tots, he wrote out a cheque for £2 which the new barmaid refused to cash, explaining that it was against the

---

* As a souvenir he cherished part of the harness from Kruger's State Coach ornamented with a gold sovereign bearing the presidential head. It became a family heirloom and is preserved, among other relics, by Barney's granddaughter, Mrs Diana Barnato Walker.

rules. Barney roared with laughter and offered to leave his gold watch or his train ticket as security before the manager arrived. He assured the woman that the signature, 'Barnato', was good for millions.

Barney was oppressed by the vastness of Spencer House and took even less pleasure in the Park Lane mansion, leaving Fanny to see the decorators and furnishers who called for decisions. She worried about him, particularly when he grew morose after a drinking bout, and persuaded him to carry a stout malacca cane on his lonely late-night walks in case some irate shareholder might be lying in wait. He laughed at her fears but, for the first time since his youth, spent the whole of Yom Kippur at the synagogue and fasted the full twenty-four hours. He paid frequent visits to the graves of his parents in the cemetery at Willesden Green and also consulted a phrenologist off Queen Victoria Street who read his 'bumps' and dutifully prophesied health and longevity.

He revived when Solly came on another visit, although he was amazed that his nephew could even consider buying horses and a yacht while the stock market remained so uncertain and most people thought a South African war inevitable. Solly now hoped to spend more time in England, enjoying himself and keeping *au fait* with the London end of the Diamond Syndicate once his ambitious programme for 'Johnnies' was under way. Perhaps he also sensed that Barney was not cutting the best City figure as Chairman in his present 'bearish' mood. He therefore suggested that his uncle should build himself a house in the 'Belgravia' of Johannesburg where the firm owned a splendid piece of ground with ample space for a garden and orchard. Barney beamed approval. The weather had been damp and foggy and he yearned for sunshine and the company of old friends. He would leave at once! Solly dissuaded him as he was due to sail next day, Saturday 28 November, and had prepared himself for a pleasant voyage home in the company of Abe Bailey.

Barney arrived without warning at Southampton to see him off. He wore a pair of dress trousers and sports coat under his fur-lined coat and looked as if he had been tippling. After a few more farewell drinks he still seemed so dejected that Solly impulsively invited him to book passage as far as Madeira and stop off there

for a short holiday. Barney joyfully threw off his coat and was
soon pacing the deck, laughing and cracking jokes.

When they arrived at Funchal, however, he was handed a
number of telegrams from the Johannesburg office whom he had
informed of his trip. He at once became over-excited by what he
called 'this alarming and disquieting state of affairs' which needed
his personal attention, although Solly assured him that they were
routine matters he could easily handle. Barney disagreed roughly.
Now reinvigorated by the sea breezes, he no doubt saw his
chance for action in the friendly warmth of his boardroom in
Colonnade Building instead of having to go back to abusive
letters and the depressing daily bulletins from his brokers.

Looking spruce in a new suit bought off the peg in Cape Town
he received Johannesburg's reporters with the familiar effervescence. 'My mission in Africa is to put my house in order,' he
announced. 'I am going to peg away at it from early morning
until late at night. What's more, I'm going to reorganize the
working of the Barnato group of mines from top to bottom.
These dastardly injurious remarks which have been disseminated
have almost destroyed European faith, shattered confidence and
diverted capital. My aim will be to restore confidence, and
presently, when all this temporary disquietude shall have been
removed, I shall come to my people and put something before
them.'

Polite applause greeted this grandiloquence. The time for barnstorming had passed. Shareholders, here as in London and Paris,
were only eager for rises and dividends. Although not directed at
him personally, Barney could not help sensing a certain constraint
when he bustled 'between the Chains'. The black year, 1896, was
ending with the promise of still more conflict. De Beers shares
were at record levels, but the Company had lost many of its
cattle through rinderpest. As in Rhodesia, the native chiefs opposed
the destruction of their herds to check the disease and attacked
white settlements. With Kimberley itself threatened by murder
and pillage, the Griqualand West Brigade was ordered to relieve
the police in the outlying districts. David Harris commanded the
volunteer force which eventually restored law and order after
heavy losses on both sides.

Barney had worried over his cousin's safety. While anxiously awaiting news of him, he was distressed to hear that Groote Schuur had been completely destroyed by fire. He expressed sympathy with Rhodes whose papers, furniture and beloved collection of Dutch silver, glassware and china would be impossible to replace. Tragedy had struck while Rhodes was preparing to face what he called 'the unctuous rectitude' of his countrymen before a Select Committee appointed by the House of Commons. The Jameson Raid affair would be raked over once again and his own motives mercilessly exposed. Before sailing off for this ordeal, he could still make a wry joke: 'What with the Raid, rebellion, famine, rinderpest and now my house burnt, I feel like Job, all but the boils.' It did not prevent him from giving instructions to rebuild and refurnish his house without delay.

Barney might have benefited from a similar fighting challenge. It was his misfortune to be condemned to dullish routine and semi-redundancy. There was no scope for dazzling coups while the stock market remained unstable, and he lacked the self-discipline to sit out a crisis which was beyond his control. He had once prescribed 'money and patience' as certain cures for the false alarms that threatened the Rand. Now he imagined himself poor and had never been over-patient. Solly, of course, consulted him before every new move by 'Johnnies', but expansion was going too smoothly to require much more than the Chairman's rubber stamp.

With so little excitement on the business front, he worried incessantly about the worsening political situation. Kruger was fortifying his re-election prospects by harsher censorship and other repressive measures against the Uitlanders who would now have to register, while 'undesirable immigrants' would be vigorously excluded. But they could no longer turn to The Great Barnato who was now anything but the man who had once humbled the President with a threatened close-down.

Everyone in Johannesburg gossiped about his drinking jags and his odd tendency to start a conversation and break off in mid-sentence while he snatched a cigarette which he forgot to light or impulsively handed out diamonds to casual acquaintances from the little bag in his vest pocket. He was exhibiting symptoms of manic depression, bursting without warning from the deepest gloom into a frenzied state of elation. In both conditions he took alcohol to excess which steadily impaired his physique.

He had now practically given up social drinking. For days at a time he would climb into his bottle and pull the cork after him. He would emerge for a week or two and ration his drinks, attending to office work until some recession in stock exchange prices or an unkind newspaper reference to the defunct Bank would send him shuffling round the saloons to boast of his millions until his knees buckled and a sympathetic friend had to help him into a cab. To gain flattering listeners he began to fabricate grievances, sounding off at both Kruger and Joseph Chamberlain who were together edging the Transvaal into civil war.

Rhodes's new popularity in England, coinciding with Chamberlain's despatch of a naval squadron to Delagoa Bay, had reacted predictably on Kruger. Although forced to repeal his Immigration and Aliens Expulsion Acts, he promptly started to negotiate a treaty of 'friendship and mutual defence' with the Orange Free State, an obvious move against Britain. He also banned the Johannesburg *Star*, in which 'Johnnies' had a large holding, for poking fun at his preposterous demand for £1,677,938 3s. 3d. from the British Treasury 'for moral and intellectual damages' from the Raid.

This dangerous and bewildering game of tit-for-tat helped to pile up the chaos in Barney's already fuddled brain. He babbled curses at Kruger who was building forts around Pretoria. After so many years of effort and sacrifice, he saw himself reduced to penury as share prices continued to fall with rumours of a coming war. Lashed by alcohol, his brain could not rest.

Solly tried to divert him by unrolling his blueprints for the new Carlton Hotel. Barney made some intelligent suggestions and became enthusiastic about the big theatre block which would cost nearly £200,000 and compare with almost any auditorium in London and New York. He quickly saw himself as an actor-manager, once again dazzling audiences in *The Bells*. This optimism lasted several weeks during which he constantly visited the house he was building in Berea, near Barnato Park. Completely discarding his fears of imminent bankruptcy, he approved the architect's plans for marble columns and sanctioned an outlay of some £80,000 on rosewood panelling throughout and even a minstrels' gallery. He was delighted to learn that 25 Park Lane would definitely be completed in good time for the Diamond Jubilee, but quickly became agitated when Solly suggested that it might do him good to sail home for the festivities. He again began to rant at the shareholders who would be lying in wait for him.

His psychotic disorder pursued its zigzag course. During the early months of 1897 arms smuggling had increased across the Free State border which was being heavily patrolled. While standing on the station platform at Vereeniging waiting to change trains, Fanny Barnato was shot in the leg by a Customs officer who had carelessly lifted his rifle. She was helped into a railway carriage and given medical attention, pausing considerately on her way to the hospital to forgive the young man for what was obviously an accident. Barney had the bullet fixed to one of her bangles as a lucky escape charm and gruffly accepted the company's apologies.

By mid-April, this incident had been distorted into a Boer vendetta to destroy him and his family. He now had vivid nightmares in which he saw the Stock Exchange burning and the terrified faces of natives drowning in the Kimberley Mine. One night he awoke shrieking and ran in his pyjamas to the house of a neighbour. 'They're after me,' he stammered. 'Let me in.'

The doctor diagnosed a slight fever, recommending rest and a complete change of scene. Barney departed for the Cape's Sea Point Hotel with Fanny and the children. He went for daily drives and seemed to have made a rapid recovery. To keep his mind off business, he again took his place in the Assembly. He supported a motion to contribute funds to the Imperial Navy but rose to protest against the heavy subsidies which the Colony was being asked to pay steamship companies for a mail service. Obviously with an eye on gold shipments, he spoke very much to the point but could not resist a touch of irony. 'There seems to be so much money in this business,' he said mockingly, 'that I think I'll have a shot at it myself.' His old enemy, J. X. Merriman, jumped to his feet at once. 'Mr Barnato is apparently anxious to begin his nautical career,' he snorted. 'I do long to see him on the bridge of a first-class steamer.' Instead of sparking off Barney's latent paranoia, he reacted with surprising good humour.

He was still in benign mood when little Marie Lloyd arrived in the city to round off a very successful tour. Although they had never previously met, he presented her with a gold bracelet set with half a dozen diamonds before her benefit performance. He called often after that and took her for drives round Cape Town with her small daughter, saying how much he had enjoyed favourite songs like 'Mr Porter' and 'Wink the other eye'. Before she sailed for England, he made her promise to return soon and not sign any long-term contracts until he had his chance of booking her. 'My theatre in Johannesburg will shortly be built,' he said breezily, 'and I want you to play in burlesque for me as soon as it's ready.' He gave her a sound kiss and shouted, 'Goodbye, my girl! Come back to us soon. Don't forget to drive round to Park Lane when you get home, and write and tell me how they are getting on with my new place.' There was nothing in his manner to indicate depression or threatened suicide, she recalled later. Much improved in spirits, he soon rebooked his passage to England.

On Sunday, 23 May 1897, he had a relapse. In his delirium he began counting banknotes which crumbled to dust between his fingers, and he had to be restrained from clawing diamonds from cracks in the walls. Fanny sent a desperate telegram to Solly in Johannesburg, imploring him to come as soon as possible. He arrived on the Wednesday by which time Barney had miraculously recovered and was already resuming his daily walks. After consulting with the doctors who warned him that his uncle's condition still required complete freedom from all business anxieties, Solly arranged for a full Power of Attorney to be vested in himself and tactfully kept cheque books out of sight.

Barney was feeling better but again wished to postpone his sailing date. The old terror of facing hostile shareholders had returned, but Solly and the doctors, convinced that he would benefit from a sea voyage, won him over with a little guile. The official delegation for the Diamond Jubilee celebrations, led by the Cape Premier, Sir Gordon Sprigg, and Chief Justice Sir Henry de Villiers, would be sailing in the *Scot* on 2 June. Barney was coaxed into believing that the Chamber of Mines *insisted* on his representing the industry. He agreed at once after arranging for Fanny and the children to accompany him.

He was suddenly agog with plans for London, including a house-warming party in Park Lane on the 22nd, when the Queen would drive through the streets of her capital. Solly had to change all his own business schedules for Kimberley and Johannesburg when the doctors warned him that Barney's chances of recovery depended on a strict control of his alcoholic intake and, above all, cheerful company. On the day before sailing, Barney called at Nazareth House to ask about the new collecting van he had lately presented to the Sisters. He left them with a cheque to be distributed among the poor.

The well-tried therapy succeeded yet again. With a gently rolling deck underfoot and the sun and stinging spray on his face, Barney became more cheerful by the hour. He chatted amiably with Sprigg, who saw nothing unusual in his manner beyond the familiar exuberance, while de Villiers, who had formerly presided at the hearing of Kimberley Central's arguments against the Amalgamation, was amused by Barney's garrulous reminiscences of those exciting days.

The *Scot*, a crack mail steamer of the Union Line, was equipped like a first-class hotel with electric light everywhere and the latest refrigerating plant for a superb cuisine. All the passengers were in gay Jubilee mood. The drinks flowed, but Barney austerely sipped lemonade in the bars. To celebrate Jack's third birthday, he ordered champagne without, however, yielding to temptation himself. He talked cheerfully to George Lohmann, the cricketer, about going to Lord's with him, and kept inviting fellow-passengers to his party in Park Lane. He came into the saloon for all his meals and sat at the Captain's table with Fanny, Solly, Lohmann and Lionel Hewson, an ex-member of the Cape Mounted Police who now had extensive interests in hotels and diamonds.

According to a steward, 'he was quiet and sociable most of the time', playing dominoes and cribbage or somewhat erratic games of chess in which he rarely used the pawns. The ship's doctor did not need to be called but had Barney's cabin door closely watched at night. When he became morose, Solly would persuade him to eat in his cabin, but nothing caused him alarm apart from his uncle's odd preoccupation with the date. He would rush into the saloon before breakfast to rip off the previous day's page on the calendar, constantly asking the crew when they expected to reach Southampton. Before long he wanted to know the exact time of arrival at Madeira where they were to pick up the mail and newspapers.

He was again showing ominous concern about the stock market and his 'enemies' in London. 'How near land are we?' he kept demanding and seemed terrified of being left alone. On Sunday 13 June, only two days south of Madeira, he was chatting genially with a fellow-member of the Cape Assembly, J. L. Wiener, when he muttered something about blood poisoning but did not go into details. That evening he drifted into Hewson's cabin and suddenly took out a little bag from his waistcoat pocket. 'Here's some stones for you, boy,' he said, but Hewson declined them with a laugh.

At lunch next day, after three games of chess with his nephew, he ordered champagne for the whole table and persuaded Sprigg and de Villiers to adjourn to the smoking-room for brandies. He chattered away and seemed content with the two glasses of Guinness which Solly, after some hesitation, had allowed him. Although heavy seas were running and Solly longed to retire for a siesta, Barney took his arm and insisted on walking him up and down the promenade deck for almost an hour. He refused to go to his cabin or even sit down although Solly was near collapse from this frantic exertion after a heavy meal. Finally, completely exhausted, Solly subsided into a deckchair while his uncle walked round him, continuing his breathless monologue. 'What's the exact time?' he blurted again. Solly took out his watch and said wearily, 'Thirteen minutes past three.'

The ship's fourth officer, W. T. Clifford, was dozing off-duty a few yards away when he heard a frenzied cry, 'Murder! For God's sake, save him.' He thought he saw Solly Joel's hand clutching his uncle's trouser leg before Barney went over the side. Clifford threw off his jacket and cap and dived overboard. The *Scot* was pitching in a rough sea and steaming at about seventeen knots. Barney appeared to be swimming strongly, but Clifford could not reach him. By the time the ship's engines had stopped and a lifeboat lowered, Barney was floating head downwards. He was picked up with difficulty a few minutes after Clifford, who had managed to cling to a lifebuoy.

Artificial respiration was attempted without success. Barney's body was placed in a rough deal coffin, hastily knocked up by the ship's carpenter, and taken to Southampton where the *Scot* docked on the 18th after stopping briefly at Madeira. There the English newspapers provided an ironic footnote to Barney's forebodings. All Rand shares had picked up for the first time in months, thanks to excellent gold production figures and something like a Jubilee carnival spirit in the London market.

News of the tragedy, followed by the coroner's verdict of suicide while temporarily insane, hit all gold shares as well as De Beers. A minor selling panic started in the Barnato group with the rumour that Barney had drowned himself to avoid certain bankruptcy. A number of shareholders sent violent letters to the newspapers, and leader-writers moralized on 'the slavish worship of Mammon', but his tragic end was lamented by many in the City of London and South Africa. The Johannesburg Stock Exchange closed for a day as a mark of respect, and Sivewright, then acting Prime Minister, adjourned the Cape Assembly.

Rhodes, however, reacted with an apparent callousness which his admirers have dutifully interpreted as a cover for his deep-felt distress. He was en route for Bulawayo by train when the telegram was received. To avoid disturbing him late at night, his secretary had waited until next morning before breaking the news. 'I suppose you thought this would affect me and I should not sleep,' Rhodes snapped at him. 'Why? Do you imagine that I should be in the least affected if you were to fall under the wheels of this train?' He lost no time in appointing David Harris to replace his cousin on the De Beers board and also encouraged him to stand successfully for Barney's old Kimberley constituency. 'I always knew Barney would predecease me,' he confided later to Sir Lewis Michell, his banker friend.

Beit had never warmed to Barney, but he was much shaken and insisted on attending the funeral. He rode in one of the two hundred carriages that left Kate Joel's house in Marble Arch for the Jewish cemetery at Willesden. Every bus-driver along the Edgware Road seemed to have pinned a crêpe ribbon to his whip which he raised in salute to the plain hearse. The cortège moved slowly through four miles of streets decorated for the Queen's Jubilee until it reached the burial ground where several hundred waited, including the Lord Mayor of London and representatives of the Rothschilds and all the leading finance houses in Europe, as well as many pensioners and old friends from the East End.

William Clifford stood with head covered at the graveside. His rescue attempt was rewarded by an illuminated address and a cheque for £200 collected by public subscription, apart from a Lloyds silver medal. Woolf Joel presented him with £1,000 on behalf of the firm, while Fanny arranged for a life annuity and would later show much kindness to his children.*

She always refused to believe that Barney had deliberately committed suicide and constantly stressed young Clifford's statement at the inquest: 'Mr Barnato had a good idea of swimming as he kept up so well.' The Coroner had not pursued that point nor Solly Joel's odd remark, 'As I looked down to my watch I saw a flash, and he was over.'

Did that flash have any significance? A trick of light, perhaps, or something so menacing that Barney had rushed in terror to the ship's rail and either flung himself into the sea or fallen overboard by accident? Above all, why had Solly shouted 'Murder!' when he called for help?

Most contemporaries had accepted Barney's death, three weeks before his forty-fifth birthday, as the suicide of a man deranged by physical and mental strain and the accumulation of largely imaginary fears. A minority, however, recalled that, even during his worst spells of delirium, he had never threatened to do away with himself. Some even hinted that Solly's own rôle remained open to suspicion. Was it not possible, they asked, that the terrified cry of 'Murder! had come from Barney's own lips? Clifford, half asleep, would naturally have assumed that Solly had shouted, particularly when he saw his hand on Barney's trouser-leg. In some City clubs it was whispered that Solly obviously

---

* Barney's would-be rescuer rose to a captaincy in the Merchant Marine while his son, Vice-Admiral Sir Eric Clifford, had a distinguished career including service in the Churchill War Cabinet.

stood to gain by the departure of an unstable Chairman who had become a dangerous liability. Tongues wagged even more maliciously when, by the terms of Barney's Will, it was disclosed that his share in the business would pass to the surviving partners.

These tenuous accusations, magnified through hearsay and unsupported by any acceptable evidence, would linger mistily over the years. They were all but forgotten until Solly and Jack engaged in a bitter series of disputes with Barney's son, 'Babe', over certain claims arising from his father's Will.

Did Barney take his own life? That question is likely to remain unanswered, although a closer study of all the alternative explanations and theories suggests that 'Accidental Death' might have been a more logical verdict. One cannot ignore his obsessive fascination with the ship's calendar or his constant enquiries about the exact time while he promenaded the deck after lunch on the 14th. This pointed to the general disequilibrium consistent with a potential suicide. Once that was ruled out, however, his strange behaviour might be linked with Solly's unexplained cry of 'Murder!' And did the flash of light which had caught his eye just before Barney went over the side come from someone's pistol?

Violence again struck the house of Barnato within a few months. This seemed quite unrelated to the earlier tragedy but, paradoxically, it would add to the mystery of Barney's end by uncovering several possible clues.

On 14 March 1898, Woolf Joel was shot dead.

19

———

ALTHOUGH ALL RAND SHARES had continued to decline since the Raid, and only three in the Barnato Group stood above par, the holdings still carried a market tag at over £12m at Barney's death. Yet his personal estate was valued at only £960,119. This was mainly due to the enormous sums he had invested in his abortive attempt to bolster Kaffirs during the disastrous autumn of 1895. It is noteworthy that Woolf's fortune was almost double his uncle's. Woolf, like his brothers and Harry Barnato, had evidently given little more than moral support to that costly salvage while spreading their own investments into less spectacular fields outside the Group.

Barney had, of course, spent heavily on private and public philanthropies, while his outgoings on his stables, the Park Lane mansion and his new baronial house in Berea had all come out of capital, quite apart from Fanny's valuable collection of diamonds. Rhodes, deciding that the widow 'had not been left very well provided for', enlisted Beit's support for a generous gesture. Barnato had died only a few weeks before each of the Life Governors became entitled, for the first time under the Articles of Association, to share in De Beers' profits. This amounted to £30,000 which was voluntarily passed over to Fanny. (Had Barney survived until 1901, when the Life Governors' rights were bought out by the Company in exchange for blocks of shares, he would have participated to the tune of a further £750,000.)

Under the Will each of his three children would, at the age of twenty-one, receive £250,000 of his share in the business of Barnato Brothers and in the investments, property and other assets of the firm. Harry Barnato and Woolf Joel were appointed executors and trustees, but the former had more or less settled permanently in Nice and decided to renounce probate.

Once the first shock of Barney's death had been absorbed after a brief depression in the firm's holdings, the London finance houses turned with more confidence to Woolf who had automatically succeeded as managing partner. He had long been a popular figure with City men who preferred his quiet style to Barney's fizziness. It seemed both symbolic and auspicious that his régime would open in the new headquarters in Austin Friars with its bank-like atmosphere of mahogany, plate glass and marble.

Woolf himself looked grave and melancholy when he sailed for Africa on 15 January 1898. He drew up his Will on the previous day, after being seized with a premonition that he would never see England again. At his farewell dinner party at the Savoy, thirteen guests had 'sat down, one having fallen out at the last minute. Woolf was so upset by this omen that he almost cancelled his passage and finally insisted on his wife and baby son following him by a different boat. Perhaps as a good luck token, he made a handsome subscription to the St John's Wood Synagogue, where he often worshipped, and also took with him sacred scrolls of the law, complete with vestments, to present to various synagogues in South Africa.

His visit was scheduled to last two months at the outside. He planned to spend six weeks in Johannesburg and a fortnight in Kimberley during which he intended to streamline and co-ordinate the various companies and perhaps dispose of the troublesome Waterworks Company to the municipality. He hoped for a less convulsive business life than had been possible during Barney's last years and expected to do more yachting and develop his racing interests, having decided to take over his uncle's colours. Solly would assume control of all operations in South Africa but made it clear that he also looked forward to several months of the year in England. Meantime, he arranged to complete building Barney's house in Barnato Park which he would refurnish to his own taste.

Solly's composure was shattered by the arrival of several anonymous letters from 12 February onwards. Some were obviously cranky, but one seemed far more dangerous. 'This is how the game stands,' declared the writer who signed himself 'Kismet'. 'I must have £12,000 at once or face ruin and disgrace, which I utterly decline to do. But if my race is run so shall yours be . . . Your death shall not be murder, but your own doing really, though I will willingly admit all blame for removing you to a better world, this or the other side of the river Styx, where Barnato may be glad to see you again . . .' He was told to place an advertisement in the *Johannesburg Star*, after which he would be given instructions for handing over the money. Other letters, even more menacing, followed. Unless he were paid off, 'Kismet' threatened to kill himself and take Solly *and* his brother with him.

Solly consulted Bob Ferguson, the local chief of police, who advised him to reply in the *Star*, inviting the blackmailer to come out in the open and state his grievances. This resulted in a violent barrage of notes, again demanding the £12,000 in abusive tones and warning Solly that further attempts by the police to trap him would bring certain death. The blackmailer, however, now added the bait of valuable political 'information' which, if anything, alarmed Solly even more than the death threats.

Kruger had just been re-elected President for a fourth term, despite overt support for the rival candidate, Schalk Burger, by several mining chiefs who were rumoured to have contributed £50,000 to his campaign funds. Solly took no part in this activity and had also steered clear of the militant anti-Kruger South African League which had set up a branch in Johannesburg. By this time Kruger had grown so impatient of all opposition that he would shortly dismiss even Chief Justice Kotzé for daring to question the Volksraad's unlimited authority to legislate. After Solly's unfortunate experience on the Reform Committee, he was determined never again to involve himself in politics which would expose him to the risk of banishment. He was therefore understandably disturbed by 'Kismet's' switch in tactics.

Still much shaken by Barney's death, he turned desperately to Woolf who advised him to leave for the Cape while he himself dealt with the blackmailer. Woolf then called in Harold Strange, the manager of 'Johnnies', who agreed that the police should be kept out of the affair at all costs since any publicity would not only place Solly in jeopardy but might further damage the firm's still precarious standing with the government.

Woolf, however, became more cheerful when 'Kismet' suddenly dropped his blackmailing demands and began instead to suggest 'loans' in exchange for information of the greatest financial advantage to Barnato Brothers. He now signed himself 'Baron v. Veltheim' and respectfully asked for an interview. Woolf, accompanied by Strange, duly met him by appointment in Barnato Park where the 'Baron' confided that he had had several meetings in London and Cape Town with Barney who had advanced him various sums for organizing a plan to kidnap Kruger and create confusion among his supporters. According to him, Barney had offered up to £50,000 if the venture succeeded and had not demurred at £1,000 a month for expenses. He begged Woolf's forgiveness for almost frightening poor Solly into a nervous breakdown, but firmly insisted that he had spent considerable cash and time making arrangements which had to be abandoned because of Barney's death. If they helped him out of his present difficulties, he would show his appreciation by supplying full details of a revolutionary movement which could still be worth 'millions' to them. He boasted inside knowledge of a new plan to avert the coming war by replacing Kruger with a more liberal-minded President. Such advance information, he argued, would obviously place the firm in a splendid position to bear the stock market and make a tremendous 'killing' on the world's exchanges.

Woolf and Strange listened in astonishment to this melodramatic tale, delivered with much fluency despite a heavy German accent. Von Veltheim was 6 feet 3 inches tall, wore a high-buttoned suit and carried a silver-headed cane and lavender gloves. A diamond ring sparkled on his little finger as he lit a cigar. He might not have looked out of place in any Pall Mall club. After a few cautious questions, Woolf arranged two further meetings in Strange's office, but with pistols handy in case their visitor turned violent. However, von Veltheim's appearance and amiable manner deceived them into thinking that he could be scared off by the threat of arrest or, failing that, the offer of a little money. Significantly, he had reduced his demands to £2,500 and now spoke of departing for England and abandoning his revolutionary plan.

When he finally wrote asking for only £200 to help out an ex-member of the 'organization', Woolf grew openly contemptuous and thought he could be 'squared for a fiver'.

It was a fatal misjudgment. Had Woolf decided even then to call in the police, they would quickly have checked on the black-mailer's colourful dossier. He would then have been prosecuted or, more probably, put across the border as an undesirable alien to avoid distasteful publicity for the Joels. His real name was Karl Kurtze, born in Brunswick in 1854. After the death of his father, a forester, he ran off to sea and later joined the German Navy. He deserted, stealing an officer's gold watch and chain, together with a seal bearing the family crest of von Veltheim. Under a number of aliases he served in various British ships and finally emerged in Australia as Baron von Veltheim. He married in Perth and subsequently crossed the Pacific, settling briefly in New Orleans as a shipping agent. Soon afterwards, he drifted into various jobs in Santa Marta, Colombia, returning to the United States as its consular agent. Following a bigamous marriage, with embezzle-ment and a little blackmail on the side, he arrived in London and checked in at the Hotel Metropole early in 1896 when, it will be recalled, Barney was worried by financial losses and the very gloomy reports from the Transvaal.

Von Veltheim soon ran out of money and 'married' again, fleecing his victim of several hundred pounds. After other lucrative courtships, he sailed from Plymouth in the *S.S. Ionic* on 17 April 1897, booking passage as Franz Louis Kurt. In Cape Town he talked grandly of his prominent European connections and was then believed to have jumped 'up country' before enlisting at Kimberley on 21 July for a term of three years as a trooper in the Cape Mounted Police.

In September a body was washed up in the River Thames and identified as that of 'Captain Vincent', yet another of his aliases, by a von Veltheim 'widow'. She was mistaken, but his photo-graph and an account of his shady activities in London's dockland reached the South African authorities. That December he was asked to resign from the police. While on his uppers in Johannes-burg he stayed at a boarding house in Bok Street where he met A. E. Caldecott, a solicitor who had been a director of one or two of the less successful Barnato companies and had no love for the family. His daughter had conceived an almost pathological hatred for Solly Joel, whom she blamed for all her father's misfortunes, although 'she spoke very highly of Woolf', according to von Veltheim. If he could be believed, she had encouraged him to write the first threatening letters. When Solly departed for the Cape, she had personally delivered the rest of the 'Kismet' letters to Woolf's house.

On Sunday morning, 13 March 1898, Woolf received another note urgently demanding an interview at 10.30 a.m. next day. Strange arranged instead to meet him in the street that same afternoon and announced that Woolf would agree to discount his promissory note for £200 but declined to do anything more. Next morning von Veltheim waylaid Strange and followed him into Colonnade Building, refusing to be shaken off. He insisted on seeing Woolf, 'if only for a minute'. Disturbed by the German's agitated manner, Strange slipped a revolver into his pocket before leading him into Woolf's office.

Von Veltheim, Strange recalled, told them he was leaving at noon by the weekly mail boat train for Cape Town on his way to England and needed £2,500. He began to pace the room angrily, turning to glare at Woolf who watched him intently from behind his desk. '£200,' he repeated calmly, with a tight little smile for Strange. 'Don't you see who you are trifling with?' shouted von Veltheim. 'Mr Strange tells me you are not going to give me any money. Well, if that's your final decision, you know too much and neither of you will leave this room alive.'

Strange then reached casually for a cigar box, hoping to distract his attention while he pulled a single-barrelled Derringer from his right pocket. 'Don't you move,' snapped the German who now had a revolver in his hand and was covering Woolf. He then fired at Strange who ducked, fired back and, turning quickly, saw Woolf crumpled over the desk with three bullets in his body. He had drawn his own revolver too late from his hip pocket. It fell to the right of the desk. Strange, having discharged his only barrel, dived for Woolf's pistol, but von Veltheim stepped on his thumb and again shot at him just as some members of the staff burst in and overpowered him.

Von Veltheim was charged with murder on an indictment drawn by Jan C. Smuts who, however, handed over to Dr F. Krause on being appointed State Attorney soon afterwards. The prosecution uncovered the accused's colourful past but proved inadequate in dealing with his plausible plea of self-defence. He claimed that Strange had fired the first shot which snicked him under the right eye, leaving a scar which he exposed for the jury's benefit. They were not reminded by the prosecution that it dated back to his boyhood when he had accidentally exploded a pistol stolen from his schoolmaster. He insisted that, after seeing Strange with the smoking pistol still in his hand, he first noticed that Woolf had also drawn a revolver.

'I then realized that for some purpose they meant to shoot me. My hand flew to my pocket. I had a little ·32 calibre revolver which I always carry. I fired at Strange and . . . then fired in quick succession three shots at Mr Joel . . . I then saw Strange was not trying to shoot, and I forebore to fire at him again, but told him to be quiet . . . I saw Joel fall against the wall, and that he was sinking. I picked up his pistol and walked to the door.'

The jury of burghers was obviously well-disposed. Remembering Solly Joel's part in the Jameson affair and his uncle's bullying campaign to release the prisoners, they were more than prepared to swallow the accused's story of a plot to overthrow the régime. Everyone knew that the Republic had enemies sworn to destroy it, and who more suspect than this notoriously pro-British clan? By comparison, the strapping German ex-trooper cut an almost heroic figure, representing a country which had so warmly supported the Boer cause.

After a trial lasting nine days they took precisely three minutes to find him 'Not Guilty', a verdict with which Mr Justice Morice expressed strong disagreement. Defence counsel refused to shake hands with von Veltheim who was consoled by the crowd's hysterical ovation outside. However, Kruger promptly had him rearrested and expelled from the Transvaal as 'a public danger'.

Despite its unsatisfactory conclusion, the hearing left several new leads to the mystery surrounding Barney's death. Woolf had obviously acted with remarkable stupidity in not exposing the blackmailer to the police, and still more by parleying with him. His offer of £200 in hush money was almost as uncharacteristic as Solly's panicky reaction to the 'Kismet' letters. No doubt they were both over-anxious to absolve the firm of any suggestion of anti-Kruger activity, but they may possibly have considered von Veltheim's account of his meetings with their uncle not wholly fanciful, although highly suspect.

He claimed to have first met Barney in the smoke-room of the Hotel Metropole in London in the summer of 1896, having been introduced to him by a mutual friend whose name he refused to give and who never appeared in Court. Barney was supposed to have advanced him £500 to act as a secret agent in overthrowing the Transvaal Government, but nobody ever saw them together in London, and there was no record of any written communication between them. The 'payment', if any, had been conveniently made in untraceable banknotes.

Von Veltheim had arrived at the Cape towards the end of April 1897. Before leaving England, he was said to have been handed another £500 by special messenger at the Grand Hotel, Eastbourne, with a pencilled note from Barney: 'I expect you by the first boat. Meet me at Cape Town before I sail. You will receive all instructions then.' On the very day he landed, Barney had apparently invited him to lunch at the Sea Point Hotel ('He was strange, and I thought he had been drinking'), and said he was going to England ('If you want any money, apply to Woolf Joel'). Solly had then come into the room and been jovially introduced as 'my other nephew, Solomon. He's a good boy, but he must not know anything about this business'. The only difficulty about this homely touch was that Solly happened to be in Johannesburg at the time and swore that he had never set eyes on von Veltheim until he saw him in the dock. Against this, however, was the blackmailer's vividly detailed account of the alleged plot to depose Kruger. He reproduced Barney's style and accent to the very life: 'Money is of no consequence. If it could be done within a million pounds it would be cheap at the price.'

This story was uncorroborated by a single living person or the smallest scrap of documentary evidence. It was riddled with dis-

crepancies as to times and places and could be dismissed as an
elaborate tissue of lies cunningly designed to extort cash from the
Joels once their uncle was out of the way. Nevertheless, it cannot be
altogether ruled out that the two *may* have met and talked, however inconclusively. Nothing was impossible in the light of
Barney's unstable condition after arriving in Cape Town in
mid-April 1897. He was undoubtedly disillusioned with Kruger,
while the alleged plot was scarcely more than a projection of what
was being whispered by many extremist Uitlanders behind locked
doors. Furthermore, Barney was not then under supervision and
had gone for walks and drives alone before his serious collapse on
Sunday 23 May.

His history of alcoholism and bouts of severe depression supports
the suicide theory without, however, completely excluding the
possibility that he might have been threatened by someone on
board the *Scot*. If so, could it have been von Veltheim or some
accomplice? It is self-evident that, if Barney had been unwise
enough to part with even small sums or hint grandiosely at
'millions' to such a predatory blackguard, he would at once have
exposed himself to more pressure and even a threat of violence. His
preoccupation with the ship's calendar and the exact hour of
arrival in Madeira then takes on rather more significance than the
nervousness of an imaginary bankrupt terrified of his shareholders.
Moreover, his repeated questions to Solly about the time, as they
walked up and down the deck, also become consistent with an
appointment with someone on board who had issued an ultimatum.

The *Scot* had sailed from Cape Town on 2 June. Von Veltheim
enlisted in the Cape Mounted Police on the 21st of the following
month which would still have given him time, although on a very
tight schedule, to have made the return trip, particularly if he had
disembarked at Madeira. He *could* have gone aboard the steamer
either as a passenger or more likely as a member of the crew. He
was a master of disguise and an experienced seaman. His brutality
towards Solly and Woolf is proof enough that he would not have
scrupled to threaten their sick and unnerved uncle for much-
needed cash. It then becomes equally feasible that Barney might
have confided his fears to Solly whose panic on receiving the
'Kismet' letters thereby becomes more explicable.

If Barney indeed had a rendezvous with von Veltheim or an accomplice for around 3 p.m. on 14 June or considered himself threatened, then Solly's indistinctive cry of 'Murder!' becomes almost intelligible. It will be recalled that von Veltheim always carried a pistol. One then has to ask whether Barney and his nephew both caught a glimpse of it simultaneously at 3.13 that afternoon. If so, one need perhaps look no further for an explanation of Solly's 'I saw a flash, and he was over'.

Solly would never comment on Fanny's strongly-worded and repeated doubts about her husband's suicide. Solly was undoubtedly oppressed by fears for his own safety when von Veltheim was arrested at Barberton soon after the trial for infringing the Order of Expulsion. He was sentenced to four months in gaol but Solly would long go around with bodyguards while in the Transvaal.

Less than ten years after Woolf's death, he received another letter from von Veltheim repeating his 'Kismet' tactics. By now, however, the whole South African situation had changed. Solly had become head of one of the world's most powerful finance houses and was very different from the man who had once fled in terror to Cape Town. He was ready and indeed eager to deal with what the blackmailer still called 'the unsettled account' between them.

EPILOGUE

———————

Cecil Rhodes died on 26 march 1902, two months before
the Boers' final surrender at Vereeniging. His body lies
beside Jameson's among the boulders of the Matoppo Hills
where they had once hunted down the Matabele. Jameson became
a director of De Beers, Prime Minister of Cape Colony, President
of the Chartered Company and an English baronet. After debts and
death duties, Rhodes left nearly £3,400,000, making ample
provision for awarding scholarships at Oxford to an élite from the
British colonies, the United States and Germany. Groote Schuur
was left as a residence for future Prime Ministers of the Union
Government of South Africa.

His old enemy, Kruger, fled to Europe where he found sanctuary
in Holland after being turned away by his one-time ally, the
Kaiser. He breathed his last near Montreux on 14 July 1904, true to
his vow to General Botha, 'born under the British flag, I shall not
die thereunder'. The £5m in gold which he was supposed to have
hidden from the British invaders attracted a horde of treasure-
hunters, among them the sinister von Veltheim. While in Trieste,
he raised capital on bills of exchange amounting to half a million
kronen (£20,000) by claiming to be the sole survivor of a small
body of men, 'sworn to secrecy', who knew 'exactly' where the
treasure was buried. After the Boer War he had travelled about,
living on his wits and the fruits of bigamy, until by June 1907, he
was desperate enough to write to Solly Joel again, this time
demanding £16,000.

Since Woolf's death, Solly's fortunes had advanced in inverse
ratio to the blackmailer's. He had succeeded his brother as
managing partner of Barnato Brothers and head of 'Johnnies'. He

was also a director of De Beers and the outstanding leader of the Diamond Syndicate. Alfred Beit had died in July 1906, tortured by fears of the synthetic diamond as well as the discovery of competitive fields like the Premier Mine, just north of Pretoria. The shock of first seeing this new find, home of the Cullinan diamond, brought on a fatal haemorrhage.

Solly was of stronger fibre. He master-minded the plan by which the Premier did not compete with De Beers who eventually acquired a controlling interest. Solly went on the Board and was responsible for arranging to sell the Cullinan, the largest diamond ever found, to the Transvaal Government who presented it to King Edward VII on his sixty-sixth birthday. After being cut, the four largest stones became part of the crown and sceptre of the British regalia.

Although diamonds would always remain his absorbing love and passion, Solly's dynamism actuated all the firm's varied activities in the first decade of the new century preceding the Union of South Africa. He disposed of the Waterworks Company to the municipality for over a million sterling. Johannesburg's new Carlton Hotel and theatre were built, and 'Johnnies' quickly re-established itself as the largest real estate combine in the Transvaal, apart from a mining finance house in the first rank. As more gold fields were tracked down in a huge area stretching far beyond the original reefs, rights were leased from the Government on a profit-sharing basis in the rich Modderfontein area which gave Barnato Brothers an enormous return on their initial investment of £1m. Several other valuable holdings were taken over, including Van Ryn Deep and Ferreira. By now, the Johannesburg house had also outgrown its head office and moved into the far more imposing Consolidated Building in Fox Street. Within a few years the Group was producing an annual £10m in gold.

Solly did not become enslaved by office routine. Visitors who turned the massive silver front-door handle in Mayfair's Great Stanhope Street entered luxurious salons hung with paintings by Lawrence, Gainsborough, Romney and Reynolds, interspersed with the owner's favourite Morlands. He hated to part with a picture even for exhibitions, and never forgave himself for once presenting a Landseer to a museum in South Africa. The curator placed it on show but, finding himself pressed for wall space, briskly cut the canvas down to size.

Solly was particularly proud of his diamonds which he kept in a vast safe, not even his wife and family being entrusted with the key to its combination lock. The rich carpets, the Chippendale upholstered in rose silk damask and his rare early Dresden rivalled those of Sir Edward Sassoon who had bought Barney's neighbouring house. But even that enormously wealthy Anglo-Indian family did not compete with Solly's expenditure on thoroughbreds and yachts. He bought Maiden Erlegh, a country estate of 750 acres in Berkshire, and established a racing stud there, soon followed by another at Newmarket, Sefton Lodge. He took almost as much delight in his yachts, successively named *Doris* after his favourite elder daughter. He liked to take his family on long Mediterranean holidays but found it easier to impress the children than his mother who had remained very down-to-earth. When they put in at Venice during her first cruise, she pinched her nose in distaste. Glancing critically at the crumbling *palazzi*, she observed, 'If you ask me, this place won't last long.'

The firm's prosperity was reflected in booming share values which proved so beneficial to the partners that Harry Barnato left some £3m when he died in London of a cerebral paralysis in November 1908, at the age of fifty-eight. His daughter, Lily, was left a million, plus £10,000 a year, and £250,000 was bequeathed for medical endowments, notably at the Middlesex Hospital, in memory of Barney Barnato and Woolf Joel. The testator's considerable holdings in the firm passed to his nephews.

All the Continental newspapers had reported details of the Will. Readers were also regaled with Solly's negotiations for the sale of the Cullinan Diamond and stories about the special coach which he grandly attached to trains in South Africa to enable 'Black Nanny' to travel about with his children without any embarrassment.

Tales of such magnificence could not fail to reawaken the bitterest animosity in von Veltheim who had temporarily run out of 'wives' and cash. Stranded in Antwerp, he postmarked a letter as from Odessa and addressed it to Solly at the Austin Friars offices in London. Dated 6 June 1907, it included such menacing phrases as: 'I will be satisfied once and for all with a purely financial settlement of my outstanding account against you . . . I must remind you to recall to your memory the character and grievances of the man addressing you. You have every reason to know from the history of the past that he keeps his word under all circumstances, *regardless of consequences*. Had you known this in Johannesburg and acted accordingly, the history of your house and S.A. would have been a different one. Let me see now if you have learnt anything from the past or not, *or again regret when too late*.' It was followed by a similar letter posted in St Petersburg and sent to Sefton Lodge. This time von Veltheim announced that his 'proxy' would shortly call on Solly. He duly arrived in London with a remarkable document: 'At sight pay to my order £16,000 sterling, value received as per advice, to Solomon B. Joel Esq., 10 and 11, Austin Friars.' It was signed, 'Franz von Veltheim.'

The envoy was watched by the police and followed back to Antwerp, but the blackmailer had by then moved on to Paris where he was arrested in September. After being extradited, he was committed for trial at the Old Bailey in February 1908. Solly gave evidence, again denying that he or Barney had ever engaged in any anti-Kruger plot with the accused. The latter then went into the witness-box where his story was mercilessly riddled by prosecuting counsel. He still maintained, however, that Woolf had promised him £12,000 and then attempted to shoot him with Harold Strange's help. He further declared that, after his acquittal, two attempts had been made on his life by Solly's agents while he was in Delagoa Bay. According to him, a bomb had been delivered to him in a parcel which exploded. A few weeks later the hotel was burned down and he was lucky to escape in his night clothes.

The British jury regarded him with far less sympathy than Kruger's burghers. He was found guilty and sentenced to twenty years' penal servitude. After serving seven years he was released on licence for saving a warder's life during a prison break.

He returned to Germany but again made his way back to South Africa, still hopefully seeking subscribers to his prospectus for 'Kruger's treasure'. Deported for the last time to his Fatherland, he received another term for false pretences and died penniless in Hamburg in 1930.

St. Petersburg, June 1907

Solly B. Joel, Esq.
  Maiden Erleigh
      Reading.

Sir,

I enclose copy of letter
sent you from Odessa.
There is nothing to add to
it. I shall shortly be in England
and will soon communicate
with you by proxy. The
Gentleman who will call
on you has no inward
knowledge of the issue
between us, but considders

the whole matter an every day business one. So you need not fear any trap. Now act as you think proper but remember your decision is a final one

J von Veltheim

One of the two blackmailing letters received by Solly Joel in mid-1907. They led to the arrest of von Veltheim who was later sentenced to twenty years' penal servitude at the Old Bailey.

Solly's unhappy experience with von Veltheim was soon blotted out by his triumphs in the financial world. The opening up of the Transvaal Government Areas in 1910 took courage on the firm's part when many prominent companies, including even the Corner House, had hesitated to tender. These claims in the Eastern Rand would distribute a profit between the Government and shareholders of over £80m during the next half-century.

An even more stunning coup, comparable in scale with the historic De Beers-Kimberley amalgamation, was the Barnato Group's purchase in 1917 of Robinson's Randfontein and Langlaagte companies for £4,500,000. The properties had been so grossly mismanaged and allowed to run down that enormous sums were essential to make them productive. Even so, it would be several years before Randfontein paid its first dividend. During the costly period of reconstruction which eventually resulted in returns of over £2m per annum, Solly's auditors discovered that, several years earlier, Robinson had made illicit and undisclosed profits for himself by selling land and options to his own share-holders at inflated prices. Solly instituted proceedings which dragged on for several years and were contested with the bitterest acrimony on both sides until Robinson was ordered to repay £462,000 and foot legal costs of over a quarter of a million. He had become a baronet but the unsavoury disclosures over the Randfontein deal robbed him of the ermine he had long coveted. Not even Lloyd George's notorious tolerance in such matters could prevail against the Upper House's indignant refusal to welcome such a candidate.

By contrast, Solly Joel's public image was now bright and shining. The firm's bold and successful operations in gold and diamonds had proved so beneficial to the Union together with its own shareholders, that few questioned General Smuts's flattering tribute, shortly after the Armistice: 'The two men who saved South Africa were the brothers Joel.' Solly sported an honorary colonel's uniform during the war, fitted out a fleet of motor ambulances and dipped deeply into his pocket to entertain British and American soldiers on leave. The racing public followed his salmon pink and green colours in which he won a wartime 'substitute' Derby, St Leger and 2,000 Guineas with Pommern. He did not become too popular in the City by forming a company to insure diamonds in transit for a 3% premium, sharply under-cutting Lloyds's standard 5%, but partly redeemed himself by patriotically lending his 1,000-ton steam yacht, *Eileen*, to the Royal Navy. She served as a flagship for patrol boats and carried four six-pounder guns and two twelve-pounders.

The yacht had been renamed in honour of his younger daughter when he disowned her sister, Doris, who had given him mortal offence by marrying a stockbroker of whom he disapproved. He even went so far as to issue a Press statement: 'So keenly does Mr Solly Joel take the secrecy of his daughter's wedding that neither Mr Arthur Walter nor his wife may expect forgiveness.' As a sign of mourning, he grew a beard which he wore to the end of his days and had Doris's name removed from the yacht down to the very linen and cutlery. There was a brief reconciliation when the marriage broke up and Doris presented him with his first grandson. After the baby died, however, Solly refused to see his daughter again and forbade any mention of her name, although continuing to sign cheques for her allowance. When Doris, a gifted composer of light music, wrote some pieces for a Charlot revue with lyrics by Noël Coward, her father paid an incognito visit to the theatre but still could not bring himself to congratulate her.

His patriarchal severity was soon directed at his eldest son, Woolf, on whom he had placed extravagant hopes. After Eton and a brief spell at Cambridge, he made some pretence of starting his business career in Johannesburg but welcomed the outbreak of war as a chance for more excitement. He joined the Natal Light Horse as a trooper, won a commission in the field and saved three of his men from drowning in the Orange River. Later he transferred to the Royal Flying Corps and flew as an Observer with his friend and idol, Capt. Albert Ball, V.C. On one unauthorized skylarking flight, he crashed a plane and suffered a severe head injury which may have contributed to his odd behaviour on returning to civilian life.

Installed behind a big empty desk in Austin Friars, he rapidly drifted to gayer circles where his champagne parties and practical jokes, including a frivolous impersonation of his father in a false beard, made him a favourite at the Embassy Club and other haunts. Although Solly restricted him to a relatively modest allowance, he behaved like a Crown Prince which inevitably attracted a crowd of spongers and confidence men. After a series of luckless ventures in films and other doubtful enterprises, he was trapped into late-night gambling parties and lost heavily while 'under the influence'. When moneylenders presented their discounted bills and I.O.U.s, Solly settled up but took stern vengeance by making his son bankrupt, naming himself as the principal creditor. Woolf was packed off, with withering sarcasm, to start fruit-farming in Egypt but, on board ship and with Solly's farewell cheque nestling in his wallet, succumbed to a last game of poker for very high stakes. After losing yet again, but with his usual gay nonchalance, he fell down a companion way while reeling back to his cabin. The autopsy disclosed a skull wound which was consistent with either a fall or a heavy blow from some blunt instrument.

Solly's attitude towards his children estranged him further from his wife who had long tried to shield them from his Old Testament wrath. They separated. Some months after her death in August 1919, he married Mrs Phoebe Juta, a former musical comedy actress whom he had met while she was touring South Africa. Their Riviera honeymoon was postponed because Solly was then busily involved in attempting to steady the diamond market during an international trade depression. With Ernest Oppenheimer he strengthened the Diamond Syndicate and ensured that the newly-developed deposits in Angola, South-West Africa and the Belgian Congo did not topple De Beers from its world hegemony.

   Solly's most spectacular achievement in this field was to prevent the Bolsheviks from flooding the market with a hoard of jewels 'confiscated' from the Tsar's family and other members of the Russian aristocracy. He sent envoys to Reval and offered a quarter of a million pounds for the stones which had been roughly tossed into fourteen cigar boxes. The Russians demanded a million, part of which could be payable in British coal, but Solly held firm. While the negotiations stretched into months, the price of diamonds continued to decline and De Beers had to stop mining. In the end Solly secured the whole Russian collection for under £400,000. 'I still overpaid,' he said afterwards, 'but our shareholders saved themselves the million at least they would have dropped if those diamonds had gone loose on the market.'

Guests at fifty-bedroomed Maiden Erlegh could enjoy lakes

stuffed with trout, a magnificent aviary, a cricket field, polo ground and the loveliest deer park in Berkshire, but the £12,000 Pompeiian marble pool was always the main attraction for Solly's gayer City friends. He once invited some pretty chorus girls from Drury Lane to join them for an evening swim. They were provided with some very chic-looking bathing suits which shrank to nothing on impact with the water. Solly explained gravely that he was only trying out some new waterproof material which he hoped to market.

After his second marriage he was so often the smiling host at first nights in the West End that a music hall star, Clarice Mayne, once sang out to him, 'Here comes Solly Joel. Isn't he a jolly soul?' But his passion for the theatre had its business side. He went into partnership with Sir Alfred Butt who had enormous flair and managerial experience in the theatre, although Solly's financial genius sealed most of the deals. Together they bought the Queens, the Globe, the Gaiety and the Adelphi, disposing of them later at a splendid profit. When it was arranged to pull down the old Empire Theatre in Leicester Square and replace it by a luxury cinema in association with M.G.M., Butt agreed to put up £300,000 but still needed £400,000 to complete the deal. Solly, who happened to be in Johannesburg on business, simply cabled his brother, Jack, at Austin Friars, 'Give Alfred £400,000', without vouchsafing a word of explanation.

He was equally direct in finalizing the purchase of the Meux Brewery site in Tottenham Court Road on which the Dominion Theatre was later built. His ebullient Lancashire friend, 'Jimmy' White, with whom he would later fall out, was handling the deal which he was so anxious to complete that he accosted Solly at Goodwood where they both happened to have rival horses running. To avoid missing the race, Solly quickly signed a cheque for £500,000 for the property over a glass of champagne in the paddock bar. Nevertheless, he had the millionaire's traditional weakness for petty thrift. Although a kindly and generous employer, he once flew into a rage on discovering that a clerk had carelessly over-stamped a letter to Johannesburg.

Like Barney, he prided himself on an excellent memory for the smallest business details. Looking down the list of returns for one of his theatres during a most successful run, he spotted that a box was producing little or no revenue despite 'House Full' notices. He discovered that his own son, Stanhope, who had recently left Eton for Trinity College, Cambridge, was so taken with one of the actresses that he had booked the box night after night for himself and fellow-undergraduates. Solly did not find it at all amusing and soon stopped the issue of 'complimentary' vouchers.

After one theatre deal which did not turn out as profitably as he had expected, he glumly inspected his cheque for a half-share in the balance of £23,840 11s. 10d. due to the partnership. Tossing it angrily across the table, he snapped, 'This is five and elevenpence short'. Butt handed him the extra small change without a word. Predictably, they also quarrelled in the end, despite Jack Joel's efforts as a peacemaker, a rôle he had increasingly to undertake on behalf of his nephews and nieces.

But the Joel-Butt partnership made theatrical history while it lasted. Solly had a controlling interest in the Drury Lane Theatre, investing thousands—for a huge return—on record-breaking productions like *Rose Marie*, *The Desert Song*, *Show Boat* and *The New Moon*. After the final performance of *Show Boat* he arranged a party worthy of Ziegfeld. The vast stage was transformed into a miniature replica of the host's yacht, complete with mast and funnel. Two miles of cable were laid for the lighting effects, with foghorns, sirens, a gently rolling stage, and even a mock Customs office to provide 'atmosphere'. Waiters, dressed as stewards, served caviare, truffles and champagne for hundreds of guests who included Royalty as well as most of 'Debrett'.

Such generous hospitality became habitual to Solly who was ranked, at least by the popular Press, as one of the half-dozen wealthiest business magnates in Britain. It was an exaggeration fostered by his sybaritic tastes and reports of mammoth deals like the purchase of the Speyer interests in the London Underground railways on behalf of Barnato Brothers for a price running into several millions. He also financed a £5m deal for Horrockses, Crewdson and Co., the great Manchester firm of cotton spinners and manufacturers, apart from acquiring major holdings in the A.B.C. group of cafés and the valuable Covent Garden Estate.

Although on the boards of at least thirty flourishing companies, headed by De Beers and 'Johnnies', he had to take some heavy losses from the mid-twenties onwards. He invested substantially in South African platinum mines but was defeated by huge working costs and a market which did not recover during his lifetime. He was also premature in sinking vast sums in the Northern Rhodesian copperfields just before the price of ore was catastrophically hit by the world depression of 1929. 'Johnnies', thanks to the Government Areas and Randfontein, produced about one-quarter of the Rand's total gold output. From 1926 onwards, the Diamond Syndicate had to face a critical situation, not only through the discovery of new mines far beyond Kimberley, but as a result of uncontrolled alluvial production in the Lichtenburg area of the Transvaal and in Namaqualand. The diggers dumped vast quantities of diamonds on the market which made it necessary, in 1927, for the Syndicate to take over and hoard huge stocks to the value of £8m.

Such stockpiling was too costly to be continued indefinitely. The problem was finally solved by forming the £5,500,000 Diamond Corporation (superseding the Syndicate in 1930). It soon became an integral part of the Diamond Producers' Association, together with the Union Government, De Beers and all the other leading companies. The result was effective control of virtually the whole of the world's diamond production and marketing through one central body. Solly and Sir Ernest Oppenheimer were the mainsprings of the Corporation which almost certainly saved the industry from collapse. Solly, following Uncle Barney's precedent during the first Rand crisis, had refused to consider the possibility of failure. 'Women are born every minute,' he reminded gloomy stockholders. 'As long as women are born, diamonds will be worn.' He is credited with originating De Beers' celebrated slogan, 'A diamond is forever.'

His second wife provided a dazzling showcase for this philosophy. At Deauville, Le Touquet and Monte Carlo, where Solly played for enormous sums in the casinos, she more than held her own with the flashing Dolly Sisters and the Begum Aga Khan. On *Eileen II*, with its miniature putting green on the quarterdeck, they entertained the wealthy Cowes set, returning the hospitality of old friends like Sir Thomas Lipton and Gordon Selfridge. With his yachting cap, cigar and trimmed beard, Solly was looking more and more like a slender version of the late King Edward VII, although infinitely more abstemious. He constantly sipped Veuve Clicquot but was never seen the worse for drink. With a twinkling eye he would tell American reporters that he was strongly in favour of Prohibition but refused to confirm or deny that he was making half a crown on every case of bootleg liquor run into American ports from Bermuda.

He was offered the gambling concession at Monte Carlo, but found it much more attractive to try and defeat the house at roulette or chemin-de-fer. He played coolly for high stakes and usually emerged a winner, always getting up when the play was running against him. In the end, he grew bored with the tables. Sitting on the terrace of the Hotel de Paris with his panama over his eyes, he was pestered by a young man to enter the Casino for a few hands of 'chemmy'. 'What's the good?' he grunted. 'If I win a thousand pounds it makes no difference. If I lose it, I'm miserable for the rest of the day.' He then lit a fresh cigar and murmured casually, 'However, if you're so keen on losing your father's money, I'll be happy to toss a coin for £10,000.' The offer was hurriedly declined.

He subscribed liberally to synagogues, schools and many other Jewish causes, but on a far smaller scale than Barney. His non-Jewish benefactions were more munificent. Noting the lack of recreation grounds around Reading, he lopped twenty acres off his estate, adding a gift of £10,000 for the National Playing Fields Association. Together with his brother, Jack, he endowed a University Chair of Physics at the Middlesex Hospital Medical School with the sum of £20,000. On Solly's visits to South Africa, where it was said that his appearance on the Johannesburg Stock Exchange would send most shares up several points, he always found time to visit the Bowling Club, whose freehold had been presented by 'Johnnies', and the park at Houghton Drive built on the forty acres also donated by the firm. He gave Joel House, the mansion in Barnato Park he had completed after Barney's death, to the Transvaal Government. (It later became part of the site of the Johannesburg High School for Girls.) He would also visit the firm's Polana Hotel in Lourenço Marques but never tarried there.

After spending a fortune on draining the swampy land and building the hotel to the highest luxury standards, with the implied understanding that he would be given a gambling concession, this was refused (on moral grounds!) by the virtuous authorities who promptly granted it to a Portuguese syndicate.

He often stayed with his kinsman, Colonel Sir David Harris, who had won fame in command of the Town Guard during the Siege of Kimberley. Knighted by King George V, he was a respected member of the Cape Assembly for a quarter of a century and a Senior Director of De Beers, usually presiding at the Annual General Meetings. He liked to talk over old Whitechapel days and practise his cockney rhyming slang, but never quite warmed to Solly whom he found less endearing than Barney. A passionate gardener himself, he admired the palm court at Maiden Erlegh but privately thought that twenty-thousand flowers planted in the owner's racing colours a trifle ostentatious. In addition to his studs at Maiden Erlegh, Solly had scores of horses in training at Moulton Paddocks, Newmarket, formerly the racing headquarters of Sir Ernest Cassel. He liked to spend weekends there, whenever possible, and used to watch all the early-morning gallops on the Heath, often giving shrewd pointers to his own trainer. He spent far less on bloodstock than the Aga Khan, Lord Derby and the Astors, but was rarely behind them in the list of winning owners and breeders. He won over £350,000 in stake money, often with horses which turned out to be wonderful bargains.

His greatest disappointment was never to win a peacetime Derby, an honour which Jack Joel carried off twice, together with practically every other major event in the calendar. At Childwick Bury, near St Albans, Jack bred superb horses and had a more natural instinct for racing than Solly although rather less of the 'Joel luck'. His greatest owner-bred colt, Humorist, won the Derby in 1921 and looked set for a rich future at stud. A month after his Epsom triumph, however, he bled to death in his box from an internal haemorrhage.

The turf rivalry between the brothers was carried into all their relationships. According to Solly's son, Stanhope, they would frequently have bitter stand-up arguments, 'like Potash and Perlmutter', but angrily closed ranks against any strangers who dared to attack one to the other. Although both were almost fanatical about racing and also enjoyed playing for high stakes at Deuuville or Cannes, they remained as different as champagne and port, as Barney had shrewdly judged when they first came out to Kimberley together.

Solly was the human dynamo, while his brother was temperamentally more suited to act as a balance-wheel. Jack took pride in the Rubens and Romney that adorned the study of his mansion in Grosvenor Square, but outside his office preferred to live like a country squire, devoting himself to farming and horse-breeding. At Childwick Bury he cherished his 145 prize racing pigeons, never having lost his love of this sport since the far-off days when he and his brother had turned a few nimble shillings in their loft over The King of Prussia.

He was reserved and far less flamboyant than Solly who thought nothing of luring away the Embassy Club's chef to cook meals aboard the *Eileen* or impulsively buying a silver gilt dinner service, weighing a mere 4,000 ounces, from the Belgian Royal House. And only Solly would order two zebras to be shipped from Cape Town, as well as some white donkeys from Egypt, to amuse his children during their school holidays.

Solly's Ascot-eve stag parties at Maiden Erlegh became a glittering annual fixture in the social diary. He would invite about three hundred friends and acquaintances, greeting each of them by his Christian name or nickname, as they filed in to a sumptuous champagne luncheon served in a marquee decorated with the host's racing colours. His two sons dutifully assisted him at this party. The younger, Dudley, was somewhat shy and had to contend with a slight speech impediment which always worsened in his father's presence. He tried manfully to master diamond-sorting with a view to entering this side of the business, but showed no aptitude. Instead, he decided on a political career and began nursing a Midlands constituency. He dared not risk Solly's displeasure by marrying during his lifetime, but Stanhope fell in love with a charming American girl, Gladys Mcfadden of Philadelphia, and refused to come to heel.

Solly carried anti-nepotism to extremes. Disappointed in his eldest son, he was determined that the others should occupy only menial positions in the firm, conveniently forgetting how Uncle Barney had treated him and his brothers. Stanhope had done well enough at school and university to justify something better than an office boy's stool. He read for the Bar and was well advanced with his studies when he first met Miss Mcfadden. Solly at once objected that marriage was out of the question until he had been 'called'. The couple parted reluctantly, but Solly was equally intractable when his son qualified and promptly asked his consent. He now insisted that Stanhope should marry a girl of the Jewish faith, preferably English, and threatened to cut him off unless he saw reason. He was supported by Phoebe who did not get on at all well with her stepson.

Stanhope married at a register office in Littlehampton. Solly did not disown him, but vented his displeasure by refusing to add a penny to his allowance, 'as presumably would have been the case,' recalls Stanhope, 'if I had married a girl of whom he approved—though it is doubtful if anyone human could have met his specifications.' He augmented his 'comparatively slim family income' by building up a modest though steady practice at the Bar. Solly proved an affectionate and generous grandfather when 'fillies', as he called them, were born.

Free of such a crushing magisterial handicap, his nephews showed a far keener aptitude for the family business than his own boys. Woolf's son, Geoffrey, settled smoothly into Consolidated Building. He won the M.C. on wartime service and later became a director of both 'Johnnies' and De Beers, while Jack Joel's son, Jim, acted as his father's right-hand man at Austin Friars in handling the London firm's investments and its diamond trade.

Solly lavished most affection on his daughter Eileen who was vivacious and shared his passion for yachting and horses. He was the proudest man in England when, in 1925, she became the first woman to win the Newmarket Town Plate, the only race open to both sexes under Jockey Club rules. She won under a considerable handicap since her father considered riding breeches unladylike and stubbornly refused to buy her a pair. She rode astride but had to compromise with an adapted habit. Solly forgave her after her triumph, but he would always remember it for another reason. He had staked £2 on Eileen at 4 to 1, but the

Silver Ring bookmaker disappeared when the horse passed the post. Solly used to laugh about the incident although he took the most energetic steps to track down the welsher. The loss of £10 weighed as much with him as £100,000.

Although he chose 'Facta non verba' as his family motto, 'Nemo me impune lacessit' might have been more appropriate. Few men can ever have been engaged simultaneously on more lawsuits either with ex-friends like James White or mine-owners who dared to question the hegemony of the Diamond Syndicate, not to mention dozens of business rivals, J. B. Robinson among them, who had unwisely crossed his path. One of his rare defeats in Court—and certainly the most expensive—was suffered at the hands of his cousin, Barney's younger son.

Fanny Barnato, who turned more for advice to Jack Joel than his brother, had brought up her children in comfort but without luxuries like Eton, yachts and retinues of servants. She had a spacious flat near Marble Arch, a house in Upper Colwyn Bay and a pleasant villa at Brighton where her offspring, always immaculately turned out, would be promenaded rather primly during their school holidays. The two boys were educated at Charterhouse and Cambridge, and Leah had the upbringing of a young heiress without, however, being spoilt in the process. After being briefly engaged to her playboy cousin, Solly's eldest son, she married Alfred Haxton, a concert violinist. Her second marriage to Carlyle Blackwell, the film star of Hollywood's silent era, was a particularly stormy union and may have contributed, apart from heredity, to her history of alcoholism.

Barney's first son, Jack, had his mother's quiet charm and geniality to balance the Barnato dash. Barely out of his teens on the outbreak of the Great War, he served as a pilot in the Royal Naval Air Service and subsequently the R.A.F. A member of the first squadron to bomb Constantinople, he was mentioned several times in despatches. He died from bronchial pneumonia in October 1918, aged twenty-four, after being married less than two years. (His widow, Dorothé, later married Lord Plunket.)

His brother, Woolf, better known as 'Babe', had modestly

joined up as a private, serving in the ranks for a year before winning a commission and an eventual captaincy. He owed his nickname to remarkable physique and stamina. A laughing, mahogany-tanned cavalier with wavy dark hair and his mother's brown eyes, he stood over six foot but looked shorter because of his stocky and muscular build. At Cambridge he was already flooring the heaviest of boxing Blues and soon established himself as one of the greatest all-round athletes of his generation. He excelled equally at shooting, foxhunting and ski-ing, and earned his place as wicket-keeper for Surrey. He even played plus-two golf, but super-charged cars were his true passion. After one race he celebrated with an original party at the old Kit-Kat Club. All the waiters wore racing kit, complete with crash helmets, and the table décor reproduced the track at Brooklands. Pinned to the menu was a friendly warning from the host: 'Before parking his or her chassis, each driver should ensure that his or her carburettor is flooded with at least two cocktails.'

Like his father, he could never resist a bet. He backed himself to race the Blue Train from Cannes in his Bentley and won by four hours, driving non-stop. While his wife was awaiting a baby in her Dorchester suite, he passed the time by arranging a sweepstake on the date and hour of the happy event. The arrival of his first son stimulated him to do a solo victory dance round the foyer, followed by drinks for the entire hotel staff of close on five hundred. This boy, Peter, was the product of Babe's second marriage, together with another son, Michael.

He married three times. The first wife, Dorothy Falk, daughter of a prominent Wall Street figure, presented him with two daughters. His second, Jacqueline Claridge Quealy, came from a wealthy Californian family with colliery interests. They were married in San Francisco by a Bishop of the Mormon Church to which the bride belonged. Babe took her on a gay 10,000-mile honeymoon tour of America in the largest Bentley ever made, an eight-litre, six-cylindered sports model which exactly matched his outsize flamboyance.

In many ways he was a throwback to the Regency bucks. He had his father's tremendous appetite for fun but also inherited some of his little peculiarities. He had something of a phobia about lending even small sums of money although spending an average of £800 a week on his racing cars and parties. On returning by boat from one of his American trips, he was asked by a close friend (later a distinguished Air Marshal) for the loan of £100 in dollars. Babe hesitated but could not refuse. Back in his flat in Grosvenor Square, the man pulled out his cheque book and, with a perfectly straight face, asked if he might give him 'something on account', and the balance in the near future. Babe looked most unhappy, but growled agreement. The leg-puller then wrote out a cheque for £99 19s. 11d.

On coming of age, Babe agreed to dissolve the partnership between himself and the Joels in accordance with the discretion provided for in Barney's Will, under which he had inherited a quarter of a million sterling, and a similar amount from Woolf Joel's estate. With ample means and a boisterous disposition, he was ideally cast for a playboy rôle in the roaring 'twenties. At Arden Run Hall, near Lingfield, he organized races along the drive and round the lake, the huge cars hurtling towards each other at suicidal speeds. When the house burned down, he spent over £100,000 on his ranch-style home near Englefield Green. Designed by Lutyens and standing in twenty Surrey acres, it had a magnificent swimming-pool, twenty-five bedrooms and a dozen bathrooms fitted with gilt taps, as well as a 'talkie' cinema, squash courts and stables. A £10,000 plant supplied electricity to the mansion, including a drive lit by secret rays.

His cash helped to stave off bankruptcy for the original Bentley Company for which he also became a more than dashing shop-window. Driving his huge six-and-a-half-litre model, he won the gruelling Le Mans twenty-four-hour endurance trial three times running from 1928–30, an achievement never equalled. Many still consider him the finest road-driver in all racing history, and his victories over the supercharged seven-litre Mercedes are acknowledged as classic performances of strategy and daring.

He revelled in the champagne glamour surrounding the 'Bentley Boys', Tim Birkin, the Dunfees, Kidston, Jack Barclay, Dick Watney and other idols of the Brooklands track. 'He loved to win and to be in the limelight,' recalls one of his racing mechanics, 'but he was a good sport if anyone beat him—though that didn't happen often.' He drove everywhere at hair-raising speeds, reminiscent of Barney's exuberant cross-country dashes in his gilded coach, and needed no excuse to give a party. Unlike his father, however, he had a strong professional sense of team spirit and did exactly as he was told by mechanics and pit crews who found drivers like Tim Birkin far harder to control.

'He was a formidable man, behind a glass of whisky, behind a driving wheel and behind a boardroom table,' recalls W. O. Bentley who, like all Babe's friends, soon discovered that he would gladly hand out cigars at home, but, like Barney, had some aversion to offering his cigarettes outside. 'It was the ambition of many of us to get our fingers inside the gold cigarette-case which he always carried in a long specially-tailored pocket in all his suits!'

He made shrewd investments in the commodity markets and a variety of paying companies ('I know nearly a hundred thousand pounds went down the drain in Bentley Motors,' he once told a friend, 'but on one diamond deal during that time I made a hundred and twenty thousand, so I can't grumble'), but he benefited by keeping clear of the family business which was so sharply hit by the economic blizzards of the early 'thirties.

Babe proved himself anything but a playboy in the decade of litigation following his coming-of-age. In addition to the cash left to him by his father and Woolf Joel, he was also entitled to a share of the profits in Barnato Brothers proportionate to those sums between 1897 and his majority in September 1916. This account was most strenuously disputed on his behalf by his lawyers and, in particular, by his first father-in-law, Herbert Valentine Falk. The latter gave up his seat on the New York Stock Exchange—for an agreed percentage of the proceeds!—to engage in some very acrimonious negotiations with the Joels. According to him, they were less than helpful in producing books and accounts.

Solly, always a last-ditcher in money matters, showed characteristic resentment at any attempt to question his statements. It was not until May 1925, after arbitration, that an 'amicable' settlement was reached by which Babe received some £900,000 with agreed costs at £50,000. Among the battery of counsel, Norman Birkett acted as leader for the plaintiff with a brief marked at 1,000 guineas. He always treasured a gold cigarette case on which

Babe had inscribed the words, 'Little acorns into oak trees grow.'

The strain of litigation, followed by a catastrophic fall in securities due to the world depression, affected Solly's health. He died at Moulton Paddocks of a heart attack in May 1931. He had spent his last days propped up in bed with a forbidden Havana in his mouth, studying 'Ruff's Guide to the Turf'. Among the wreaths at the Willesden Cemetery was one from Doris with a note, 'I loved you, Daddy'. He had provided generously for his family, including an annuity for Doris, but the share slump hit his estate which was valued at little over a million. He did not live to see his son, Dudley, enter Parliament or the tremendous boom in Rand shares after Britain and South Africa went off the gold standard. 'Johnnies' floated several new mining companies and, by 1938, was producing gold worth £18m a year, also developing several more townships in the Transvaal. The firm's heavy investments in copper and platinum had justified Solly's faith, while De Beers, under Sir Ernest Oppenheimer, gradually emerged from stagnation.

The family business had come under the control of Jack Joel who managed the difficult transition period up to the outbreak of war with a quiet but most productive efficiency. When he died in 1940, leaving an estate of £3,600,000, the chairmanship of 'Johnnies' and Barnato Brothers passed to his bachelor son, Jim.

Dudley Joel joined the R.N.V.R. on the outbreak of war and was drowned while trying to rescue his comrades when their ship was sunk. His brother, Stanhope, served as a Squadron-Leader in the R.A.F. and afterwards settled on an eight-acre estate in Bermuda bought from Babe Barnato. He has devoted himself to his investments, including considerable real estate development in the West Indies, but continues the family's racing tradition by maintaining studs in England and Ireland. Several of his horses have won important races in his father's old colours. His sister, Eileen Rogerson, and her husband are also prominent owners.

The younger generation did not inherit the prejudices of their fiercer and more combative sires. Once the bitter lawsuit was over, Babe showed a generous spirit which was fully reciprocated by his cousins. For some years he and Stanhope Joel shared the same block of offices in Mayfair, and the old clannishness pervaded a huge celebration at Claridge's for Fanny Barnato's eightieth birthday in 1939.

As a Wing Commander in the Second War, Babe helped to organize the defence of aircraft production factories. He died of cancer at fifty-two only six months after his third marriage. The six-and-a-half-litre Bentley in which he won Le Mans was laden with flowers and wreaths to lead the funeral cortège.

He was always enormously proud of his daughter, Diana, who had learned to fly at Brooklands and won wartime fame with Air Transport Auxiliary, ferrying planes to R.A.F. bases. She married Derek Walker, a fighter-bomber pilot who crashed to his death in a Mustang. She later won membership of the exclusive 'Ten Ton' Club by piloting herself at over 1,000 m.p.h. A brilliant horsewoman, she has survived two operations for cancer and hunts regularly with the Old Surrey and Burstow of which she is a Joint M.F.H.

The whole Barnato-Joel dynasty has thinned out in the direct line of male succession. One of Babe's two sons, Peter, is dead, and the younger, Michael, lives in Nevada where he has real estate interests. His heir is named 'Barney' after his great grandfather. Woolf's only son, Geoffrey, died in Johannesburg in 1959. The last significant family link with the business is Jim Joel, a bachelor now in his late seventies. He retired as Chairman of 'Johnnies' in 1962 on being appointed Honorary President, but gave this up on relinquishing his seat on the Board seven years later. Thus ended the clan's association with a Company founded by Barney eighty years before. A quiet and reserved millionaire, he is a racing owner with many famous horses in his stables, including Royal Palace whom he bred for a Derby victory in 1967.

On New Year's Day 1963, the control and management of 'Johnnies' was formally transferred from London to Johannesburg, and Barnato Brothers became a wholly-owned subsidiary which

now conducts the firm's investments and other business in the
United Kingdom. The market value of Johannesburg Consolidated
Investment's shareholdings is today over £200m. The Company
has benefited from gold prospecting in the Western Areas and the
new Elsburg mine, its substantial investment in De Beers and the
British South Africa Company ('Chartered'), and the boost in
uranium and copper production. Although still a major finance
house, it is dwarfed by the mammoth Anglo-American Corporation which, with its numerous subsidiaries, is directed by Harry
Oppenheimer, Sir Ernest's son and successor. Through a network
intricately meshed with holdings in most other mining concerns,
this group now controls 40% of South African gold, an important
slice of De Beers' output, in addition to copper, Rhodesian nickel
and a strong minority interest in the vast American industrial
complex headed by C. W. Engelhard.

Kimberley has become a pleasant tree-lined city of some fifty-
five thousand people. Residents of the Hadison Park suburb have
remembered the little pioneer by calling one of their thorough-
fares, 'Barnato Street'. Although diamonds at deep levels continue
to be drawn from Dutoitspan, Bultfontein and Wesselton, the only
major relic of its colourful past is the famous 'Big Hole' now half-
full of water and abandoned since 1909 after producing over
£50m worth of diamonds. Richer areas have since been located
in Angola, Sierra Leone and Tanzania.

By contrast, Johannesburg is a sophisticated modern city, the
largest and most dynamic in Africa with over a thousand miles of
busy streets. The Carlton Hotel was demolished in 1964 and the
theatre completed after Barney's death is now a cinema. The
Barnato Park district of Berea now has a Place, a View and a Court
which also bear his name. But the city's skyscrapers, department
stores and elegant suburbs offer few reminders of the frontier town
to which he drove up from Kimberley only ninety years ago. His
faith in the Rand's potential has been dramatically realized, although even he could not have anticipated that all the free nations'
monetary reserves would be backed by its mined gold or that a
300-mile mineral reef would one day stretch from Johannesburg
and with still-undetected goldfields confidently predicted by
surveys. The firm's Consolidated Building still looks solid enough

if less impressive than Anglo-American's headquarters on Main Street. The present generation is perhaps more intrigued by the great stone lions which dominate the entrance to Kruger's old house in Pretoria, now a museum.

Barney's portrait by Tennyson Cole occupies an honoured place in the boardroom at Austin Friars within walking distance of the Whitechapel alleys where he ran about as a boy. His Park Lane mansion has long since passed out of the Sassoon family. Its site has been transformed by the London headquarters of the Playboy Club. Spencer House, the scene of so many glittering receptions during his brief heyday, is now rented by the more austere Economist Intelligence Unit.

With all his faults, Barney Barnato left too big a mark on his adopted country during its fermenting years to be relegated to a squalid footnote in South African history. It should not be altogether forgotten that he was both the impresario and the victim of an age hardly more rapacious and share-hungry than our own.

When Jacob C. Schiff, the railroad magnate, once questioned whether he had had any true ability apart from a get-rich-quick opportunism, John Hays Hammond reminded him angrily that Barnato had qualities of heart and mind lacking in many of America's robber barons. He added, in scathing parenthesis, 'If he were penniless, I would have grubstaked him to a few hundred dollars and in no time he'd have taken all your money away from Wall Street.'

Despite his sentimentality and weakness for self-deception, Barney might have relished that blunt epitaph far more than those which piously recall his clan in their lonely corner of Willesden Green.

BIBLIOGRAPHY

In addition to newspaper files, letters and other records to which the author has been given access, special acknowledgement is due to Harry Raymond's *B. I. Barnato: A Memoir* (Isbister & Co., 1897); *Barney Barnato* by Richard Lewinsohn (Routledge, 1937); Louis Cohen's *Reminiscences of Kimberley* (Bennett, 1911) and *Reminiscences of Johannesburg* (Holden, 1924); *The Story of 'Johnnies'* (privately published, Johannesburg, 1965); *The Story of De Beers* by Hedley A. Chilvers (Cassell, 1939); *Ace of Diamonds* by Stanhope Joel, as told to Lloyd Mayer (Frederick Muller, 1958); Paul Emden's *Randlords* (Hodder & Stoughton, 1935); *The Uitlanders* by Robert Crisp (Peter Davies, 1964); *The Corner House* by A. P. Cartwright (Macdonald, 1965); *Rhodes* by J. G. Lockhart and C. M. Woodhouse (Hodder & Stoughton, 1963); and J. X. Merriman's *Correspondence*, ed. by Phyllis Lewsen (Cape Town, 1960).

Other sources consulted or quoted are listed below under authorship in alphabetical order.

Bentley, W. O. *An Autobiography* (Hutchinson, 1958)

―――― *The Cars in My Life* (Hutchinson, 1961)

―――― *My Life and My Cars* (Hutchinson, 1967)

Calder-Marshall, Arthur *Prepare to Shed Them Now* (Hutchinson, 1968)

Cartwright, A. P. *Gold Paved the Way* (Macmillan, 1967)

Cole, P. Tennyson *Vanity Varnished* (Hutchinson, 1931)

Colvin, Ian *Life of Jameson* (Edward Arnold, 1922)

Fitzpatrick, Sir James P. *The Transvaal from Within* (Heinemann, 1899)

―――― *South African Memories* (Cassell, 1932)

Green, Timothy *The World of Gold* (Michael Joseph, 1968)

Gross, Felix *Rhodes of Africa* (Cassell, 1956)

Hahn, Emily *Diamond* (Weidenfeld & Nicolson, 1956)

Hammond, John Hays *Autobiography* (Farrar & Rinehart, Inc., 1935)

Hammond, Natalie *A Woman's Part in a Revolution* (Longmans, 1897)

Harris, Sir David *Pioneer, Soldier and Politician* (Sampson Low, 1931)

'Imperialist' *Cecil Rhodes* (Chapman and Hall, 1917)

James, Robert Rhodes *Lord Randolph Churchill* (Weidenfeld & Nicolson, 1959)

McDonald, J. G. *Rhodes: A Life* (Phillip Allan, 1927)

Matthews, J. W. *Incwadi Yami* (Sampson Low, 1887)

Monnickendam, A. *The Magic of Diamonds* (Hammond, Hammond, 1955)

Newton, H. Chance *Cues and Curtain Calls* (John Lane, 1927)

—— *Idols of the 'Halls'* (Heath Cranton, 1928)

Pakenham, Elizabeth *Jameson's Raid* (Weidenfeld & Nicolson, 1960)

Sims, G. R. *My Life* (Eveleigh Nash, 1916)

'Vindex' *Cecil Rhodes* (George Bell, 1900)

Weinthal, Leo *Memories, Mines and Millions* (Simpkin, Marshall, 1929)

Wilson, G. H. *Gone Down the Years* (Allen and Unwin, 1947)

Young, Francis Brett *City of Gold* (Heinemann, 1939)

Index

INDEX